Reflective Teaching and Learning

A guide to professional issues for beginning secondary teachers

Reflective Teaching and Learning: A guide to professional issues for beginning secondary teachers

Edited by Sue Dymoke and Jennifer Harrison

Reflective practice is at the heart of effective teaching. This core text is an introduction for beginning secondary teachers on developing the art of critical reflective teaching throughout their professional work. Designed as a flexible resource, the book combines theoretical background with practical reflective activities.

Developing as a Reflective Secondary Teacher Series

These subject-specific core texts are for beginning secondary teachers following PGCE, GTP or undergraduate routes into teaching. Each book provides a comprehensive guide to beginning subject teachers, offering practical guidance to support students through their training and beyond. Most importantly, the books are designed to help students develop a more reflective and critical approach to their own practice. Key features of the series are:

- observed lessons, providing both worked examples of good practice and commentaries by the teachers themselves and other observers
- an introduction to national subject frameworks including a critical examination of the role and status of each subject
- support for beginning teachers on all aspects of subject teaching, including planning, assessment, classroom management, differentiation and teaching strategies
- a trainee-focused approach to critical and analytical reflection on practice
- a research-based section demonstrating M-level work
- a comprehensive companion website linking all subjects, featuring video clips of sample lessons, a range of support material and weblinks.

Teaching Mathematics
Paul Chambers

Teaching History
Ian Phillips

Forthcoming:
Teaching Science
Tony Liversidge, Matt Cochrane, Bernie Kerfoot and Judith Thomas

Teaching ICT
Carl Simmons and Claire Hawkins

Teaching English
Alyson Midgley, Peter Woolnough, Lynne Warham and Phil Rigby

Reflective Teaching and Learning

A guide to professional issues for beginning secondary teachers

edited by
Sue Dymoke and Jennifer Harrison

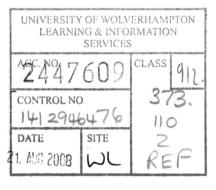

SAGE

Los Angeles • London • New Delhi • Singapore

First published 2008

SAGE Publications Ltd
1 Oliver's Yard
55 City Road
London EC1Y 1SP

SAGE Publications Inc.
2455 Teller Road
Thousand Oaks, California 91320

SAGE Publications India Pvt Ltd
B 1/I 1 Mohan Cooperative Industrial Area
Mathura Road
New Delhi 110 044

SAGE Publications Asia-Pacific Pte Ltd
33 Pekin Street #02-01
Far East Square
Singapore 048763

Library of Congress Control Number: 2007940063

British Library Cataloguing in Publication data
A catalogue record for this book is available from the
British Library

ISBN 978-1-4129-4646-9
ISBN 978-1-4129-4647-6 (pbk)

Typeset by C&M Digitals (P) Ltd, Chennai, India
Printed in Great Britain by T.J. International, Padstow, Cornwall
Printed on paper from sustainable resources

CONTENTS

FIGURES

TABLES

ACKNOWLEDGEMENTS

The writing team wishes to thank Clive Sutton and Mel Vlaeminke, who originated the *University of Leicester Secondary PGCE Teacher Development Pack,* together with past and present colleagues Jane Adams, Richard Aplin, Denise Burn, Wasyl Cajkler, Chris Comber, Wendy Curtis, Karen Garland, Ian Godwin, Morag Gornall, Roy Kirk, Roger Knight, Sylvia McNamara, Marlene Morrison, Tony Mummery, Mike Price, Sarah Raynes, Gabby Ramos, Rosemary Sage, Hugh Starkey, Adrian Stokes, Alan Sutton, Megan Thirlaway and David Whale who have all contributed to the development and revisions of the pack since its inception. Thanks are also due to Steve Woods for his help during the final draft stage.

Sue Dymoke would like to thank the University of Leicester for granting her a period of study leave in 2007 during which two chapters were redrafted.

INTRODUCTION
Jennifer Harrison and Sue Dymoke

CONTENT, ORGANIZATION AND UNDERPINNING APPROACH

This book has been written for beginning teachers who are preparing to teach in secondary schools. It covers a range of core professional studies which all graduate teachers need to address, whatever their subject or curriculum specialism. The impact of national government policy to raise educational standards in England, and the wider academic research that informs and underpins new approaches to teaching and learning, have *both* contributed to a continuing expansion of a curriculum for professional studies in most education courses.

The latest of these political initiatives is the *Every Child Matters* agenda, which requires multi-agency professionals, including all teachers, to work together to support children and young people. The remodelling of the workforce in teaching is also leading to new relationships between teachers and para-professionals, including teaching assistants, classroom assistants and other support staff within schools. Furthermore, there are many new approaches being deployed in schools and classrooms involving information communication and technology advances such as virtual learning environments and interactive whiteboards. In addition to such novel aspects, there are the important and traditional priorities for beginning teachers, such as knowing how to teach.

The organization of the book is as follows. Chapter 1 aims to develop your understanding of reflection as a critical activity, provides opportunities for focusing on core competences such as communication skills, and examines the relationship between 'reflective practice' and professional learning.

Chapter 2 introduces you to theories of learning and explores the implications of these for your preparation for teaching and learning.

Chapter 3 considers the way learning and inclusive environments can be structured in secondary schools. It also explores how educational policy has shaped teaching, curriculum content and the qualifications framework, as well as some of the impacts of e-learning.

Chapter 4 covers the many aspects of managing learning within classrooms (and other learning places) both in and out of school. It provides you with the chance to reflect upon the dynamics of classroom life and the ways in which you can influence learning through systematic planning and evaluation of your practice.

Chapter 5 focuses on key issues concerning monitoring, assessment, recording, reporting and accountability. It provides some of the theoretical background to assessment, the terminology you will need to use and provides ways for you to reflect on your early experiences of assessing your students.

In Chapter 6 the focus widens to consider the impacts on the education system, particularly in England, from the start of the twentieth century. It provides a chance for you to reflect on your own professional values and perspectives, for example on the many aspects of social exclusion and inclusion, and to consider the role you will wish to play as your teaching career develops.

Chapter 7 opens out a range of issues to do with the pastoral care and the many tutorial responsibilities of all teachers. It examines the links between pastoral tutoring and the academic and personal–social curricula and provides you with a chance to think critically about your own tutorial roles in the future.

Each chapter provides an academic approach to these same studies that teachers need to address in order to reach Master's (M) level. While this book complements the separate subject studies that form part of all secondary initial teacher education (ITE) courses, each author in the writing team for this book is from a different subject specialist area and working on a secondary postgraduate certificate course. Each author has been able to bring to the separate chapters of this book some particular perspectives from their subject area. This should help you, also, to make the bridges or connections necessary for integrating your knowledge and understanding of both professional and subject studies.

We believe this book and the reflective approaches embedded within it, will find a place in the various routes for initial training, in induction and the early professional development of new teachers. It provides a flexible learning resource for use by beginning teachers in private self-study, when working in group seminars (tutor-led) at the university, when working with mentors during school placements, or in more informal groupings in twos or threes.

Teaching is a professional activity. In learning how to teach we need to explore three important questions in becoming a teacher:

- What do teachers do?
- What affects what they do?
- How do they do it?

However 'knowing about teaching' is much more than acquiring a set of skills and accomplishing technical expertise. It is about asking a further question:

• How do teachers improve their practice?

In exploring this question, beginning teachers have to exercise originality of thinking and critical judgement, use educational research strategies, draw on educational theories and develop professional values and practices to support professional learning and development. These are rooted in the several forms of 'enquiry learning'.

When we ask the very important question, 'What *kind* of teacher do we want to be?' we have to recognize four core characteristics of teaching. The first is that teaching is an *intellectual activity.* This includes the ability to process knowledge and understanding, together with a capacity to communicate it effectively. A second characteristic is forging and maintaining effective *personal interactions.* A third area is the forming of *ethical judgements.* The fourth characteristic is the *social significance* of teaching. The book incorporates reading and activities and attempts to take account of all of these areas of teaching within each chapter.

Reflective practice as a dynamic developmental process in initial teacher education is at the heart of the book. We have incorporated a first chapter to explore what is meant by 'the reflective practitioner'. Although reflective practice has become a standard in initial and continuing professional education and development, it is actually a state of mind as well as an educational approach for all professionals to examine both non-critical and critical incidents in our working lives. We present it as a pedagogical approach – one in which you can begin to learn through professional enquiry.

Reflective practice provides a way of examining your personal experiences in the workplace. Thus, it is psychologically useful but, more than this, it is situated within the wider political and social structures of education. Therefore we believe that, through reflective practice, you can be encouraged to examine the values that underpin all your practice in teaching.

This book should also help to raise a beginning teacher's awareness of the particular role of their teacher-mentor. A mentor helps you to step 'outside of the box' of your job and personal circumstances, and look in at it together. Clutterbuck and Megginson describe this as 'like standing in front of a mirror with someone else, who can help you see things about you that have become too familiar for you to notice' (1999: 17). A mentor can contribute to your learning in a number of ways: as teacher, coach, encourager, supporter, enabler, role model or critical friend. A mentor should be able to offer: empathy and non-judgemental critique; to challenge your behaviour (not you); to challenge your assumptions (not your intellect), to challenge your perceptions (not your judgement); and to challenge your values (but not your value). They should be able to help you evaluate the available evidence from your practice. Many of the activities in this book can involve other teachers and mentors with you and can stimulate the wider professional discussions that are so important in your early training.

TERMINOLOGY

We have adopted the term 'beginning teacher' to describe the trainee or student teacher, or new entrant to the profession, who is learning how to teach. We have therefore chosen to avoid the use of the term 'student teacher' in order to distinguish clearly the term school 'student'. The word 'student' in this book, therefore, refers always to the young person, pupil or child whom the beginning teachers will teach.

We have used the word 'mentor' in relation to the designated teacher in your own subject or curriculum area, who is likely to have been given a particular *supporting* and *mentoring* role in relation to you and your initial training in the school. In some cases the mentor may be the same person as the school 'tutor' and therefore have multiple roles in connection with your training and its assessment.

There is much jargon used in education and there is terminology that often has specialized meaning in educational settings and which differs from its everyday use. These are emboldened at their first appearance in the chapters. A glossary of key terms is provided at the end of the book to provide you with an extra referral point for important terminology.

WAYS OF USING THE BOOK

This book has been written in such a way that it should allow you to read and think more widely about education and teaching, and to work with other beginning teachers and tutors in higher education institutions (HEIs) and in schools and colleges. You are encouraged to read the early parts of each chapter as an introduction to the seven professional areas of study. As you read further into each chapter you will find an extension to the area of study, and the references to wider reading and associated activities for the most part will become more complex.

Reading and using a textbook can be a rather passive and lonely experience, with the expectation that you will assimilate all the ideas within it. We sincerely hope that this will not be the case with this book. It has been written in such a way that will allow you to read and think more widely about education and teaching, and to work with other beginning teachers and tutors in higher education institutions and in schools and colleges. A wide variety of activities and links to web-based materials are embedded within each chapter. We hope these approaches will challenge and stimulate you to think for yourself about teaching, and in ways that will provide you with opportunities for direct 'conversations' with yourself and with others.

ITT STANDARDS FOR QTS

We have provided on the website (www.sagepub.co.uk/secondary) a chart (see also Appendix) of the main Standards areas and an indication of where in the book you might find topics and tasks that relate to particular areas. The recently revised professional standards for teachers make explicit the level of critical thinking required for progression within the teaching profession.

POSTGRADUATE CERTIFICATE IN EDUCATION (PGCE) M LEVEL

Study at Master's level requires a level of critical reflection which is not always achievable by the already packed programmes of most PGCE courses. This book should go a long way towards providing you with some independence in learning, particularly if you are embarking on this route. For example, it provides flexible materials and tasks so you can use your non-contact time effectively. Each chapter provides you with references to high-quality, current theoretical literature, some of which can be accessed through online links. University libraries should have access to key texts as well as a range of e-journals. Your institution's virtual learning environment (VLE) may also provide you with valuable opportunities for beginning teachers and tutors to share and develop ideas, and to communicate with each other in discussion forums. This book can be used to assist and inform critical reflection in preparation for assessed units of work.

The range of tasks in each chapter of this book has been selected to provide explorations of topics at both H and M levels. All the tasks address *general pedagogical issues*. We have recognized the progression that will be needed to move towards M level. There is at least one substantive task which allows for a more in-depth 'professional enquiry' within each chapter. Tutors and teachers in both school-based work and taught sessions will have a role to play in helping you relate your M-level study to your work in schools, and thereby link theory, research and practice. The Master's level work in our book is integral to all elements of the general or professional part of a PGCE programme – it has not been conceived as a 'bolt-on' to the traditional PGCE course structure.

Jennifer Harrison and Sue Dymoke
31 July 2007

REFERENCES

Clutterbuck, D. and Megginson, D. (1999) *Mentoring Executives and Directors*. Oxford: Butterworth-Heinemann.

1 PROFESSIONAL DEVELOPMENT AND THE REFLECTIVE PRACTITIONER

Jennifer Harrison

By the end of this chapter you will have :

- developed your understanding of reflection as a critical activity
- gained an overview of the relationship between the reflective practitioner and developing professional knowledge
- been introduced to the core competences of the reflective practitioner
- understood the role of learning conversations and the mentor in supporting reflection on practice.

AN INTRODUCTION TO THE REFLECTIVE PRACTITIONER

Perhaps, by the time you open this book, you have already come across ideas such as *reflective writing* or *evaluation of teaching and learning* or *problem-based learning*? You may already have found reflective practice to be an eye-opening experience in your teaching or, indeed, in other workplaces in which you have been able to consider and evaluate an aspect of your work. Some of us, as keen promoters of reflective practice, can point to its particular role in professional activities and how reflective practice can contribute to teacher learning and development (Harrison, 2004). As authors of this book, we certainly anticipate that it will help you make sense of what you do and to place value on the knowledge and experiences that you have gained, and will gain, in your training.

A few others, rather more critical of the process, might already think that engaging in reflective practice can be a somewhat superficial activity – another hurdle to jump, or a bit of a chore. If it does seem to have become a somewhat repetitive exercise in your training programme, then we hope that, by reading this chapter and engaging in some of the activities, you will be helped to refocus on its benefits.

What is reflective practice?

What is a reflective practitioner and what is **reflective** practice? These seem to be simple questions and, initially, the answers might appear to be rather obvious to the reader. Surely all professionals think about what they do and adapt their ways of working as a result of such thinking? Certainly reflective practice is talked about in teacher education (and other professional settings such as nursing and social work) and so it has gained credibility as well as being criticized as a much overworked expression.

Thinking about *reflective practice* as a concept is crucial since we do need to be clear about what it means. Whether we are beginning teachers, university education tutors or school mentors involved in school-based training, it is important that all of us have a chance to clarify what we understand by it and what we expect it to entail. Our starting point is that it is much more than just *thinking about teaching*. It can be thought about in terms of asking searching questions about experience and conceptualized as both a state of mind and an on-going type of behaviour. Zeichner and Liston (1996) provide a helpful overview of the traditions of reflective teaching. Being a reflective practitioner at any stage in teacher development involves a constant, critical look at teaching and learning and at the work of you, the teacher.

Reflecting on aspects of teaching practice is usually fairly instinctive for most beginning teachers. You will focus mentally on particular problems or dilemmas that are to do with how a particular teaching session went. Often, perhaps with the aid of a lesson evaluation form, you will identify what went well during the teaching session, and what did not go according to plan. You will then be encouraged to go on to think about what might need changing in the next teaching session, or to identify what could be tried out in other types of teaching sessions. This takes you from an essentially *technical* kind of reflection towards a more *practical level*, in which you begin to examine the interpretative assumptions you are making in your work. The highest, *critical* level of this hierarchy of reflective practice (van Manen, 1977) is where you critically reflect on the ethical and political dimensions of educational goals and the consensus about their ends.

The practical and critical levels are less instinctive to most beginning teachers. Indeed you may feel frustrated that, while you are being encouraged to discuss theoretical issues, you have a more immediate need to master the day-to-day aspects of teaching: for example, how to get your students to listen to you, how to establish authority, how to teach about *cells* as the basis unit of life in a meaningful and engaging way, and so on. This is why we would encourage you to try the training activities in this particular chapter and consider critical reflective practice as part of your professional study. The practical levels of reflective practice, and the sorts of skills and attributes we would wish you to develop during this training year, are explored later in the chapter.

Reflective practice and professional knowledge

It is in its relationship with professional knowledge and practice that deeper reflection becomes such an important feature of the reflective practice. If reflective practice stays at the technical level, restricted to the evaluation of teaching and learning strategies and classroom resources, it would be difficult to stress its overall importance in teacher development. However, as reflective practice is used to explore more *critically* the underlying assumptions in our teaching practices, then we can begin to build our understanding of learning and teaching and add to our professional knowledge. Teachers who are unreflective about their teaching tend to be more accepting of the everyday reality in their schools and 'concentrate their efforts on finding the most effective and efficient means to solve problems that have largely been defined for them by some collective code' (Zeichner and Liston, 1996: 9). In other words, such restricted ways of thinking do not allow problems to be framed in more than one way.

There are a number of eminent writers and researchers who have contributed to the complex thinking that surrounds reflective practice. Dewey's (1910) book *How We Think* was seminal and clearly influenced the later work of both Schön and Kolb. Dewey's view was that reflective action stems from the need to solve a problem and involves 'the active, persistent and careful consideration of any belief or supposed form of knowledge in the light of the grounds that support it' (1910: 6). He proposed a five-step model of problem-solving, which included suggesting solutions, posing questions, hypothesizing, reasoning and testing. These together form a sequential process for reflective thinking.

Dewey's work has been extended by others. Van Manen, as we have noted, highlighted, at the highest level of reflection, a moral dimension to reflective action in which the 'worthwhileness' of actions can be addressed (1977: 227). Carr and Kemmis also speak of this higher-level reflection as involving teachers as the central actors 'in transforming education' (1986: 156). More recently Pollard has stated, 'reflective teaching implies an active concern with aims and consequences as well as means and technical competence' (2005: 15).

There are clearly particular skills and dispositions associated with being a reflective practitioner. Dewey drew our attention to particular qualities that could be linked to ways of thinking. These include open-mindedness, responsibility and wholeheartedness (1933). Others such as Brookfield (1987) have tried to describe critical thinking in relation to pedagogy and have advocated ways of provoking critical thinking.

Brookfield (1995) coined the term *critical lenses* and identified four perspectives that such lenses might provide when reflecting on practice:

- the practitioner (you, the beginning teacher)
- the learners (your students)
- colleagues (for example, your mentor)
- established theory (as found in the educational and other academic and professional literature).

Brookfield explored all those things that we do, the things that influence what we do, the things we never stop to think about or ask questions about, and asked that we should try to unpack the assumptions about what we do in the classroom. Through such critical reflection on practice we should then be able to examine not only the *technical* aspects of our teaching, but also look *practically* and *critically* at issues, both within the school as a whole, and outside, that might impact on the quality of teaching and learning in the classroom.

Some forms of **action research**, **professional enquiry** and **self-study research** have grown out of these roots of reflective practice. As beginning teachers you might wish also to observe your own university tutors in their work as teacher educators. How do they create experiences for you to gain access to their thinking about, and to their practice of, teaching?

Alternative conceptions of reflection

Schön (1983; 1987) recognized that professional knowledge lies in the *doing* of the job. Many experienced teachers cannot actually articulate what they know – they just *do it*. Schön argued that in these situations professionals use their knowledge and past experiences as a frame for action – it is a form of 'knowing in action' which comes with experience, and therefore differs from Dewey's conception of routinized action. Schön argued that if professionals can begin to separate out the things they know when they do them, then they become more effective in their work. Part of this reframing involves *setting* as well as *solving* problems, 'a process in which interactively we name the things to which we will attend and frame the context in which we will attend to them' (Schön, 1983: 40). He proposed two sorts of reflection: reflection-in-action and reflection-on-action. It is useful to explain these terms further.

Reflection-in-action is the almost unconscious, instantaneous reflection that happens as a more experienced teacher solves a problem or dilemma. Schön described this as drawing on their *repertoire* of knowledge, skills and understanding of a situation so that he or she can change direction and operate differently in the classroom. In other words, rather than randomly trying any other approach, the teacher is using the accumulated experience and knowledge to seek alternatives in the classroom in response to the needs of the pupils.

Reflection-on-action takes place after the event or teaching session and is a more deliberative and conscious process. There is more critical analysis and evaluation of the actions and what might have happened if a different course of action had taken place. Since it involves looking back at an event, it is a form of retrospective reflection. It can involve the actual writing down of what happened and why (critical analysis and evaluation) as, for example, on a lesson evaluation form.

However, in attempting to separate *thinking* from *doing*, Schön gained a number of critics. Day (1993) and Solomon (1987), with others, have pointed to his lack of attention to the role of conversation or dialogue in teachers' learning, arguing that reflection is also a social process requiring the articulation of ideas to, and with, others to allow the development of a critical perspective. The importance of detailed conversation with a mentor in order to jointly analyse and evaluate what happened provides further opportunity to examine professional knowledge and theories-in-use. Time is also needed for separate reflection *on* action. Carr and Kemmis (1986) argued that Schön's narrow focus on the *individual* neglects any consideration of wider social settings. Thus we need to find ways of tapping into, and supporting, time available for such learning conversations and improving the quality of these.

Experiential learning and the role of a mentor

There are several theoretical approaches which have been used to try to explain the relationship between experience and learning – sometimes referred to as *experiential learning*. One of the best known models is that of the experiential learning cycle (Kolb, 1984), which forms the basis of several mentor-training manuals (see DfES, 2004; Harrison et al., 2005; Moon, 2004). Kolb's theory is that people learn from their experience, and the way this happens is through (1) *reflection* on the things we do (concrete experiences); and (2) experimentation (action) in similar situations at another time, in order to gain further experience; *reflect* again, and so on. As shown in Figure 1.1 it is this cyclical process of reflection that allows us to learn from experience.

Experiential learning also acknowledges that much informal learning takes place outside formal educational settings and this is as true for learners in initial teacher education as it is for students in schools. In this way reflective practice allows the learner to make sense of all learning, both formal and informal, and to organize and evaluate it.

The knowledge and theories that beginning teachers learn in the workplace (in this case, schools and colleges) are as valid as the knowledge gained through

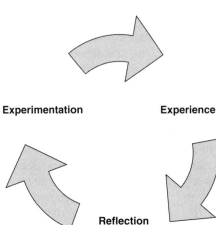

Experimentation   **Experience**

**Reflection
Learning**

Figure 1.1 The cycle of reflection (Kolb, 1984)

more formal qualifications (such as in a first degree in a specialist subject area, or a professional qualification). In saying this, Argyris and Schön (1975) argued that there are two types of theories that professionals use in their workplace and distinguished the two as follows. First, there are the *official* theories of the profession, to be found in textbooks, codes of practice and so on. There will be plenty of these examples in the subsequent chapters of this book. Such theories gain an established place and are endorsed by professionals – teachers, and others. Then there are the theories-in-use – the *unofficial* theories of professionals, which are the ideas and concepts that professionals actually draw on. They are the professionals' own ideas and theories about learning and teaching.

Activity 1.1   'Official' and 'unofficial' theories in education

Work on this within a small, mixed curriculum group of beginning teachers. Look at the *theories* listed as bullet points below.

a) First, each of you should work on your own. Try to annotate each theory with either 'U' or 'O':

- 'U' is an 'unofficial' theory of a teacher
- 'O' is an established 'official' theory in education

b) Then, compare your annotations and the reasons for your choices, with other members of the group.

- Boys don't enjoy writing as much as girls.

- People with dyslexia are lazy and don't attempt to overcome the difficulty of acquiring and using literacy skills.

- Teachers don't eat in the classroom in the presence of the boys and girls – it gives the students the wrong idea.

- The parents I need to see most at parents' evenings are the ones that stay away. They lack the motivation or skills to support their children's education.

- The main point of 'constructivism' is that humans actively construct their knowledge rather than receive it fully formed from external sources.

- Children learn in different ways. That is why we need different ability 'sets' for subject teaching. Mixed-ability classes just don't work.

- Intelligence is fixed and is something that can be measured.

- Caring relationships in a classroom are an important medium for supporting students' learning and socio-emotional development.

- Collaboration is essential for an inclusive climate in school.

- The 'zone of proximal development' is the difference between what the child can do by himself or herself and the more he or she can do with assistance from an adult, or a more knowledgeable peer. There are sensitive periods in a child's development for learning particular skills.

- Vocational courses are for students who are ill-equipped for academic courses.

Thus, it is through reflective practice that teachers can begin to tease out the different types of theories, select and apply them to advantage. The pedagogy of **constructivism** (see Chapter 2 for more on this concept) forms an important part of most teacher education courses and professional expectations are that, 'knowledge is … created rather than received, (is) mediated by discourse rather than transferred by teacher talk, (and is) explored and transformed rather than remembered as a uniform set of positivist ideas' (Holt-Reynolds, 2000: 21). This acquisition of knowledge is similar to the process of building or construction and Vygotsky's work (1962; 1978) is important, not only in identifying the particular role of discourse of practice, but also in pointing towards the particular importance of mentoring or learning conversations in support of experiential learning (see also Chapter 2). Structured suggestions for ways of exploring and transforming ideas and promoting critical reflective practice during formal mentor conversations can be found in Harrison et al. (2005).

There are many issues raised in the rest of this book which should provide you with opportunities for critical reflection in this widest sense. For example, you might start with your own classroom practice and examine how well your students responded to your use of *small group* activities within a particular lesson (see Chapters 3 and 4 for more on aspects of group work). Afterwards ask yourself some specific questions such as:

- To what extent did the activities empower independent learning or a more democratic approach in the classroom?
- Did all students respond in the same way?
- Was your class briefing satisfactory?
- Were all students ready for a lesson that was less structured and expected independent learning?

What now follows in this chapter are a further four sections to help you develop the skills of reflective practice, each with activities for you to try out. The first section explores what we might mean by professional identity with tasks to help you develop your self-awareness and engage in the use of *storytelling*. The next section provides tasks for you to consider the five core competences for a reflective practitioner: observation, communication, judgement, decision-making and team working. Within the fifth competence (teamworking), there is also a brief introduction to forms of professional enquiry and action research. A further section presents particular features of critical reflection on practice and illustrates these as a two-stage process: (1) changes in awareness, followed by (2) changes in practice. The final section provides a summary of the whole chapter, with important words of caution about the use of reflection as a disciplinary regime, as well as identification of its potential emancipatory power as a form of learning in the workplace.

In summary we hope that, by engaging with the work in these next sections, you can gain the confidence to use critical reflective practice in your everyday work in classrooms, and can embed it in your wider professional training covered by the remaining chapters of this book.

IDENTITY MATTERS FOR TEACHERS

Looking in the *looking glass*

Teaching is a public practice which bears some similarities with the process of acting. This is because teaching involves constant vigilance of the audience, with the teacher making regular efforts to imagine how he or she is coming across, and regular on-the-job evaluations of whether attempts at communication are being understood by students as intended. This comparison with acting stresses the *looking-glass* nature of teaching. It is one in which Cooley, as early as 1902, emphasized the essentially reflective nature of identity in his articulation of the *looking-glass self*. You will find yourself reflected in a variety of mirrors: your colleagues, your learners, their parents, the government and media, all of whom provide multiple, often idealized, images of teachers' professional identities. These images may compete frequently with your personal identity, may distort your self-image, and bring about a need for self-reflection. It is now recognized that identity in the workplace is not fixed and singular but is multiple, changing and provisional in nature (Weick, 1995). Identity construction is always a social activity; it involves a continual constructing and reconstructing of relationships with others in the workplace.

Nias (1989) has also made important contributions to the debate about teachers' developing identity. In her longitudinal study of primary school teachers' lives and identities, she identified a distinction between the personal and the professional elements. She found that incorporation of the identity of 'teacher' into an individual's self-image was accomplished over long periods of time. It follows that it is highly likely that you, as a beginning secondary school teacher, are experiencing a *substantive identity* (that is, your stable, core identity – *you*) as relatively independent of your presentation of yourself within professional setting such as a school (that is, your *situated identity*, or professional self – *teacher*). Drawing from this research work, you may be into your second decade of teaching before you will have fully incorporated your professional role into your self-image and can identify your substantive identity as *teacher*. Nias concluded that being yourself in school was less to do with the practical aspects of teaching young learners skills and information, and more to do with generating a sense of community and integrating personal and professional connections between teacher and learner.

Thus the central idea is that constructing identity (here, your professional or situated identity) involves you, first, in *making a pattern of experiences* that have consistency over a period of time. You gradually acquire, and accept, characteristic patterns of decision which, in turn, determine your choices and decision-making in the workplace. This second process of *integration* which Nias describes is very challenging particularly to beginning teachers because there are so many mirrors available in which to examine your professional identity. While each of these mirrors may have a distorting effect in terms of providing competing messages about teachers' professional lives, it is important to begin the process of describing each new professional self throughout the training process. The third part of the process involves a *disruption* or *inconsistency* in identity (see Warin et al., 2006). There will be plenty of instances that you, and your peer group, will experience in this training year where your own pedagogical beliefs (for example, about the importance of learner-centred education) may not coincide with another teacher's beliefs in more teacher-centred methods; or where your perceptions about your subject's status may differ from those of teachers of other subjects.

For further reading, you should look at publications arising from the *VITAE* project (Day et al., 2006), a four-year study of variations in teachers' work and lives and their effects on students (Universities of Nottingham and London); and the *Teacher Status Project* (Hargreaves et al., 2007), a national four-year study of the status of teachers and teaching profession in England, carried out by researchers at the Universities of Cambridge and Leicester, between 2002 and 2006.

Self-awareness

Rogers noted that, 'if I can form a helping relationship to myself – if I can be sensitively aware of and acceptant towards my own feelings – then the likelihood is great that I can form a helping relationship toward another' (1967: 57). Developing your self-awareness is therefore an essential tool for teachers and is central to developing your reflective practice. At this early stage let us think about the **reflexive** practitioner as the teacher who is attentive to himself or herself in practice.

Activity 1.2 Developing your self-awareness as a new teacher

This is an individual/small group activity.

a) You are very new to the teaching profession.

 After some very early experiences in the classroom, think about your answers to the questions below. Then share your thoughts with other beginning teachers after attempting to answer the following questions:

 - What kind of status does teaching have?

 - What does it mean to you, personally, to take on the mantle of 'teacher'?

 - What public images are there of teachers with which you can identify?

 - How might new teachers begin to combine their personal and professional identities? (Accept that, for some, this might be experienced as the inability to be oneself.)

 - What is your overall philosophy of teaching and learning?

 - What assumptions (implicit or explicit) about the nature of students' learning are inherent in your approaches to teaching?

b) Try to return to the final two questions in three and, then, six months' time and answer them again.

- What changes to your philosophy and your assumptions have taken place?
- Specifically, have there been any changes to your general approach to teaching and learning, for example, in terms of you 'reaching out' to *all* the students in your classes?

To begin developing your self-awareness, try using metaphors in your *story-telling* about your teaching experiences, or in your journal writing. You could start this with a sentence which begins, 'Teaching is like … '.

Francis provides examples from her beginning teachers' reflective journals which illustrate the mismatch for some, between their espoused theories of practice and their choice of metaphor. Here is one from a beginning teacher who claimed to have adopted a constructivist approach to teaching and learning:

I see myself as a teacher who is like the current flowing through an electric circuit. Each student causes a resistance and a subsequent withdrawal of energy from the teacher … The source of energy which the teacher relies on eventually runs down and needs to be recharged if the light bulbs are to continue to glow brightly … (Francis, 1995: 238).

The flow, or movement, metaphor used here is clearly at odds with notions of constructivism. Thus, by forming such metaphors, beginning teachers can become more aware and be helped to examine any inconsistencies between their teaching beliefs and their actual practice.

Some beginning teachers struggle to understand teaching and to know how to work in realistic ways. Schools, as workplaces, often provide complex contexts that can produce confusion and stress. They can generate, very quickly, feelings of vulnerability. There is an urgent need for you to learn about self and how to best engage with your students and their difficulties and there will be many questions about the precise role of schools, for example within multicultural communities. Activities (such as 1.2) can provide a bridge between feelings and realities, and can open up questions about difficult experiences. This is reflective practice. The place of emotional intelligence is as important in teacher education as it is in student learning. To read more on this concept of emotional intelligence also go to www.funderstanding.com/eq.cfm.

The following exercise grows out of the work of Luft and Ingham in the 1950s. They created the *Jo-Hari Window* for their work on group processes (1963). The Jo-Hari Window is a technique that allows people to understand themselves better, and to learn more about themselves from feedback given by other people and from the types of information communicated to others. It is a four-section

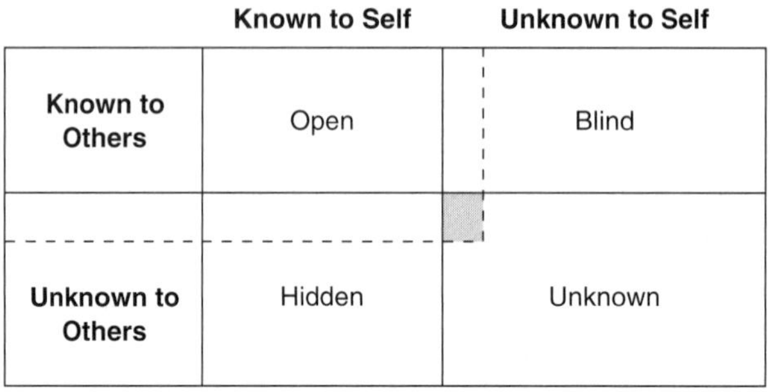

	Known to Self	Unknown to Self
Known to Others	Open	Blind
Unknown to Others	Hidden	Unknown

(Figure based on the original work on
group processes of Luft and Ingham 1963)

Figure 1.2 The Jo-Hari Window

window that helps the person to map out different aspects of the self in the following categories (Figure 1.2).

The first area in Figure 1.2 is the *open* area. These are the things both you and others know about you; these are public and are also obvious to you. Where there is a lot of feedback from others, together with sharing with others, this window would be large in proportion to the other three areas.

The second area is the *blind* area. These are things that others know about you, but things of which you may not be aware. The blind area can be reduced by asking others for more feedback.

The third area is the *hidden* area. These are things that you know about yourself, but that others do not know about you. The hidden area can be reduced by letting others know more about your self.

The fourth area is the *unknown* area. Neither you nor others are aware of these things here. Some things in an unknown area can be reached by offering more feedback or providing for more disclosure among people; group interaction often brings up old memories and experiences that were forgotten. However, there will always be some unknown and secret area of our selves.

Activity 1.3a   Representing your Jo-Hari Window

This part is an individual activity.

a) On paper, create an intuitive map of your own Jo-Hari Window. Arrange the squares as they appear in Figure 1.2, but adjust their actual sizes once you have explored part (b).

b) Think about yourself and ask yourself if you have a large open (public) area or hidden area. Give some general proportions to your own window, and consider what it indicates about the public and private aspects of your life.

If you have a large *unknown* area, this clearly offers you the least potential for self awareness, since you may not be accustomed to much interaction about yourself with others. Conversely, a large *open (public)* area offers great potential for self-awareness that is based on your open sharing and receiving feedback that has happened in the past.

Activity 1.3b   Examining your Jo-Hari Windows

This is best carried out with some beginning teachers who tried Activity 1.3a.

Work with at least two, but not more than five peers.

a) First, have a look at the four types of personality types listed below, which reveal themselves when working within a group.

Open area: *Open and attentive* (that is, gives and takes feedback)
Blind area: *Bull-in-a-china shop* (that is, gives, but does not take feedback)
Hidden area: *Interviewer* (that is, takes, but does not give feedback)
Unknown area: *Ostrich* (that is, does not give or take feedback).

A personality type is represented by each window (as shown in Activity 1.3a). Some people characterize each area as a set of *attitudes* that will show up when a group is interacting.

b) Referring to your own representation of the *size* of each of your windows (based on Activity 1.3a), work out the degree to which *you* are capable of exhibiting each one of these four types of personality. Share your thoughts with others in the peer group.

c) This should follow any further group discussion. On your own, you should try to explore the degree to which you are willing to know and learn things about yourself from others. Distinguish between your willingness to learn from *giving* feedback, and your willingness to learn from *asking for* feedback. Consider the importance of the intention behind feedback (here, sharing information for a professional learning process), and how it can be done directly, honestly, and as concretely as possible. Remember, too, that feedback is not final and absolute. Further feedback can always be sought later as part of your developmental learning process.

This initial representation of your framework of windows is not static. The general proportions of your windows are likely to change with time, depending upon your actions. As you share more information with people, both the *hidden* and *unknown* areas should decrease. As you receive more feedback from people, the *blind* and *unknown* areas should decrease. The shaded area in Figure 1.2 represents the uncovered creative potential that you have. The aim would be to reveal as much of this as possible through self-disclosure and feedback from others.

It is worth noting at this point that the person-centred approach of Rogers (1980) has been very influential in education. His focus on the development of the learner led to a model of learning that places the learner at the centre of the learning and teaching process. The role of the teacher in this approach is to facilitate learning.

Reflective practice in workplace learning

Notions of reflection and reflective practice are now well established in a number of areas of professional education. As has been demonstrated already in this chapter, reflective practice is essential in the capacity to integrate and make sense of the ongoing story of self in the face of the many images of the profession today.

Schön (1983) saw the risk that reflection-in-action could become stale and routinized and argued that *reflection–on-action* prevents this by revisiting previous judgements in a more analytical way designed to make hidden knowledge more explicit. It also allows for more deliberative judgement after the event: decisions (in your teaching) that were made quickly, in the heat of the moment, are revisited, and a wider range of options and theories can be considered.

Reflective practice has been readily accepted since the late 1980s because it provides for an individualistic view of learning and provides a useful framing device to help conceptualize some important processes in professional learning. The use of *individual action planning* involves a systematic *review* process with another, more experienced teacher, and ends with some agreed *plan* and target-setting (Figure 1.3). It is a formal structured process which can provide the time needed for reflective practice. It forms the basis of our own initial teacher education course. It also forms the basis of termly review meetings with the induction tutor that you should encounter during your first year of teaching (induction year) in England. The Career Entry and Development Profile which you will assemble at the end of your training year is in effect an Exit Action Plan ready for your first year of teaching (TTA, 2003).

In the 2000s, there is a questioning of the nature of professional practice, and in turn of the types of education and training that support developing professional practice. Dreyfus and Dreyfus (2005) provide a description of the several stages they have identified through which someone moves from being unfamiliar to

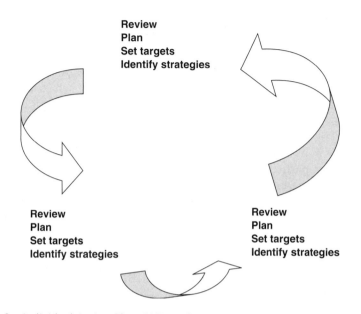

Review
Plan
Set targets
Identify strategies

Review
Plan
Set targets
Identify strategies

Review
Plan
Set targets
Identify strategies

Figure 1.3   Individual Action Plan (IAP) cycle

becoming an experienced practitioner. Some professional educators now wish to view reflection within the context of those settings that have more orientation towards a group, or a team of professionals. Think how you might collaborate with other staff inside a classroom, inside the whole school, or between staff, parents and other professionals in the community. For example, where students with 'special needs' are in regular classrooms, the regular teacher can begin to consider with these other staff (teaching assistants, support staff or other adults) how effective the system of individualized support for these children is in practice in this classroom.

As the contexts for professional practice change, teachers will rarely work alone. New teachers will be expected to be part of collective decision-making rather than making autonomous decisions in the classroom. New teachers will also be expected to work as part of an inter-dependent group of people, often containing participants from different professions or occupations. Cressey and Boud (2006) have described the particular concept of *productive reflection*. They argue that, on the basis of insights into what happened previously, productive reflection leads to interventions into work activity that change what is happening. In other words productive reflection leads to *organizational* as well as individual action.

In teaching, therefore, not only do professional practices change, as we shall see when working with other adults in classrooms, but also the professional identities of the partners in such settings are subject to change. As our professional identity shifts, we might also begin to regard our own students as involved in the co-construction of knowledge about themselves and their own situation within the developing *personalized learning agenda* in education today. (See Chapters 3 and 4 for more on personalized and student-centred learning.)

In conclusion, as teachers in the next decade you will find yourselves increasingly working in mixed settings that change over time, and in groups that form and re-form for particular purposes related not only to the school but other organizational settings. These groups will require you to be able to work collegially with others, not simply as multidisciplinary groups but as groups that cut across traditional disciplines in an attempt to place children and young people at the very heart of everyone's practice.

DEVELOPING THE SKILLS AND ATTRIBUTES OF A REFLECTIVE PRACTITIONER

This section explores in more detail the practical aspects of reflective practice. The five core competences thought necessary for good practice as a reflective practitioner are presented in turn: observation, communication, judgement, decision-making, teamworking. All are important professional competences and are applicable to *all* stages of teacher learning, including initial teacher education.

Observation

The skills of observation take account of noticing your own feelings and behaviours (see also the section, 'Self-awareness', in this chapter), and include *noticing, marking and recording* in order to distinguish some *thing* from its surroundings. You can find numerous practical exercises for developing these skills, designed for both individual and small group work, in Chapter 2 of Mason's book (2002) *Researching Your Own Practice*.

Noticing involves recording brief but vivid details which allow you to recognize the situation for itself. There are various ways in which you might do this: through writing, drawing, or video- and audio-recording, and even photographing an artefact or product of your teaching. As Mason writes,

> so all that is needed at first is a few words, literally two or three, enough to enable re-entry, to trigger recollection. Then the incident can be described to others *from* that memory, together with any significant further detail that may be needed. Brevity and vividness are what make descriptions of incidents recognisable to others. (2002: 51, italics represent original emphasis)

In learning how to teach, the noticing and recording of *critical moments* can be helpful in relation to developing the skills of reflective practice. Some practical suggestions are given in Activity 1.4 for you to try. One method may be more appealing to you than another. Try a few ways and then stick to ones that you enjoy and find useful.

Activity 1.4   An autobiographical approach: noticing and recording your critical moments

Try this activity on your own.

a) Describe a brief and vivid significant moment from your new life in teaching and learning your subject. Most people tend to record critical moments that are negative incidents. You don't have to choose one of these.

b) If you plan to keep a *learning journal* the following guidance might be helpful to you. A *diary, a blog or electronic discussion forum* might also be used to contain isolated fragments of critical incidents.

When first asked to keep *personal accounts in a journal*, there are three standard formats that you might employ, in various mixtures and levels of detail:

• *Critical moments summarized in a few, rather generalized words*

Remember, if you make a general summary, you might quickly lose contact with the incident itself. All that remains are generalities. Find a way to follow this up in a more detailed *oral* description to someone else.

• *Critical moments recounted in detail, including actions, feelings, thoughts*

Be wary, however, that excessive details, with attempts to justify or explain what actually happened, can block your further development. You should try to record immediate 'trains of thought'.

• *Critical moments recorded as conversations*

If you record dialogues, you may be replaying 'talk in the head' after the event, often over and over. Bear in mind that there may be other important details to add, such as gestures, postures and tones of voice.

One frequently used activity in teacher training programmes to encourage reflection is the use of reflective writing assignments. These allow you to draw from and enlarge upon examples of the critical moments which you might have recorded in your journal or diary. Sometimes these reflective assignments might involve the writing and analysing of a *teaching case*. You could be asked to identify a dilemma you are experiencing in the classroom and write a narrative or story about this event or situation. Its intention is to help you highlight the complexity of problem-solving and decision-making in learning and teaching. It also provides a way of observing and analysing your own teaching, rather than relying on relatively infrequent observations by others. Another purpose is to help you uncover beliefs and assumptions about teaching.

Written case study accounts such as these might then be shared with others through a *case conference*. This allows collaborative analysis and discussion of *the case*. A group of beginning teachers reflects together on the embedded dilemmas, identifies the range of possible solutions and, in so doing, each can relate another's case to their own teaching experience. There is some research evidence (Lundeberg and Scheurman, 1997) to show that beginning teachers do benefit from a second reading of a case analysis in that it helps them connect theoretical knowledge with practice.

Another possibility is for you to stop a moment and step into another person's shoes (for example, a student, parent, social worker) and consider how that person's perspective might be different from your own. What differences might there be? How does knowing about the differences change your own perspective on a situation or event? In this way you can start to consider the role of race, class, ethnicity and gender with regard to teaching dilemmas.

To encourage critical reflection you might identify two students on whom to focus your reflection – one for whom the lesson and being in school is a positive experience; one for whom the lesson content and being in school is a problem. In addition, one of the students could be of a gender, race or culture that is different from your own. Each student can then 'sit on your shoulder' and 'whisper' what went well and what did not.

You will find it helpful to audit your strengths and areas for further development from time to time during the training year. Such self-observation can be supported by systems such as the strengths, weaknesses, opportunities and threats (SWOT) analysis or sentence completion – see Activities 1.5a and 1.5b for frameworks to support these approaches.

Activity 1.5a   Assessing your strengths, weaknesses, opportunities and threats (SWOT analysis)

This is an individual activity. Conduct a SWOT analysis for your own professional development.

a) Arrange on paper a table of four cells, labelling each as:

(S) STRENGTH	(W) WEAKNESSES
(O) OPPORTUNITIES	(T) THREATS

You can do this analysis using bullet points to provide the key information. Within each cell, try to identify at least one critical moment which has, in turn, provided you with evidence for your judgement. This activity also provides opportunities:

- to make explicit *to yourself* how you perceive your current state of preparation for the teaching to be done, with your goals, aims, desires and so on

- for your self-assessment of the level of support and possible courses of action of which you are aware.

You will express your frustrations as well as noting things that appear to be hindering your progress.

Activity 1.5b   Assessing your likes, hopes and fears using sentence completion

Part (a) is an individual activity. Part (b) can contribute to a discussion with a mentor or peer.

a) Complete a sentence for each of the sentence stems below:

What I most like to do (in my work) is ....

My biggest difficulties (in my work) involve ....

My greatest successes (in my work) are ....

My greatest pleasures (in my work) are ....

My greatest strengths (in my work) are ....

My biggest weaknesses (in my work) are ....

b) You will need to be prepared *to share the evidence* you have that underpins each of your completed statements (remember, these are your judgements). Think of particular critical moments that will have provided you with evidence, insights and feelings that gave rise to your completed sentence.

Once you have made your own judgements and selected the evidence on which you have based these, you need to conduct a reality check with a teaching colleague or your mentor. For example you could ask them to complete the same sentences in order to indicate their judgements about *your* progress. You can then compare how your perceptions of your own progress actually match another's perceptions of your work.

Finally, do ask yourself if you might be setting yourself too high a standard for 'good enough work' at this stage of your teaching career. Any gap between your current state and your personal and professional goals does provide the *window of opportunity* for further development. That gap needs to be wide enough to be sufficiently disturbing that you want to do something about it. However it should not be so wide that it feels impossible to achieve.

Communication

Your communication skills in relation to reflective practice can be developed in a variety of ways: through the keeping of a personal learning journal or diary, or through a more formal professional portfolio, supported by a system of formal tutorials with a mentor.

Learning journal, diary or professional portfolio

Since critical reflection on practice is an active and conscious process (see Schön, 1983; 1987; 1991), you can start by asking yourself a series of open questions about a particular teaching episode or a critical incident within that episode, and jotting down your impressions using one of these ways of recording:

- What have I been doing?/What am I doing?
- What has happened?/What is happening?
- What led up to this?
- And why?

By doing this regularly you will be helped to reflect on and learn more about your practice. By sharing some of your reflections with others, you will learn more about yourself and your practice, your strengths and your limitations.

As we have noted already, reflection can also be a *critical activity*. If you ask yourself, 'How do I improve my practice?' you are actually questioning what you do, how you currently do things and the value of what you are doing. Asking a fundamental question like this will assist you in thinking more critically about why a particular practice of yours is a success (or a failure, or something in between). Remember that *being critical* is not a negative activity. It is about trying to see things differently and doing alternative things.

Formal tutorials with a mentor or university tutor

A key issue for a mentor, working in ITE, is how they can develop the beginning teacher's expertise in engaging in *reflective conversations* in more structured ways. The **General Teaching Council in England (GTCE)** has referred more broadly to the role of the *learning conversation* in bringing about teacher development, claiming that it can 'encourage access to a diverse range of opportunities and activities ... It is designed so that all teachers through performance management review and in other ways, may choose a route that matches their professional needs' (2004: 8).

We have seen that, through engaging with Activities 1.4 and 1.5, there is the opportunity for a follow-up dialogue to assist reflection on practice. Activity 1.4, with its focus on critical moments or critical incidents, provides a route in which professional development can be supported through a reflective conversation with a teacher, or mentor, who has a good working knowledge of the contexts or situations in which the described event has taken place. For Activities 1.5a and 1.5b, the dialogues might be more general and based on more open-ended questions such as 'How far are these observations ... about what actually happened? ... about your personal feelings? ... about your personal and professional identities?'

A reflective conversation is therefore a process of bringing improvement forward. Crucially, it is the *quality of the conversation* that is important and so you and your mentor might need some structure for the best use of this conversation time. A 30-minute review meeting might be arranged along the following lines.

Guidelines for a structured reflective conversation with a mentor

- Look back and review significant features in a recent critical moment or event.
- Share some of your remarks in your own records of practice such as your learning journal, or diary.
- Celebrate some recent success.
- Identify one thing that you could still improve whatever your level of achievement.
- Decide together how best to bring the further improvement forward.
- Agree more precisely your next step.
- End by setting a date for your next review meeting.
- Aim to keep your own brief record of the conversation and the main agreed targets.

All learning conversations are two-way dialogues where meaning is being constantly negotiated by both participants. At best they become learning and teaching situations for both parties. Sometimes, for the beginning teacher, the dialogue can be potentially both supportive and threatening since the power relations with the mentor may be imbalanced. Beginning teachers often feel that they would like more opportunities to explain their views and perceptions of a lesson, and that they prefer the tutor's feedback to be constructive, and delivered in a friendly, supportive and encouraging way, rather than in a more challenging way. The dialogue will quickly close down if they feel powerless to intervene.

Tutor interventions may be thought of as either *directive* or *non-directive*. Table 1.1 illustrates these categories further. It can be a useful reflective exercise for mentors, occasionally, to record on tape or digital recorder (with your permission) their dialogues with you. This will allow them listen to recordings analytically, to ask to what extent the beginning teacher has been given a chance to make their own views known and to explore any other agendas of their own. In other words, reflection on practice is important for teacher educators too.

Although it is clear that different interventions can be used at different times and for different purposes, the *catalytic* category (see Table 1.1) has been shown to be crucial for professional learning. Heron suggests that 'it is the linchpin of any practitioner service that sees itself as fundamentally educational' (1990: 8).

Judgement

In order to analyse a classroom event or situation, we should try to be absolutely clear what that event or situation consists of. If we, too, are involved in that event or situation then this view of the event needs to be impartial. This is a difficult process – to see ourselves as others see us. Remember also, that we often see in others what we dislike in ourselves.

Just describing what happens during the event can be problematic as well. We might, rather skilfully, combine details of the event with our judgement, or with additional explanations and theories. It would then be difficult for another person to begin to discuss our analysis and say whether they agree with the analysis, or not. Mason (2002: 40) has helpfully distinguished between an account *of* a situation and an account *for* it. Thus, if we wish to *account for* an occurrence, and particularly if we expect another teacher to agree with our analysis, we must first explain precisely the thing that we are trying to analyse (the *account of*). By doing this we can begin to recognize that when we give an *account for*, we are also giving a justification, a value judgement, a criticism, or an attempt at an explanation.

Accounting for means, first, asking 'why' and, second, providing an inter-pretation. Mason draws on an example from Tripp (1993: 18) and this note from Tripp's reflective diary, kept as a practising teacher, is useful to include here:

> 'John didn't finish his work today. Must see he learns to complete what he has begun.'

What are the possible answers if we begin to ask why John is apparently not finishing his work today? That first sentence might have to be rewritten,

> 'John finished work on parts one and three whereas most others worked on parts one through seven; John was still working on part three when I stopped them working' (Mason, 2002: 42).

The crucial issue in the account above is about what constitutes 'finishing work'. Mason argues that, by asking further questions about how students see classroom tasks, and by thinking about the student experience of engaging in the given task (as opposed to the teacher's perceptions), then we are more likely to find out about the personal circumstances for a student such as John before we label him as a 'non-finisher'. Tripp (1993: 19) suggests asking the following line of questions:

- Why did John not finish his work?
- Why should he finish it?
- What was his view of the tasks demanded of him?
- Are the tasks of the right kind, quality, and quantity?

Table 1.1 Types of (A) directive and (B) non-directive tutor interventions

(A) Types of directive intervention	Its purpose	Example of tutor intervention
Prescriptive (telling)	Directly informs beginning teacher about what to do; gives instructions or suggestions	'When you want the class to measure out the chemicals accurately, stop the class work. Ask them to watch you do a demonstration, focus on the careful use of the dropping pipette and use of the measuring cylinder … That is why I asked you, "What are you trying to achieve?" If it is the development of the practical skill of measuring accurately, ask them to count how many drops they use to get 10 ml. of water into the measuring cylinder.'
Informative	Provides information to the beginning teacher	'A double lesson is crucial for conducting some practical activities; you wouldn't be able to get the class to do these otherwise.'
Confrontive	Challenges beliefs or behaviour of the beginning teacher; asks for a re-evaluation of some action	'I observed one task throughout that part of the lesson. It was just "question and answer", and it went on too long. I was expecting something else. What else could you have done on your plan to help bring about deeper learning?'

(Continued)

Table 1.1   *(Continued)*

(B) Types of non-directive intervention	Its purpose	Example of tutor intervention
Cathartic	Allows the beginning teacher a chance to express thoughts and feelings	'You let me see the lesson plans for that class for the whole week. You had some broad aims for the whole set of lessons. Some things did happen differently in the lessons. How do you feel now you have taught these lessons?'
Catalytic	Helps the beginning teacher become more self-aware and reflective	'We have agreed that managing behaviour in a practical lesson is very important. Is there anything else you could have tried, in terms of control?
		What were some of the students doing while the others were taking the measurements? Did you notice, at each workbench, what was happening?'
Supportive	Tries to boost beginning teacher's confidence by focusing on what they did well	'I have noticed some crucial things in the lessons this week. You have dealt very well with some students when they give you certain answers. Shall we try together to summarize what was working so well?'

Source: adapted from Heron, 1990

Activity 1.6   Developing your skills of judgement

This can be carried out with a small group of your peers (maximum, three).

a)   Each chooses a recent segment of their teaching (such as the one about *John*, described on p. 28).

Use the prompts or questions given in columns one and two of Table 1.2. These will allow you to focus on the events that might have led up to the situation (before or during the lesson), to think about the judgements and actions you had to make or take, and to note what happened afterwards in any discussions about the situation.

Write in the third (blank) column of Table 1.2 your answers to the key questions given in column two.

b) Join two other beginning teachers and, in turn, share what each of you has written. While one speaks (*Talker*), one other can use appropriate prompts to elicit meanings and thoughts which underpin your writing (*Critical Friend*). The third should keep brief notes of the key discussion points (*Observer-Scribe*) and share these for further discussion after all three have taken each role.

c) Plenary. In your trio, draw some conclusions about the process you have just engaged in:

- How far were the conversations about 'what happened'?

- How far were the conversations about 'feelings' and emotional reactions?

- How far were the conversations about teacher identity and the extent to which you were able to distinguish between your personal and your professional identities in this situation?

Table 1.2   Some key questions for 'Learning Conversations'

Area for exploration in a learning conversation	Key questions(for you to use to critically reflect with peers; or for your mentor to use to help your critical reflection on practice)	Your answers
Stimulus	What led you to make this judgement? What went on beforehand?	
Responsibility	Who made (or did not make) the judgement? Was it you, or was it made by a group?	
Ethical Issues	How far was your judgement made in someone's best interest? Did you take steps to safeguard their privacy, or gain their informed consent to share information?	
Information	To what extent was your judgement based on sound and valid data or information?	
Consequences	How far were the consequences of your judgement justified?	
Consensus	To what extent was there agreement on your judgement? Or was there disagreement, or conflict?	

Skills of decision-making

It is important to think about how you make sense of your learners and classrooms events. From a constructivist point of view Uhlenbeck et al. described teacher learning as 'organizing and reorganizing, structuring and restructuring a teacher's understanding of practice. Teachers are viewed as learners who actively construct knowledge by interpreting events on the basis of existing knowledge, beliefs and dispositions' (2002: 243).

There are, as we have noted already, several types of activities that can encourage reflective practice: reflective writing assignments form one of these. Another involves the writing and analysis of a *teaching case* (see earlier in Chapter 1). These, as we have discussed, has the potential to exert tremendous influence on your perceptions of teaching and learning. The following analysis is taken from a research study (Alger, 2006) in which the author classified six types of classroom-based *case* presented by her beginning teachers, and concerned with behaviour management in the classroom. The solutions which the beginning teachers described in their cases were categorized as follows: 'teacher behaviours for seeking compliance' (28); 'curricular and pedagogical solutions for gaining student compliance' (15); 'help-seeking strategies to gain student compliance' (8); and one 'other'. Table 1.3 provides examples of the sorts of solutions offered by beginning teachers. They are grouped into three columns which illustrate particular types of teacher behaviours: (1) telling; (2) talking with; and (3) managing /providing behaviour strategies.

The author followed up her analyses with interviews with these beginning teachers at the end of the year, in order to track the development of their reflection over time. The beginning teachers were asked to reframe, or restate, the original behaviour management problem they had described, and re-evaluate the strategies they had tried in order to solve the problem. She found that these beginning teachers' understanding of the solutions to the problems (that is, the way they made their decisions) had changed substantially, as did their nuances of the dilemmas. There were shifts:

- away from *behaviourist* approaches
- towards greater *relationship building*
- involving greater use of *effective classroom strategies* to manage behaviour.

You will find more discussion on behaviourist approaches in Chapter 2.

For many of the beginning teachers in Alger's study reflection was a two-step process. The first step occurred at the planning stage when, for example, they tried to *visualize the lesson* based on the plan, asking themselves,

Table 1.3 Classroom 'cases': types of solutions offered by beginning teachers to their dilemmas of practice

Teacher behaviours (to gain student compliance)	Curricular/pedagogical solutions (to gain student compliance)	Help-seeking solutions (for gaining student compliance)
Telling Tell learner Warn/threaten	*Telling* Give additional instructions Give more time to finish	*Telling* Contact parent/carer
Talking with Talk with learner Negotiate	*Talking with* Explain relevance of content	*Talking with* Meet with learner and senior member of staff
Managing/providing behaviour strategies Move closer Ignore Give detention Keep back after class Loss of 'good behaviour' points Make example of learner Refer to another member of staff	*Managing/providing behaviour strategies* Separate learner Place learner with motivated others Give learner responsibility for leadership in task	*Managing /providing behaviour strategies* Talk with Special Needs Co-ordinator

Source: (adapted from Alger, 2006: 292)

'What might work, what might not?' This process clearly involves drawing on previous teaching episodes to speculate on the effectiveness of the lesson plan in question. This is a form of reflection. A second step took place after the teaching, by asking oneself, 'What went well; what did not go so well?' This reflection might involve a mental review only, or recording in note form the evaluation, with further ideas for changes that might be made on the next occasion.

Thus, these types of reflective practice strategies are important in that they should allow you to see, and cope better with, the complexities of teaching and you make decisions for further actions. In addition the reflective practice itself is helped, through case analysis, to promote analysis and evaluation at a deeper level. The approach taken by Alger allows reflective practice to be both *deliberate and intentional*. Its power, as with other reflective practice strategies, hinges on the support provided by a mentor to help you probe the strengths and weaknesses of a lesson more deeply through dialogue and critical reflection on practice.

Teamworking

We know, increasingly, that schools as institutions and the individuals within them have to be flexible to respond to rapid paces of changes. Etienne Wenger, a socio-cultural theorist, focused on notions of networking in the workplace and developed a key concept with Jean Lave – **communities of practice** (Lave and Wenger, 1991; Wenger, 1998). As we have noted in an earlier section of this chapter on workplace learning, we can no longer think about a teacher or a school existing in isolation. For more on this see Chapters 6 and 7 and the discussion on emerging agendas in schools and their communities in connection with the national policy of *Every Child Matters*.

It is now recognized that professional expertise has to be networked, integrated or joined up. You will find yourself working in a number of teams from the start of your teaching career: your subject or curriculum team, your pastoral team and cross-curricular groups working on particular issues such as personalized learning and aspects of assessment, and so on. The following sub-sections introduce you briefly to some collaborative ways of working in schools.

Co-teaching

This way of working provides experiences which revolve around collaboration and the sharing of ideas and perspectives on practice to help in the reframing of earlier ideas (Schön, 1983). Co-teaching provides two teachers (mentor and beginning teacher; two beginning teachers) with access to possibilities for learning that are not so likely when working alone. This can have the advantage of providing a safer haven for more risk-taking and experimentation, such as introducing new types of practical activities into a science lesson; managing a role play; taking students for out-of-classroom activities. As Loughran has written, 'collaboration and teaming in ways that provide professional support for one another leads to improvements in practice as the sharing with, and learning from, one another offers meaningful ways of framing and reframing existing practice' (2006: 57). In other words all partners, experienced and inexperienced, can benefit. Co-teaching offers the opportunity to ask much of your partner:

- What is the purpose of this teaching session?
- How does what we do today link with last week's lesson?
- Why are you choosing to use that teaching strategy with this class?

Questioning one's own learning or thinking about one's own thinking is a form of **meta-cognition** (see Chapter 2). Co-teaching provides a vehicle for becoming more aware of one's thoughts and actions that influence the development of understanding of a situation. It also offers the possibility of insights into teaching and learning which might be very different from just being told what to do and how to think.

Collaborative practitioner enquiry

Enquiry is the response we make to a desire to find something out. Kelly (2006) has argued that teachers who identify closely with instrumental practices are likely to have **cognitivist** views of expertise and learning. In contrast, teachers with more reflective and discursive identities may, through an ongoing conversation with their practice, adopt stances which respond to their learners' difficulties, and seek to collaborate with learners and colleagues. They *look for ways forward* in professional guidance and through research, using their learners and colleagues as starting points in their enquiry, and adopting complex measures of success.

There are some parallels here with the ways of conducting *academic research*. These also require systematic enquiry but are done less for oneself and more for reporting to other people so that conclusions can be criticized, challenged or taken up by others. This is a form of constructivism. For any research to be convincing the research questions have to be well formulated (these may be the hypotheses to be tested), and the chosen methodology (types of observations, other types of data collection and methods of analyses) has to conform to accepted standards.

Action research

This way of working tends to fall between 'academic researcher' researching other people and 'teacher practitioner' researching their own actions. **Action research** is an approach that has become widely used in research into education and schooling. It takes several different forms, one of which is systematic enquiry. Often beginning teachers, regular teachers and support staff working together and the enquiry designed to produce practical results which can improve an aspect of, say, learning and teaching. It is a well recognized form of social science research.

Your choice of research topic with colleagues can be affected by your combined interests, values, any funding you have available, and so on. Using descriptive approaches, you might support, observe and study the effects of other people. In some cases you may be the *actor–researchers* using a more analytical approach to make a strategic change in your collective practices. You might start by asking, 'What can we do to improve our practice?' You could then pursue one of the action research routes illustrated in Figures 1.4a and 1.4b.

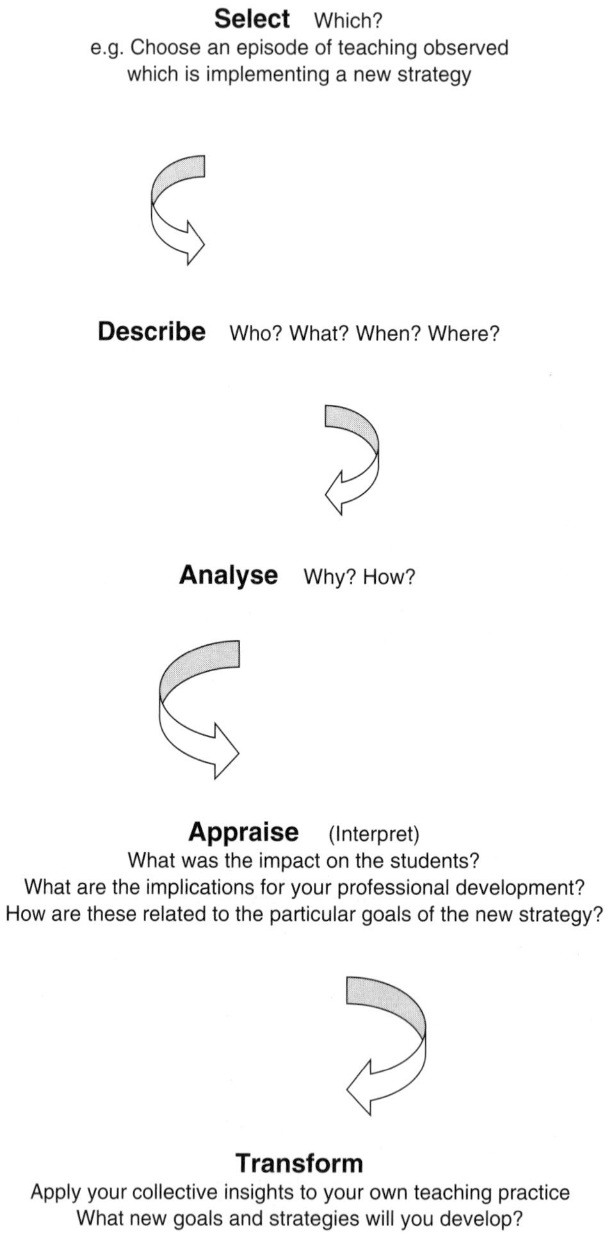

Select Which?
e.g. Choose an episode of teaching observed
which is implementing a new strategy

Describe Who? What? When? Where?

Analyse Why? How?

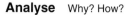

Appraise (Interpret)
What was the impact on the students?
What are the implications for your professional development?
How are these related to the particular goals of the new strategy?

Transform
Apply your collective insights to your own teaching practice
What new goals and strategies will you develop?

Figure 1.4a An evaluative approach to action research (adapted from Levin and Camp, 2005)

You may prefer a more methodical, formal problem-solving sequence.

Pose the problem ⇨   **Propose the method** ⇨

⇨ **Find a solution**   ⇨ **Look back**

Figure 1.4b   A problem-solving approach to action research (based on Polya, 1945)

When you begin to research classrooms and schools in these ways, and small action research activities may start in your training year, you will probably need to read more widely about some of the concepts associated with these ways of researching classrooms. The *Handbook of Action Research* (Reason and Bradbury, 2005) and *Action Research: A Guide for the Teacher Researcher* (Mills, 2000) are good reference books for Master's students. By using action research approaches in these ways we are acknowledging the long-standing value of collaborative approaches to critical reflection on practice (Stenhouse, 1971; 1975) and teacher research in general (Elliott, 1991). Such approaches provide for close partnerships between schools and higher education institutions. On a more cautionary note, Kelly (2006) reminds us of government-led initiatives, such as the Best Practice Research Scholarships (DfEE, 2001; DfES, 2002) through which, he argues, the policy-makers were exploiting the particular purpose of implementing some central policy. With a few exceptions, the wider research outcomes of such practitioner research do reside largely within the target school, and are not generally widely shared elsewhere.

It is also clear that, by enabling teachers and beginning teachers to work alongside each other, we can provide for shared knowledge and collaborative learning. All parties can benefit. Finally, it is possible through ongoing initiatives for all teachers in their professional development to provide forms of support to develop teacher identities that are more rooted in reflective, discursive, collaborative ways of working, and which allow teachers to be more deliberate in their actions in their working lives.

REFLECTION AS A CRITICAL ACTIVITY

One of the serious pitfalls with the idea of reflective practice is that it has tended to become a catch-all term. The terms *reflection* and *reflective practice* are now seriously overused buzzwords, and are likely to mean different things to different people. Zeichner, in 1994, was already pointing out the separate and distinct interpretations of reflective practice, only some of which could be called *critical*.

The process of reflection can be in danger of reductionism – to a set of procedures; a skill to be learned. So far this chapter has tried to show what reflective practice can look like, but with a caution that it should not be reduced to some standardized competence. If that were the case, reflection would become an end in itself.

The questions that must remain are those concerning the purpose or focus of the particular reflection. It is these questions that are important for critical reflection. We have talked about reflection as a habit; one that is deliberative. Reflection and action run together if you wish to change the world around you. Therefore, critical reflection can create the conditions under which you as teacher, or your students as learners, can become more aware of the power of agency and the possibilities for action.

The sorts of questions that can progressively unearth deeper assumptions, illustrate the process of critical reflection on practice. The process is transformative because it focuses on dominant assumptions which may influence our practice unwittingly (Brookfield, 2000: 126). From this perspective, critical reflection on practice enables an understanding of the way (socially dominant) assumptions may be socially restrictive, and has the potential to bring about more empowering ideas and practices. Critical reflection on practice provides a freedom to the individual and to groups to change the operation of the social environment at the level of their personal experiences. The process of critical reflection on practice can be thought of as a two-stage process, moving from changed awareness to changed practice. Activity 1.7 is designed to link with the sort of enquiry or action research approaches you might be using in order to reach M level.

Activity 1.7   Seminar to prepare for an action research project

a) In a seminar setting (5–8 people) each participant brings a description of a piece of their practice for reflection in two stages: a reflective stage, and a clear linking with the next stage with the intention of changing professional practice.

Example A:

Stage 1. How can I help my students improve the quality of their learning?
Stage 2. I would like the improvement to focus on the particular action:

Example B:

Stage 1. How can I respond to pupil diversity in my class?
Stage 2. I will present to the seminar a particular incident in my classroom experience as a new teacher which involved issues of diversity.

b) Group members can help each person reflect on their chosen situation, by using a set of questions, such as selecting from those listed below:

- What does your current practice imply about ...?

- What are you assuming when ...?

- How do you influence the situation through your presence/your perceptions/your interpretations/your assumptions?

- What are your beliefs about power and where do they come from?

- What perspectives are missing?

- What types of language do you use and what do these patterns imply?

- What is your own thinking and what is the result of any power relations (for example, gendered, cultural, structural)?

c) Following this probing and discussion with others, work out in detail how you personally intend to bring about some changes in practice. Use the following example to help you.

To move to the next stage (that is, planning for changes in my practice) I decide to take the following steps through action research:

- Focus on responding to the diversity of student strengths and needs as a teaching concern. I will examine the positive and negative impacts of student diversity on their learning. I will aim to understand better the importance and skill of adapting the curriculum and the learning environment to include every student.

- Develop ideas and skills during teaching practice. I will plan ways of getting to know each student better and of adapting the curriculum to meet their particular needs. I will reflect on the various methods of learning and teaching that I try, and evaluate the impact that these have on the students' learning.

- During the process of implementing and reflecting, I will collect evidence of the effectiveness (or otherwise) of my particular attempts to respond to diversity. I will ask two key questions. How well are all the students engaged in the new lessons? What progress does each student make?

- Critical evaluation using theoretical frameworks. I will access and use wider academic reading on models of teaching and learning and research literature in connection with pupil diversity.

Fook (2000) has shown that, in a social work setting, this process of critical reflection on practice within a deliberatively reflective group structure is one of *critical acceptance*. It is conducted in a climate which balances safety and challenge. It is participatory, non-judgemental, and open to new and other perspectives. It involves the responsibility not to blame, the right to draw limits, and acceptance of multiple contradictory views. It provides a focus on the *story*, not the person, and on the *why*, not the *what to do*. It is non-directive.

Two very accessible texts for you to read further in this somewhat complex area are by Stephen Brookfield (1995) *Becoming a Critically Reflective Teacher*, and Jennifer Moon (2004) *A Handbook of Reflective and Experiential Learning*.

BEING A REFLECTIVE PRACTITIONER: SUMMARY

The notion of the reflective practitioner is an enticing one. It starts with messy, unpredictable practices, unpicks what is going on, generates **inductive hypotheses**, asks for analysis and attempts to reveal more about the nature of expertise within the professional setting and the judgements upon that. It provides an important counterbalance to current emphases in policy making on evidence-based practice, in which certainty and technical rationality are the ideals.

Reflective practice asks us all to weigh up the scientific evidence base against competing versions of events. Thus it can take account of the richness and creativity of our practice and lead to new notions of professionalism based on diversity and flexibility. At its heart is the unsettling of hierarchies (for example, the gendered nature of teaching) and traditional working practices. Loughran refers to this phenomenon as *disturbing practice* and argues persuasively that 'it does not divorce feelings from the actions associated with confrontation or challenge; it creates powerful learning episodes ... Working with colleagues ... (provides the opportunity) of gaining advice and feedback on such episodes and of continuing to push to make the tacit explicit' (2006: 57).

Reflection implies that you can see one thing in another – the external world in your mind and, as such, it provides a powerful metaphor which also deserves a word of caution. It describes and is performative, since the act of reflection can give back some improvement in professional practice (Biggs, 1999) – it may be expected that it leads to action and change. This is a persuasive feature of reflective practice. In addition, professional portfolios can be used as vehicles for the assessment process in professional training and you can position yourself to present your material to make a convincing claim that you (as a professional) are competent. Reflection in this situation might become a self-measurement and provide for self-evaluation against standards or other appropriate performance measures.

In contrast to such highly instrumental practices in professional education there must be deeper forms of reflective practice as well as criticality in learning. These require freedom from the gaze, in the Foucauldian sense, of the institution in which we work (see Foucault, 1980: 155). Thus, research and auto-biographical approaches in professional education do provide the freedom to think more about self in context, personally and socially, and in potentially radical ways. Truly reflective practice involves trust and relative autonomy; schools today are steeped in cultures of accountability and audits, involving measurements (for example, the number of students in school receiving free school meals) and managerialism (for example, through the publicity of league tables of performances). However, in today's rapidly moving society, the reflective practitioner cannot and should not be seen as a practitioner freed of the constraints of the reality in which he or she practises. As Wenger's (1998) approach shows, professional work is influenced by participation and by the fixed and solid environment we all work in.

Very broadly, in workplace learning, professional development becomes the formation of professional identity. It provides a process in which to translate the practices, values and attitudes of the *teacher* (the worker) with those currently part of *teaching* (the profession), and in some situations with the goals and mission of the *school or college* (the organization). However there are additional important words of warning. One of the current difficulties you will encounter with generic statements of professional standards in teaching is that they allow for multiple interpretations of meaning. In addition, the learner (you, the novice teacher) becomes the pre-existing objective within the competence statements. Professional (expert) teachers are presented in such a system as subjects who understand how the learner learns and how to support you as beginning teachers in your learning. If we are not careful, reflection could become simply a self-measurement and self-evaluation against these teaching standards. More than this, the rhetoric of technical expertise, competence and reflective practice is used to promote changes in professional practices and identities in particular ways, and can on occasions be used to identify certain practices and dispositions of the teachers as specifically *professional*.

Therefore in the remaining chapters of this book we anticipate that you will begin to recognize that workplace cultures can be very powerful and may be hidden to you in their operation (see Chapter 2 in Rogers, 2006, for an introduction to the nature of school cultures). The range of tasks we provide in each chapter should allow you to examine some of the assumptions implicit in all sorts of professional practices that you will encounter in your training year. By the end of the year you should have a better understanding of what we might mean by a *teaching profession*, what we might mean by *professionalism* in teaching, and the range of *professional values*. In this way you can be helped to recognize the particular professional values and practices that are within the Initial Teacher Training (ITT) Standards, discover for yourself what these might mean for you, and in turn make your own links to the GTCE Code of Professional Practice. Overall this book is designed to support what Yinger

(1990) has described as the 'the ongoing conversation of practice' in which you are beginning to participate.

REFERENCES

Alger, C. (2006) '"What went well, what didn't go so well": growth of reflection in pre-service teachers', *Reflective Practice*, 7(3): 287–301.

Argyris, C. and Schön, D. (1975) *Theory into Practice: Increasing Professional Effectiveness.* San Francisco, CA: Jossey-Bass.

Biggs, J. (1999) *Teaching for Quality Learning at University.* Buckingham: Open University Press.

Brookfield, S.D. (1987) *Developing Critical Thinkers: Challenging Adults to Explore Alternative Ways of Thinking and Acting.* Milton Keynes: SRHE/Open University Press.

Brookfield, S.D. (1995) *Becoming a Critically Reflective Teacher.* San Francisco, CA: Jossey-Bass.

Brookfield, S.D. (2000) 'Transformative learning as ideology critique', in J. Mezirow (ed.), *Learning as Transformation.* San Francisco, CA: Jossey Bass. pp. 125–48.

Carr, W. and Kemmis, S. (1986) *Becoming Critical: Education, Knowledge and Action Research.* Lewes: Falmer/Deakin University Press.

Cooley, C.H. (1902) *Human Nature and Social Order.* New York: Charles Scribner.

Cressey, P. and Boud, D. (2006) 'The emergence of productive reflection', in D. Boud, P., Cressey and P. Docherty (eds), *Productive Reflection at Work: Learning for Changing Organizations.* London: Routledge. pp. 11–26.

Day, C. (1993) 'Reflection: a necessary but not sufficient condition for professional development', *British Educational Research Journal*, 19(1): 83–93.

Day, C., Stobart, G., Sammons, P., Kington, A., Gu, Q., Smees, R. and Mujtaba, T. (2006) *Variations in Teachers' Work, Lives and Effectiveness: VITAE Report (DfES Research Report 743).* London: Department for Education and Skills.

Department for Education and Employment (DfEE) (2001) *Best Practice Research Scholarships.* Nottingham: DfEE publications.

Department for Education and Skills (DfES) (2002) *Best Practice Research Scholarships.* Nottingham: DfES Publications.

Department for Education and Skills (DfES) (2004) *Mentoring and Coaching Capacity Building Project.* London: CUREE/DfES. www.tda.gov.uk/upload/resources/pdf/m/mc_frame work.pdf (accessed 28 June 2007).

Dewey, J. (1910) *How We Think.* London: D.C. Heath.

Dewey, J. (1933) *How We Think: A Re-statement of the Relation of Reflective Thinking in the Educative Process.* Chicago, IL: Henry Regnery.

Dreyfus, H.L. and Dreyfus, S.E. (2005) 'Expertise in real world contexts', *Organization Studies*, 26(5): 779–92.

Elliott, J. (1991) *Action Research for Educational Change.* Milton Keynes: Open University Press.

Fook, J. (2000) *Social Work: Critical Theory and Practice.* London: Sage.

Foucault, M. (1980) *Power/Knowledge: Selected Interviews and Other Writings 1972–1977.* New York: Pantheon.

Francis, D. (1995) 'The reflective journal: a window to preservice teachers' practical knowledge', *Teaching and Teacher Education*, 11(3): 229–41.

General Teaching Council for England (GTCE) (2002) *Code of Professional Values and Practices for Teachers*. London: GTCE.

General Teaching Council for England (GTCE) (2004) *The Learning Conversation. Talking Together for Professional Development*. London: GTCE.

Hargreaves, L., Cunningham, M., Hansen, A., MacIntyre, D., Oliver, C. and Pell, A. (2007) *The Status of Teachers and the Teaching Profession in England: Views from Inside and Outside the Profession. (DfES Research Report 831A)*. London: Department for Education and Skills. www.dfes.gov.uk/research (accessed 28 June 2007).

Harrison, J.K. (2004) 'Encouraging professional autonomy: reflective practice and the beginning teacher', *Education 3–13*, 32(3): 10–18.

Harrison, J.K., Lawson, T. and Wortley, A. (2005) 'Facilitating the professional learning of new teachers through critical reflection on practice during mentoring meetings', *European Journal of Teacher Education*, 28(3): 267–92.

Heron, J. (1990) *Helping the Client: A Creative Practical Guide*. 4th edn. London: Sage Publications.

Holt-Reynolds, D. (2000) 'What does the teacher do? Constructivist pedagogies and prospective teachers' beliefs about the role of a teacher', *Teaching and Teacher Education*, 16: 21–32.

Kelly, P. (2006) 'What is teacher learning? A socio-cultural perspective', *Oxford Review of Education*, 32(4): 505–19.

Kolb, D. (1984) *Experiential Learning: Experience as the Source of Learning and Development*. New York: Prentice Hall.

Lave, J. and Wenger, E. (1991) *Situated Learning – Legitimate Peripheral Participation*. Cambridge: Cambridge University Press.

Levin, B.B. and Camp, J.S. (2005) *Reflection as the Foundation for E-Portfolios*. www.aace. org/conf/site/pt3/paper_3008_455.pdf (accessed 28 June 2007).

Loughran, J. (2006) *Developing a Pedagogy of Teacher Education. Understanding Teaching and Learning about Teaching*. Abingdon: Routledge.

Lundeberg, M. and Scheurman, G. (1997) 'Looking twice means seeing more: developing a pedagogical knowledge through case analysis', *Teaching and Teacher Education*, 13(8): 783–97.

Luft, J. and Ingham, H. (1963) *Group Processes. An Introduction to Group Dynamics*. Palo Alto, CA: National Press Books.

Mason, J. (2002) *Researching Your Own Practice. The Discipline of Noticing*. London: RoutledgeFalmer.

Mills, G.E. (2000) *Action Research: A Guide for the Teacher Researcher*. Engleniod Cliffs, NJ: Prentice Hall.

Moon, J. (2004) *A Handbook of Reflective and Experiential Learning*. London: RoutledgeFalmer.

Nias, J. (1989) *Primary Teachers Talking*. London: Routledge and Kegan Paul.

Pollard, A., with Collins, J., Simco, N., Swaffield, S. and Warwick, P. (2005) *Reflective Teaching*. 2nd edn. London: Continuum.

Polya, G. (1945) *How to Solve It*. Cambridge, MA: Princeton University Press.

Reason, P. and Bradbury, H. (eds) (2005) *A Handbook of Action Research*. London: Sage.

Rogers, B. (2006) *I Get by with a Little Help ... Colleague Support in Schools*. London: Paul Chapman Publishing.

Rogers, C.R. (1967) *A Therapist's View of Psychotherapy*. London: Constable.

Rogers, C.R. (1980) *A Way of Being*. Boston, MA: Houghton Mifflin.

Schön, D.A. (1983) *The Reflective Practitioner. How Professionals Think in Action*. New York: Basic Books.

Schön, D.A. (1987) *Educating the Reflective Practitioner*. San Francisco, CA: Jossey-Bass.

Schön, D.A. (ed.) (1991) *The Reflective Turn: Case studies in and on Educational Practice*. New York: Teachers College Press.

Solomon, J. (1987) 'New thoughts on teacher education', *Oxford Review of Education*, 13(3): 267–74.

Stenhouse, L. (1971) 'The Humanities Curriculum Project: the rationale', *Theory into Practice*, 10: 154–62.

Stenhouse, L. (1975) *An Introduction to Curriculum Research and Development*. London: Heinemann.

Teacher Training Agency (TTA) (2003) *Career Entry and Development Profile*. London: TTA.

Tripp, D. (1993) *Critical Incidents in Teaching: Developing Professional Judgement*. London: Routledge.

Uhlenbeck, A., Verloop, N. and Beijard, D. (2002) 'Requirements for an assessment procedure for beginning teachers: implications from recent theories on teaching and assessment', *Teachers College Record*, 104(2): 242–72.

van Manen, M. (1977) 'Linking ways of knowing with ways of being practical', *Curriculum Inquiry*, 6: 205–28.

Vygotsky, L.S. (1962) *Thought and Language*. Cambridge, MA: MIT Press.

Vygotsky, L.S. (1978) *Mind in Society: The Development of Higher Psychological Processes*. Cambridge, MA: Harvard University Press.

Warin, J., Maddock, M., Pell, A. and Hargreaves, L. (2006) 'Resolving identity dissonance through reflective and reflexive practice in teaching', *Reflective Practice*, 7(2): 231–43.

Weick, K. (1995) *Sensemaking in Organizations*. Thousand Oak, CA: Sage.

Wenger, E, (1998) *Communities of Practice: Learning, Meaning and Identity*. New York: Cambridge University Press.

Yinger, R. (1990) 'The conversation of practice', in R.T. Clift, W.R. Houston and M.C. Pugach (eds), *Encouraging Reflective Practice in Education*. New York: Teachers College Press. pp. 73–96.

Zeichner, K.M. (1994) 'Research on teacher thinking and different views of reflective practice in teaching and teacher education', in I. Carlgren (ed.), *Teachers' Minds and Actions: Research on Teachers' Thinking and Practice*. Bristol, PA: Falmer Press. pp. 9–27.

Zeichner, K.M. and Liston, D. (1996) *Reflective Teaching: An Introduction*. Mahwah, NJ: Lawrence Erlbaum Associates.

2 AN OVERVIEW OF LEARNING
Sue Dymoke

By the end of this chapter you will have :

- been introduced to theories of learning and the key figures who have researched, written and influenced theoretical developments in this field
- reflected on your own experiences as a learner
- explored the implications of learning theories for your classroom.

INTRODUCTION

This chapter considers the nature of learning and learners. It explores theories of learning and the influence of key academic figures including Vygotsky, Bruner and Gardner. It considers debates about the nature of learning including: learning styles; multiple intelligences; accelerated learning and thinking skills and the impact of these debates on classroom practice. This chapter leads you to reflect on your own learning in ways which can inform your developing classroom practice and awareness of the learners with whom you are working.

How do learners learn?

There are many contrasting and complementary theories about the ways in which young people and adults learn. These are constantly refined as new research is carried out and reported on. No single theory to date is able to describe neatly the complexities of the learning process. Learning is not just a discrete, school-based event. It occurs in many different contexts but, as Wood argues, the school environment engenders new and distinct forms of learning: school-based learning includes a series of 'contrived encounters' or 'social interactions that come about as a result of explicit educational goals' (1998: 16). Aspects of many different theoretical perspectives can inform the classroom practices you observe and begin to adopt for yourself during your training. Learning and teaching are, in many respects, closely allied. Successful teachers are those who want to continue learning and to reflect on and refine their practices throughout their careers. In exploring what it means to be a teacher, it is therefore vital for you to consider your own learning processes and what is also understood by the term 'learner'. The learning theories which you are introduced to in this chapter do not represent an exhaustive overview of all of them but they do include those which have influenced educational practices in the past hundred years and are frequently acknowledged within discussions of learning and teaching. Each is outlined in a simplified form. For more detailed information, you should consult the further reading and web links embedded within the activities and the titles on the reading list at the end of this chapter.

AN INTRODUCTION TO THE MAIN LEARNING THEORIES

Learning theories developed in the twentieth century fit into two broad groupings – those concerned with behaviours (how people respond or react to different kinds of stimuli) and those linked with cognition (how people interact with stimuli and construct their own learning).

Behaviourist theories

Behaviourist theories have been developed through observation of how behaviours can change as a direct result of the learning process. **Behaviourism** is concerned with: modelling appropriate behaviours; creating environments that enable or condition students to respond in what are deemed appropriate ways; rewarding positive responses; and learning through repetition. A key figure in this field is Burrhus Frederic Skinner.

Skinner's laboratory-based experiments in the 1960s used small animals, under controlled conditions, and provided them with rewards (reinforcement) for any response that was near to the desired response. Gradually the desired behaviour was brought closer through the controlled use of stimulus–response associations, also known as *shaping*. Skinner extended his conclusions from this experimental work to consider the complex relationship between response and reinforcement in humans. He believed that learning was a process of conditioning centred on responding to particular stimuli and that reinforcement of learning (through use of an intermittently repeated schedule) and rewarding of positive achievements which resulted from this conditioned learning should be at the heart of teaching. Reinforcement made a particular response more likely to reoccur. Skinner (1968) argued that the education system favoured deficit models of teaching which were focused on punishment and exposed a learner's lack of understanding. He claimed that teachers did not shape students' learning effectively, with the result that the learning which did take place was inappropriate or of a temporary nature (see also Wood, 1998). Based on this behaviourist theory, Skinner even went to the extreme of designing teaching machines to provide further evidence to support it in human learning. These machines would break learning down into tiny error-free stages in which the learner would be uncontaminated by contact with the fallible human teacher. They were trialled in some schools but were never fully adopted.

The controlled (some would say rigid) approach to learning favoured by behaviour theorists can lead learners to take a very passive role in their own learning. It is increasingly perceived as presenting a limited view of how people learn as it does not embrace the different situations in which learning can take place or how people learn from new or one-off experiences without reinforcement. Nevertheless, elements of Skinner's research, particularly on the consequences of behaviour, have informed more recent whole-school policies and approaches to classroom behaviour management. For example, you may have already observed other teachers repeatedly using praise and positive feedback during an activity to draw as many students into a discussion as possible, or you might have reinforced previously taught expectations about putting up hands to answer questions or about how your own students should leave the room at the end of a lesson. All of these classroom events draw on aspects of behaviourism.

If you would like to know more about Skinner's research refer to Skinner (1968) and Wood (1998).

Activity 2.1　Repetition in learning

This can be carried out individually or preferably, in discussion with your mentor or another beginning teacher.

a) Try to recall two occasions in your own childhood where you asked to:

- learn something through a process of repetition, reinforcement and reward;

- learn something through participation in a 'one-off' experience.

What precisely did you learn in each case? And what do you remember now? How did you feel about these experiences at the time? How do you feel about them now?

b) Now focus on a specific topic within the subject that you are training to teach. Are there aspects of this topic which might lend themselves to behaviourist repetition and reward strategies? Why do you think these methods might be appropriate? Share your ideas with another beginning teacher in the same subject area or with your mentor. Together, draw up a table with two columns to summarise the major strengths and weaknesses of applying Skinner's approaches to educational material and teaching strategies.

Constructivist theories

Constructivist theories are concerned with the social nature of learning: how learners create their own conceptual structures in order to make sense of the world. **Social constructivism** focuses on the cognitive processes that occur as people learn through social interaction, such as listening to and working with others. The relationship between learner and teacher is a crucial relationship to consider in this regard. These learning theories are often viewed as child centred and progressive. They have informed the development of many classroom practices currently used in schools. Key figures in this field are Jean Piaget, Lev Semonovich Vygotsky and Jerome Bruner.

Jean Piaget was a psychologist. His theories were arrived at through observations of children in which he explored the qualitative development in their ability to solve problems as they reached different levels of maturity. In his view, maturation was the key influence on a child's cognitive development. He defined cognitive development as a sequential process of four phases: sensory-motor (0–2 years); pre-operational (2–7 years); concrete operational (7–12 years) and formal operational (12+ years but not attained by all). He discovered that children's modes of thinking are completely different from those of adults and they have different perceptions of reality. He argued that, as children matured, they became increasingly able to learn from their actions and to interact with other people and their environment. In turn, both of these increasing capabilities had an impact on their developing cognitive processes and their conceptions of reality. Piaget extrapolated universal statements about maturation through application of experimental psychological methods which used individual children as their subjects. His concept of four phases of maturation is now considered to be too fixed and inflexible. The phases do not, for example, acknowledge the possibility of children younger than seven years becoming logical and systematic in their thinking. They are also founded on an assumption that all young people mature at similar rates without regard to the impact of other extenuating factors such as culture, social class or well-being.

Vygotsky disagreed with Piaget's hypothesis that maturation would directly result in the development of higher level thinking skills. His own research on cognition took a different path. Work on language acquisition and development with deaf-blind children led him to conclude that speech preceded thought and, consequently, that language was the most significant factor in cognitive development. Vygotsky coined the term the **zone of proximal development** (ZPD) to define the distance which exists between the actual developmental level of learning and what potentially could be learned through problem-solving with guidance through that zone by a parent, grandparent, sibling, other adult such as a teacher or 'in collaboration with more capable peers' (1978: 86). Not everyone is educable in this way but Vygotsky's work has had a major influence on pedagogy in the latter part of the twentieth century. For examples, see the work of Barnes et al. (1972) and Britton (1974) all of whom applied Vygotsky's theories to classroom contexts and thus developed our understandings of the social functions of discourse, and the nature of co-operative learning. Nevertheless, Vygotsky's influence should still be explored with caution: his early death at the age of 37 meant that his research was under-developed; the English translations of his writings present different emphases. Gillen states that, in becoming fashionable, Vygotsky's research has been over-simplified. She questions why Vygotsky's work on ZPD has been 'so widely applied across pedagogic contexts' (Gillen, 2000: 193) when, in her reading, the original contexts of his research actually focused on assessment of learning and pretence play.

Bruner has been influenced by Vygotsky's work and to some extent by that of Piaget. For Bruner, learning centres on the search for patterns within human communication. Each human is also perceived as having their own distinct cognitive processes which vary according to subject or environment. He is particularly interested in the different processes and patterns which underpin creative problem-solving and the critical role which language plays in the development of understanding. **Scaffolding** is a term closely associated with Bruner. With Wood and Ross he conducted research (Wood et al., 1976) which investigated whether it was possible for teaching/instruction to be sensitive to Vygotsky's ZPD. Could it enable learners to move beyond their current level of competence towards achieving their potential or, conversely, might it underestimate the learner's potential? To explore this question, researchers observed how mothers taught their pre-school children to put together a pyramid of wooden blocks, pegs and holes. They used the metaphor of 'scaffolding' (Wood, 1998: 99) to represent structures (involving child–adult interaction and communication) which are perceived to surround and support a young learner in order to help shape their development to its fullest extent. Wood described the level of support as 'contingent' (1998: 100) in that it is only provided when necessary: the child is never left to struggle alone or, alternatively, given too much help which could stifle their developing independence.

Scaffolding can be seen in use in various classroom strategies where staged and structured support will enable completion of complex tasks. As a child becomes more confident with a specific task, and secure in their learning, the scaffolding can gradually be dismantled and support withdrawn. **Writing frames** are perhaps the most frequently occurring examples of scaffolding. These originated in the work of the Exeter Extending Literacy project (EXEL) (see Wray and Lewis, 1997) and are, in the twenty-first century, widely used across the curriculum in the UK. The frames usually consist of paragraph openings or sentence stems (sometimes with supporting questions) which the students complete with their own words. This structure can help them to shape their ideas or arguments in a particular form such as a news report, a piece of argued writing or a response to a literary text. Researchers are critical of the potential rigidity of a frame-based approach (Fones, 2001; Myhill, 2001). Writing frames need to be used flexibly and with care if students are to be given the chance to develop original responses and teachers are not to find themselves faced with sets of identical pieces of writing to assess. For further information about writing frames refer to Chapter 3.

Alongside scaffolding, other classroom methods closely allied to constructivist theory include self-directed tasks such as problem-solving and simulations together with those involving **inductive thinking,** Directed Activities Related to Texts (DARTs) and other small group activities which help students engage with texts and other classroom materials we want them to understand. **DARTs**, first developed by Lunzer and Gardner (1984), are activities for engaging with all kinds of texts (literary and non-literary and including visual texts) in ways which take the readers beyond straightforward comprehension and involve reflection. When used effectively, DARTs can enable learners (often working in small groups or pairs) to explore their developing interpretations of texts in creative, open-ended ways in order to make meanings for themselves. For further information about specific DARTs refer to Chapter 3.

Brain, neuroscience and learning

The brain is divided into two hemispheres – right and left. Although the hemispheres are said to have different specialist functions (see Figure 2.1) they are both used when a person is involved in complex tasks such as learning to speak an additional language or using metaphorical language, drawing a **mind map**®, learning the music and lyrics of a song.

The right and left hemispheres of the brain are said to communicate with each other via bundles of nerve fibres which cross from one side of the body to the other. This means that the left side of the brain can control the right side of the body and vice versa. With right-handed people, the logical left brain hemisphere tends to dominate the intuitive, creative right. This is known as left-sided dominance. However, it has also been argued that girls have right-sided dominance whereas boys tend to be left-sided. There is no evidence to support the idea that one type of dominance makes one individual more intelligent than another. However, there are some suggestions, which need to be viewed with considerable caution, that males and females perform better at different types of tasks which could reflect the differences in hemisphere dominance. For example, as a group, females are said to be more verbally fluent, able to read character and social cues better, manage multitasking, sequence objects and talk while they solve mathematical calculations. In contrast, males as a group, are said to be better at seeing shapes embedded within complex patterns and at solving

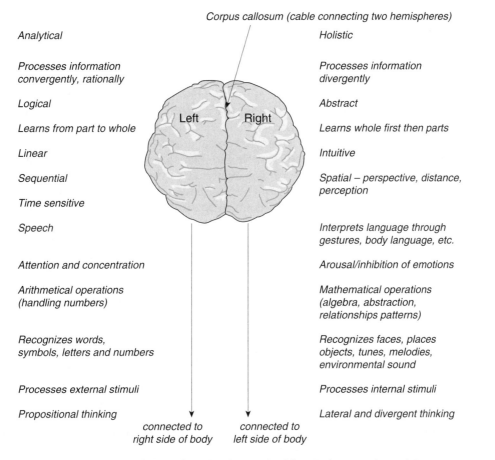

Corpus callosum (cable connecting two hemispheres)

Left	Right
Analytical	Holistic
Processes information convergently, rationally	Processes information divergently
Logical	Abstract
Learns from part to whole	Learns whole first then parts
Linear	Intuitive
Sequential	Spatial – perspective, distance, perception
Time sensitive	
Speech	Interprets language through gestures, body language, etc.
Attention and concentration	Arousal/inhibition of emotions
Arithmetical operations (handling numbers)	Mathematical operations (algebra, abstraction, relationships patterns)
Recognizes words, symbols, letters and numbers	Recognizes faces, places objects, tunes, melodies, environmental sound
Processes external stimuli	Processes internal stimuli
Propositional thinking	Lateral and divergent thinking

connected to right side of body   connected to left side of body

Figure 2.1 Functions of the left and right cerebral hemispheres (adapted from Smith, 1996 and Sousa, 2006)

mathematical problems (Moir and Jessell, 1993). Some researchers perceive that school-based learning favours right-hemisphere dominant learners. They argue the whole brain (that is, both hemispheres) supports learning through selection of a balanced and varied set of classroom activities and implementation of assessments designed to provide equality of opportunity (Sousa, 2006). Furthermore, it is said that students should be encouraged to try activities which occasionally challenge their preferred hemispheres and take them out of their comfort zones. In selecting these activities, you will also need to be very aware of your own personal preferences/ways of learning, since your personal choices, which may be revealed in your teaching plans, are unlikely to challenge everyone in your class.

Within the body of research on how the brain functions, the issue of retention of learning is another important aspect for you to consider. The level of retention can vary quite significantly during the course of a lesson. Sousa shows that potentially there are two *prime-times* for retention during a lesson. These occur during *prime-time 1* (the first 10–20 minutes, which has been shown to be the period of greatest retention) and *prime-time 2* (the final 5–10 minutes) (Sousa, 2006: 90). He argues that students will be able to recall almost any information relayed during this first period. This should then be followed up by a period of review or practice, while in *prime-time 2* students can consolidate or make sense of what they have learned. Consequently, for Sousa, the first 10–20 minutes of a lesson are not a time to engage students in speculating about what is to follow. In his view, this period should only deal with presentation of 'correct information' (Sousa, 2006: 90). In addition, he argues that teachers can tend to waste this first prime-time learning opportunity by filling it with administrative tasks such as announcements, registration and homework collection. You will learn more about lesson structures in Chapter 4. However, for the moment, think through the implications of what you have just read by completing Activity 2.2.

Activity 2.2 Using your brain to learn

This activity requires you to work in pairs, or with a small group of peers.

a) Remind yourself of the right–left brain hemisphere functions in Figure 2.1. With another beginning teacher, preferably of the opposite sex, discuss which brain hemisphere appears to dominate for each of you. Is any evidence about the way each of you learns that appears to contradict researchers' suggestions about gender and hemisphere dominance?

b) In the same pair or a small group, discuss the opening 10–15 minutes of several lessons you have observed so far. Explore what have you noticed about how experienced teachers use this period of the lesson to begin students' learning. What did the observed teachers do in this *prime-time* and when did they tend to fit in administrative tasks? In your view, what impact did the introduction of these sorts of tasks have on the learners and the learning process?

c) Now focus on the closing ten minutes of the lesson. How were the students enabled to make sense of what they had previously learned?

d) If you would like to read more about how the brain works follow the link on the companion website to sample chapters from *How the Brain Learns* by David A. Sousa.

Kolb's four learning styles

As you have read in Chapter 1, Kolb's theory of *Experiential Learning* (1984) has had a considerable influence on perceptions about how people learn. He perceives learning as a cyclical, continuous process which involves: actively experiencing a new situation; reflecting on what has occurred; theorizing about what has been experienced; and, finally, preparing for the next stage. In focusing on developmental learning, Kolb reinterpreted Piaget's four sequential phases of learning as four distinctly different learning styles with no hierarchical structure. He named these:

- *accommodative* – active learners who like to take risks, carry out plans and involve themselves in new experiences
- *divergent* – imaginative learners who are interested in people, values and feelings and like to view situations from many perspectives
- *convergent* – problem-solvers and decision-makers who prefer technical tasks to interpersonal issues
- *assimilative* – learners concerned with abstract concepts and ideas, who will create theoretical models and use inductive reasoning.

Although learners might use a mixture of learning styles, Kolb believed that essentially they would all be drawn to one of these four. Yet again, this acknowledgement of differences in the ways individuals learn suggests that a variety of teaching and learning strategies are essential in all classrooms if *all* students are to be included in the learning. Kolb's descriptions of learning styles are derived from his work with individual university students and are perhaps more relevant to an exploration of adult learners. Nevertheless his model can be successfully used to help us understand group and individual learning needs in secondary school classroom situations. Beresford (2001) provides an accessible summary of the characteristics of Kolb's four styles by exploring each type's ability to learn to use a computer:

- Accommodative learners will try out different methods in a 'hit and miss' approach, listening to other people's advice but trusting their own judgement.
- Divergent learners will initially watch others using the computer, speak to them and then try out varied approaches.
- Assimilative learners will watch, listen, make notes then try out their own approach.
- Convergent learners will refer to manuals and work on their own using a logical approach.

The existence of these different learning styles has implications on a macro level in school (in terms of curriculum structures, students' entitlements and class groupings) and, on a micro level (in terms of your own lesson planning, teaching and your expectations for individual learners' achievements). However, as educational systems begin to address issues of personalized learning (see Chapter 3), the extent to which each individual student's preferred learning style can and should be catered for within curriculum planning remains an important subject for speculation and debate.

Intelligence quotient (IQ)

Intelligence quotient is a measurement of general intelligence arrived at through completion of a set of standardized tests of deductive/mathematical reasoning.

Multiple intelligences

In *Frames of Mind*, Howard Gardner (1983) argues that learners could be said to have strengths in particular types of intelligences rather than a level of intelligence based on their IQ. Gardner's intelligences were originally arranged in seven groups of skills and abilities:

- linguistic intelligence
- logical-mathematical intelligence
- visual-spatial intelligence
- bodily-kinaesthetic intelligence
- musical intelligence
- **interpersonal** intelligence
- **Intrapersonal** intelligence.

This list of intelligences is not finite. In recent years Gardner has suggested that naturalistic and (more tentatively) spiritual or existential intelligences could also be added to the above (1999). In his view, the balance of these intelligences within an individual will affect their preferred way of learning. Gardner has also become bolder in his claims about how these seven or nine multiple intelligences (**MI**) could lead to new definitions of human nature. The work of Gardner and his *Project Zero* team is increasingly influential in school improvement worldwide, particularly in terms of:

- understanding about students' aptitudes
- development of differentiated approaches to learning and teaching
- curriculum content.

In some schools, decisions about students' *intelligences* are arrived at through completion of questionnaires (for examples, see Activity 2.3). In others, learners appear to have been made very aware of their *intelligences* and preferred learning styles to the extent that they may even carry labels identifying them from class to class. In addition, Gardner's terminology has triggered identification of other *intelligences* within some specific school contexts. For examples of how MI has been embedded and adapted in school improvement policies refer to case studies and papers posted at www.tda.gov.uk which include an account of implementation of a new staffing structure and an advanced skills strategy at the Thomas Lord Audley School and MacGilchrist's paper on 'Leading the intelligent school' (2006).

Although it has been acknowledged by Davies that use of methods based on MI can lead to a rise in students' self-esteem and a potentially more liberal approach to curriculum planning (2006), the concept of MI is not without its critics. One of the most vocal is John White who questions how the artistic/subjective and non-empirical nature of Gardner's research has generated the 'myth of multiple intelligences' (2004: 1). In his view, intelligence has always been linked with the notion that humans need to be flexible to achieve their desired goals and he argues that, in this respect, Gardner offers nothing new to the debate. White suggests Gardner's theory confuses the development of social intellectual activity with a system predicated on a set of biologically based characteristics (drawn from Piagetian developmentalist theory). He also questions whether the adoption of an MI 'shrink wrapped' (2004: 2) approach by educators could lead students to develop potentially damaging (or even limiting) false perceptions about their own capabilities.

Gardner's theory of multiple intelligences underpins the principles of *accelerated learning* developed by Alistair Smith. Smith suggests that by encouraging the development of a full range of intelligences a teacher can promote lifelong learning. He argues for a supportive classroom environment which enables learners to be receptive to new ideas and to set themselves high personal targets. Teachers need to be alert to the physical state of their students to ensure that their basic needs are met and they are alert and ready to learn. He suggests music might be played to help students achieve a state of 'relaxed alertness' (1996: 10). Students might be able to drink water during the lesson as dehydration is thought to be bad for the brain. They will occasionally participate in 5-minute *brain gym* activities designed to stimulate thinking by connecting left and right brain functions. Learners are also encouraged to regularly review and reflect on their learning methods.

The **accelerated learning** methods of Smith centre on a range of visual, auditory and kinaesthetic (often referred to by teachers as **VAK**) strategies which are designed to support the three types of learner identified by neuro-linguistic programming (**NLP**). NLP models of communication indicate that people have specific sensory preferences for how individuals make sense of the information which their brains receive from their five senses. The three types are defined as follows.

The visual learner

This is the person who learns most effectively through visual means, preferring to receive information through charts, diagrams, visual images or demonstrations and (in some cases) written texts. Such people prefer to demonstrate their learning through visual representations such as: turning a short story into a digital **storyboard**; drawing a cartoon which shows their interpretation of a historical event; making a collage of a poem they have studied; describing a chemical process as a flow chart.

The auditory learner

This person learns most effectively through listening and prefers to listen to recorded interviews, lectures, discussions or teacher explanations than to other methods of delivery. They demonstrate their learning best by, for example, giving an oral presentation, performing a rap or contributing to discussion.

The kinaesthetic learner

This is the person who learns most effectively if they participate physically in their learning and demonstrate this learning through *doing*, for example, role plays, activities in the field and other types of visits, practical investigations, perfecting free kicks on the football pitch, or making models or other objects. (It is important to be aware that active learning of a practical nature does need to be supported by discussion and opportunities for reflection on what has been learned if the activity is to have a lasting impact.)

Some strategies used to support learners include the following.

Giving the 'big picture'

The teacher provides an overview of what students will learn (and participate in) during the lesson at the beginning of a session and indicates how this will connect with prior learning and intended future learning.

'Chunking down' a topic

This involves breaking down a topic into a manageable number of items – ideally between five and nine items (Smith, 1996). It can be used once the teacher has introduced the *big picture*.

Use of mind maps® and visual note-making

Mind-mapping is a graphic technique which enables both teachers (in their planning) and students (in their learning) to explore, revise and summarize ideas about a topic in a very visual and creative way that reflects how information is encoded in the brain. Mind maps® were first devised by Tony Buzan (2002) and are now used widely in education and in business. They can be hand-drawn or compiled using a variety of mind-mapping software programs such as *Mind Manager* and *Inspiration*. Mind maps® have a number of key elements: different categories of information are arranged in different sections of the page or screen; different categories are colour coded; key words, symbols and highlighting are used to label the categories; flowing branches, stems, arrows and links (of different thicknesses) are made between the categories to show relationships or potential connections between them.

If you have not tried mind mapping before you might want to refer to Buzan (2002) and visit

www.mind-mapping.co.uk/make-mind-map.htm or
www.ltscotland.org.uk/studyskills/10to14/understand/Mindmaps/resources/index.asp
to learn how to get started.
For further examples and an exploration of how they work go to Buzan's website www.imindmap.com/ education/#howitworks.

Visual note-making includes many of the features of mind-mapping such as symbols, arrows, flow charts, sketches, circled words, colour-coding and other features which enable the note-maker to record their notes in a way which will be memorable to them.

Use of concept mapping

These are diagrams which contain a limited number of concepts (ideas) with the propositional relationships which join them written on the linking arrows (see Osbourne, 1993). Group concept mapping provides many opportunities for students to have an enhanced dialogue about science (Sizmur, 1994) – that is, to question each other's ideas and interpret their meaning to one another. Other teaching ideas might be to present a concept map which deliberately contains some true and some false propositions. The students are asked to locate all the errors on the concept map. They then construct it correctly.

Displays of key words

Displays can be made in the teaching room on posters, word walls or hanging mobiles – these will only be effective if they are removed after use rather than

Table 2.1   Making true sentences

microbes		all	*green plants*	to get rid of	*oxygen*
animals	depend	some	*microbes*	to make	*nitrogen*
decomposers	use	on	*animals*	to provide	*water*
green plants				to recycle	*carbon dioxide*

Note: The key words are shown in italics.

becoming a permanent feature of the classroom landscape. A simple teaching strategy might involve providing a selection of the key words (to do with a given topic) and asking the students to make up five true sentences by choosing an entry from each column. The same word can be used several times to reinforce understanding and the sentences can then be displayed. Table 2.1 provides an example.

Use of jingles, rhymes and mnemonics

Mnemonics are short phrases used to jog the memory. For example, *Richard Of York Gave Battle In Vain* spells out the colours of the spectrum, as seen in a rainbow: Red, Orange, Yellow, Green, Blue, Indigo, Violet; *Friend to the end* helps you to remember how to spell the word friend correctly and to place the 'i' and the 'e' in the correct order.

Taking part in brain gym or break states

These group activities are used *for a brief period of time only* either at the beginning or end of a lesson or at a transition point within it. The intention is to improve physical and mental alertness and co-ordination. They can provide a break at a key moment in a lesson and enable students to move on, feeling re-energized and focused. Activities can include:

- rubbing hands in a circle on your stomach while patting your head (and vice versa);
- marching in time on the spot and touching a raised knee with the opposite hand;
- reading letters of the alphabet in forward or backward sequence whilst following instructions about raising right or left or both arms;
- breathing exercises;
- use of different types of music for energizing, enhancing concentration, visualization or relaxation.

Activity 2.3 What kind of a learner are you?

This is an activity which can be carried out individually.

a) Refer back to the section on Kolb's Four Learning Styles and reflect on your own preferred ways of learning. Which strategies have you found most helpful in the past when:

- making notes from your reading or from a lecture?

- revising for examinations?

- planning an essay or a presentation?

At what stage of your own education did you learn to use these strategies? What could they reveal about the way you use your brain? What could they tell you about your preferred learning style(s)?

b) Use any search engine and you will discover many websites featuring questionnaires on learning styles and multiple intelligences. For examples go to: http://www.support4learning.org.uk/education/learning_styles.cfm or Walter McKenzie's Multiple Intelligences Survey at http://surfaquarium.com

Try out one of the questionnaires. Did it help you to identify your own different strengths as a learner? Look again at the particular questionnaire with a critical eye. What do you notice about how the questions are constructed? What view of 'intelligence' is being presented and assessed?

Activity 2.4 Learning styles

This activity can be completed individually.

a) Review two lessons you have observed so far. Which learning theories may have influenced the teaching and learning strategies chosen and used by the teachers? Were the students able to learn in different ways? If so, what strategies were used and with what effect?

b) Refer to White (2004) and Davies (2006) and reflect on your own classroom observations. What do you think might be the advantages for the teacher and the students of a *learning styles* and/or *multiple intelligences* focus in the planning and teaching of a lesson? What potential difficulties could arise from this approach?

Thinking skills

This term has become an umbrella term for a range of activities including logic, enquiry, problem-solving and critical thinking. The influential psychologist Jerome Bruner believes we use different sorts of thinking strategies depending on our knowledge, the context in which we are working and the subject matter. He argues that the school context engenders distinctly new forms of learning and consequently new ways of thinking (Bruner, 1966). The development of thinking skills in school-based education has been influenced by the work of several individuals with contrasting approaches. These include Reuven Feuerstein, Matthew Lipman, Edward De Bono and Benjamin Bloom.

Feuerstein et al.'s instrumental enrichment (IE) programme (1980) was developed after the Second World War for use with traumatized and seemingly ineducable Israeli young people. This is a programme based on 'mediated learning experience', a dynamic process through which adults interact with young learners to support their cognitive development. Objects and events in their worlds are crucial aspects of the mediational encounter and are used to bring about change (Falik, n.d.). For further information and research papers on Feuerstein's work refer to www.icelp.org/asp/Aspects_of_Mediated_Learning_Experience.shtm.

Matthew Lipman et al.'s pioneering *Philosophy for Children* programme in the USA (1980) draws on the belief that children have a natural curiosity about the world and they want to ask questions about it. The programme uses novels which are read in class and have been deliberately written to guide their readers to raise questions, argue and explore ideas. This approach has been further refined and adapted for use in UK classrooms by Robert Fisher (1995) among others.

Edward De Bono's work on cognition emphasizes creative approaches to thinking which include his six 'thinking hats' strategy (1991). This is widely used both in primary and secondary schools (particularly in English teaching and personal and social education programmes) for encouraging consideration of a range of perspectives. Wearers (either individuals or small groups) of the six differently coloured hats each have to explore the same situation, argument or text from a certain perspective (depending on the colour* of hat they are wearing) and to present their ideas to the rest of the class.

* White = neutral and factual
* Yellow = optimistic, positive and offers praise
* Red = emotional, opinionated and intuitive
* Black = offers critical judgements
* Green = alternative, speculative or creative thinking
* Blue = provides overview or summary, acts as a control.

Activity 2.5   Using De Bono's hats

This activity can be completed in conjunction with your mentor.

Refer to De Bono's six thinking hats (described in this section).

Think about how you might use this approach to teach one aspect of your subject with one of your current classes.

Discuss your choices of topic and approach with your teacher-mentor. If they are appropriate, develop them into a plan, try them out and evaluate their success.

In focusing on how they learn as well as what they learn, students need to develop their **meta-cognition** – their ability to reflect on their own thinking processes. Some psychologists argue that meta-cognition is 'the one factor unique to human thinking' (Fisher, 1995: 11) and Fisher stresses the importance of meta-cognition as 'a key element in the transfer of learning' (1998: 1) if learners are to fully understand how they learn.

In the twenty-first century, thinking skills have become a more prominent feature of UK school curricula. In some schools, students' thinking skills are explicitly taught and numerous publications have been developed to support this teaching (for example, see Bowkett, 2006). However, the development of students' thinking skills can (and should) be embedded within their learning in all subject areas through selection of activities which stimulate and challenge all learners in a variety of ways. Thinking skills are promoted within the National Curriculum and National Strategy documentation. If you visit the National Curriculum website 'Personal learning and thinking skills' (PLTs) pages at www.curriculum.qca.org.uk/skills/plts/index.aspx you will find a section of the menu on the right of the screen which leads you to subject-specific sections that show how PLTs relate to the programmes of study for your subject area. Thinking skills are also a growing element of the Scottish curriculum. Go to www.ides.org.uk/Images/learningthinkingcreativi_36_tcm4-122009. pdf for an example of a *Learning, Thinking and Creativity Staff Development Handbook* devised by teachers working in Scottish primary and high schools. The National Curriculum currently identifies these skills as:

- information-processing skills – locating and collecting relevant information, sorting, classifying, sequencing, comparing and contrasting, analysing part/whole relationships
- reasoning skills – giving reasons to support actions or opinions, drawing inferences, making deductions, making judgements and decisions informed by reasons or evidence, using precise language to explain

- enquiry skills – asking relevant questions, posing and defining problems, planning and researching, predicting outcomes and anticipating consequences, testing conclusions and improving ideas
- creative thinking skills – generating and extending ideas, applying imagination, suggesting hypotheses, searching for alternative innovative ideas
- evaluation skills – evaluating information, making value judgements, developing criteria for judging their own and other people's work and having confidence in their own judgements.

Specific teaching and learning strategies such as odd one out, card sorting, cloze, sequencing, finding key words, concept mapping and hot-seating can support the development of thinking skills.

The National Curriculum for science (DfEE, 1999: 9) acknowledged the important role of science education in developing thinking skills: 'science provides opportunities to promote thinking skills, through pupils engaging in the process of scientific enquiry'. Some programmes have been developed that are subject specific (for example, science or mathematics) in which cognitive acceleration through science education (CASE) or through mathematics education (CAME) have been developed with the aim of improving general cognitive functions. CASE in particular has a focus on developing scientific thinking in Years 7 and 8. It has been promoted in many secondary schools with in-service training and support materials and thoroughly evaluated (see Baumfield et al., 2005; Shayer and Adey, 2002).

Bloom's taxonomy

Benjamin Bloom and his colleagues devised a hierarchical 'taxonomy of educational objectives' (Bloom et al., 1956). This classified educational objectives into groups in relation to their cognitive complexity and the different levels of thinking that would be required to meet these objectives. The levels extended from simple recall towards increasingly complex, higher-order thinking (Figure 2.2). The taxonomy was constructed on the understanding that higher-order skills embrace all those levels lower down the order. In other words, knowledge has to be acquired before it can be fully understood and evaluated. Its potential in providing an educational framework became widely known and it was eventually translated into 22 languages (Krathwohl, 2002).

Objectives that describe intended learning outcomes as a result of teaching are usually arranged in terms of subject matter (content) and a description of what is to be done with that content. The former would be written as nouns for

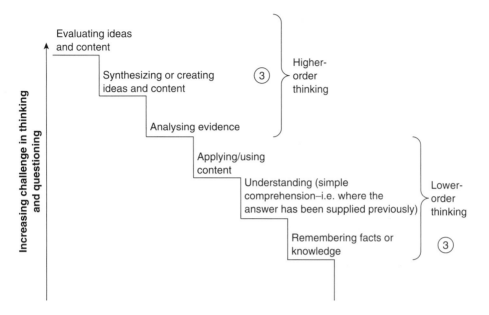

Figure 2.2   Bloom's taxonomy

example and the associated cognitive processes would be written as verbs. An example of this is: 'the student will be able to recount (*verb*) Newton's second law of motion (*noun phrase*)'. In a revised version of the taxonomy these two aspects of the learning outcome are presented as separate dimensions. It allows for a knowledge dimension (noun) and a cognitive process dimension (verb) (Anderson and Krathwohl, 2001). For a more detailed discussion of how to classify educational goals, objectives and standards, see Krathwohl (2002).

One of the challenges you will face as a beginning teacher is learning to ask questions of your students which will stimulate their higher-order thinking. You will find that Bloom's taxonomy can help you to devise learning objectives and to plan questions which offer increasing levels of challenge to all your students and should help to build their confidence. Ultimately all students should be given opportunities to work at all levels of thinking but remember that not everyone has the capacity within their working memory to sift essential and non-essential knowledge efficiently or to grasp complex ideas at the same speed. Table 2.2 provides examples of tasks and question stems from a range of different subject areas to help you think through the challenges which each level will offer. You will explore the subject of questioning further in Chapter 4.

Table 2.2 Putting Bloom's taxonomy into practice

Thinking skill	What the students need to do	Examples of questions and question stems	Task examples
Remembering	Define Recall List Match Label Name Identify Collect Describe	Describe the scene in … What do we call a …? What are the types of …? Where would you find …? What did we find out last lesson about …?	Identify the main figures in the battle. List all the characters in the novel. Match the written descriptions to the mapped locations. Pick out the prime numbers.
Understanding	Explain Interpret Outline Illustrate Summarize Discuss Distinguish	Why do you think …? What happens when …? Explain why we should …? What are the most important points? How did you …?	Explain how the nurse felt in this scene. Draw a mind map® – to show what you have learned about volcanoes.
Applying	Apply to new context Transfer Modify Use Predict Demonstrate Solve	What do you think she will do next? How can you use a quadratic equation to …? What does this reaction suggest to you?	Predict the ending of the story. Imagine you were alive in 1940s Britain. Show your partner how to hold the racket.
Analysing	Deduce Infer Explore Investigate Relate Classify Categorize Compare	How have you arrived at that evidence? Which is fact and which is opinion? What do you think this really means? What purpose does it serve?	Compare the use of colour in the two paintings. Sort the statements into agree and disagree piles. Analyse the impact of long shore drift on the beach.

Table 2.2   *(Continued)*

Thinking skill	What the students need to do	Examples of questions and question stems	Task examples
Synthesizing or creating	Design Invent Create Reorganize Compose Rewrite	What else would you add or change? What alternatives are there? How are these two different?	Write an alternative speech for the last scene. Devise an advertising campaign to promote a healthy snack.
Evaluating	Assess Evaluate Judge Appraise Justify Conclude	How successful …? Why is that valid? What do you recommend? Which is more acceptable?	Put the character or historical figure on trial. Decide which photograph is most effective.

Source: adapted from DfES, 2003 and Dobson, 2006

Within each level of the taxonomy there is also the potential for an increasing degree of difficulty of task which may be needed before learners are ready to progress towards a greater level of complexity in their thinking. Sometimes teachers can confuse complexity with difficulty but they are different. Complexity is concerned with the level of thought required whereas difficulty determines how much effort needs to be expended within each level (Sousa, 2006).

The following examples illustrate the differences: 'Tell me five facts you have learned about global warming and three points about global footprints' is *not* a more complex task than 'Recall five facts you have learned about global warming' but it is more difficult in that it relies on the recall of a greater body of knowledge. Alternatively, 'Explain what happens in the narrative poem *The Rime of the Ancient Mariner*' involves a lower-order thinking skill which requires the learner to demonstrate their understanding of the events of the text whereas 'Create an additional section in the poem written from the point of view of another character' demands more complex higher-order thinking skills to complete the task effectively. This will involve students in drawing on their knowledge and understanding of the events of the poem and their analysis of how it has been written in order to synthesize this knowledge in the creation of new verses with appropriate content and written in the same style.

Activity 2.6   Developing thinking skills

The activity is best completed as a paired activity.

a) Discuss with another teacher the examples you have seen of *thinking skills* planning and teaching in departmental schemes of work and lesson observations. In your view, which of these showed that thinking skills could be embedded within the subject teaching (rather than being in addition to the topic or concepts taught)?

b) Look again at the section in this chapter on Bloom's taxonomy. Choose a specific topic which you will be teaching. How will you ensure that your teaching promotes the development of thinking skills at all levels in this topic? Think about ways in which you can keep a check on this in your lesson planning and recording.

c) You might want to plot your ideas in brief on to a hierarchical chart. Now review the chart. Are there places where you may need to add increasing levels of difficulty to reinforce learning before moving on to the next level? Discuss your ideas with your mentor.

d) Can thinking skills be taught? Refer to Valerie Wilson's paper 'Can thinking skills be taught?' (2000) at www.scre.ac.uk/pdf/spotlight/spotlight79.pdf. Think about what you have learned so far through your reading, lesson observations, practical experience and reflections. Draw a *mind map*® in which you explore your response to this question. Share it with your mentor or another teacher.

CONCLUSION

In this chapter you have been introduced to different theories of learning and the ways in which these can shape and inform classroom practice. You have also had the opportunity to reflect on yourself as a learner, to explore your own views about theoretical aspects of learning and to begin to apply your new understandings to aspects of your subject teaching. In Chapter 3 we move on to consider the contexts in which teaching and learning take place.

REFERENCES

Anderson, L. and Krathwohl, D. (eds) (2001) *A Taxonomy for Learning and Assessing: A Revision of Bloom's Taxonomy of Educational Objectives*. New York: Longman.

Barnes, D., Britton, J. and Rosen, H. (1972) *Language, the Learner and the School*. London: Penguin Books.

Baumfield, V., Edwards, G., Butterworth, M. and Thacker, D. (2005) *The Impact of the Implementation of Thinking Skills Programmes and Approaches on Teachers*. London: University of London, EPPI-Centre.

Beresford, J. (2001) 'Matching teaching to learning', in F. Banks and A. Shelton Mayes (eds), *Early Professional Development for Teachers*. London: David Fulton. pp. 226–46.

Bloom, B., Engelhart, M., Furst, E., Hill, W. and Krathwohl, D. (1956) *Taxonomy of Educational Objectives: The Classification of Educational Goals. Handbook 1: Cognitive Domain*. Longman, London.

Bowkett, S. (2006) *100 Ideas for Teaching Thinking Skills*. London: Continuum.

Britton, J. (1974) *Language and Learning*. London: Penguin Books.

Bruner, J. (1966) *Toward a Theory of Instruction*. New York: W.W.Norton.

Buzan, T. (2002) *How to Mind Map*. London: HarperCollins.

Davies, R. (2006) *Multiple Intelligences (MI) in the Classroom: An Evaluation of the Effectiveness of an 'MI Approach' through the Teaching and Learning of History*. National Teacher Research Panel for the Teacher Research Conference. www.tda.gov.uk (accessed 19 December 2006).

De Bono, E. (1991) *Teaching Thinking*. London: Penguin Books.

Department for Education and Employment (DfEE) (1999) *The National Curriculum for England: Science*. London: DfEE.

Department for Education and Skills (DfES) (2003) *Unit 4: Questioning, Teaching and Learning in Secondary Schools: Pilot*. London: DfES.

Dobson, H. (2006) 'Thinking and reading', *Secondary English Magazine*, 10(2): 29–32.

Falik, L. (n.d.) *Using Mediated Learning Experience Parameters to Change Children's Behavior: Techniques for Parents and Childcare Providers*. www.icelp.org/asp/Aspects_of_Mediated_Learning_Experience.shtm (accessed 11 June 2007).

Feuerstein, R., Rand, Y., Hoffman, M.B. and Miller, R. (1980) *Instrumental Enrichment: An Intervention for Cognitive Modifiability*. Baltimore, MD: University Press.

Fisher, R. (1995) *Teaching Children to Think*. 2nd edn. Oxford: Blackwell.

Fisher, R. (1998) 'Thinking about thinking: developing metacognition in children', *Early Child Development and Care*, 141: 1–15.

Fones, D. (2001), 'Blocking them in to free them to act: using writing frames to shape boys' responses to literature in the secondary school', *English in Education*, 35(3): 21–31.

Gardner, H. (1983) *Frames of Mind*. Heinemann: London.

Gardner, H. (1999) *Intelligence Reframed: Multiple Intelligences for the 21st Century*. New York: Basic Books.

Gillen, J. (2000) 'Versions of Vygotsky', *British Journal of Educational Studies*, 78(2): 183–98.

Kolb, D.A. (1984) *Experiential Learning: Experience as the Source of Learning and Development*. Englewood Cliffs, NJ: Prentice-Hall.

Krathwohl, D. (2002) 'A revision of Bloom's taxonomy: an overview', *Theory into Practice*, 41(4): 212–18.

Lipman, M., Sharp, A. and Oscanyan, F. (1980) *Philosophy in the Classroom*. Princeton, NJ: Temple University Press.

Lunzer, E. and Gardner, K. (1984) *Learning from the Written Word*. Edinburgh: Oliver and Boyd.

MacGilchrist, B. (2006) 'Leading the intelligent school'. National College for School Leadership. www.tda.gov.uk (accessed 19 December 2006).

Moir, A. and Jessell, D. (1993) *Brain Sex: The Real Difference Between Men and Women*. London: Penguin.

Myhill, D. (2001) *Better Writers*. Westley: Courseware Publications.

Osbourne, J.F. (1993) 'Alternatives to practical work', *School Science Review*, 75(271): 117–23.

Shayer, M. and Adey, P. (2002) *Learning Intelligence*. Buckingham: Open University Press.

Sizmur, S. (1994) 'Concept mapping, language and learning in the classroom', *School Science Review*, 76(274): 120–5.

Skinner, F.B. (1968) *The Technology of Teaching*. New York: Appleton-Century-Crofts.

Smith, A. (1996) *Accelerated Learning in the Classroom*. Stafford: Network Educational Press.

Sousa, D.A. (2006) *How the Brain Learns*. 3rd edn. Thousand Oaks, CA: Corwin/Sage.

Vygotsky, L.S. (1978) *Mind and Society. The Development of Higher Psychological Processes*. Cambridge, MA: Harvard University Press.

White, J. (2004) 'Howard Gardner: the myth of multiple intelligences', lecture at the Institute of Education, University of London, 17 November www.ttrb.ac.uk/ViewArticle.aspx?contentId=12738 (accessed 18 December 2006).

Wilson, V. (2000) 'Can thinking skills be taught? A paper for discussion', Scottish Council for Research in Education. www.scre.ac.uk/scot-research/thinking/index.html (accessed 19 December 2006).

Wood, D. (1998) *How Children Think and Learn*. 2nd edn. London: Blackwell. (1st edn, 1988.)

Wood, D.J., Bruner, J.S. and Ross, G. (1976) 'Collaborative learning between peers: an overview', *Educational Psychology in Practice*, 11(4): 4–9.

Wray, D. and Lewis, M. (1997) *Extending Literacy: Children Reading and Writing Non-Fiction*. London: Routledge.

LEARNING AND TEACHING CONTEXTS

Sue Dymoke

By the end of this chapter you will have :

- gained greater understanding of the way learning is structured in schools and how learners are grouped and supported within inclusive environments
- explored how policy shapes teaching, curriculum content and the qualifications framework
- considered some of the impacts of e-learning.

INTRODUCTION

This chapter reviews the contexts within which learning and teaching take place, namely the overarching structures which determine how learners are grouped and how learning and teaching are organized within schools. It considers the ways in which policy translates into practice and will encourage you to reflect on *Every Child Matters*, to develop critical responses to the National Curriculum, the *National Secondary Strategy* (including literacy, numeracy and information and communication technology [ICT] across the curriculum) and the 14–19 qualifications framework. The chapter provides an introduction to special educational needs and provision for those with learning difficulties. English as an Additional Language, working with gifted and talented students and other aspects of inclusion are explored. You will also begin to consider the impact of e-learning and other topics which are revisited in more depth in subsequent chapters. Throughout Chapter 3 you are given opportunities to ask questions of those professionals you are working with and to reflect on aspects of your own developing practice.

WHAT ARE THE CONTEXTS WITHIN WHICH LEARNING OCCURS?

Types of schools

The majority of children aged 11–18 in the UK attend mainstream state secondary schools or colleges while others are educated privately in the independent sector or receive home tuition. The nature and type of these state schools are increasingly varied. There are three types of maintained state secondary schools: community, foundation and voluntary schools. Any maintained school can also be a specialist school which teaches the full National Curriculum but has a special focus on the teaching of several other curriculum areas such as sports, technology or performing arts. Other types of school include academies and city technology colleges (both of which are technically independent schools), pupil referral units (PRUs), secure training units (STUs) and, in some parts of the country, grammar schools which select the majority of their students according to their high academic ability. For a historical overview of these developments refer to Chapter 6. One of the most recent initiatives is the extended school which enables local providers and other agencies to provide access to services such as childcare (in primaries); parenting and family support; study support; sport and music clubs; ICT facilities and referral to other services including health and social care. (For more on extended schools refer to Chapter 7.) Depending on which routes they choose to follow at post-16 level, students continue their studies entirely within their own 11–18 school, or attend courses within a consortium arrangement offered by neighbouring 11–18 schools, or move on to a sixth form college or a college of further education.

Ability grouping

Within every school learners and learning processes will be organized in slightly different ways. Traditionally these could be determined by: whole-school policy; the specific nature of the school population; student–teacher staffing ratios or even the buildings themselves. In Chapter 4 you will be able to explore the different ways in which teaching spaces and specific groups/individual learners can be managed, but first we need to consider the different types of ability groupings which are commonly found in schools:

- *Streaming*: the students assignment to a class is based on an assessment of their overall ability, arrived at through consideration of their prior attainment and/or cognitive test results. Students stay in their streamed classes for most of their lessons.
- *Banding*: this has similarities with streaming in that students are assigned to broad bands across a year group on the basis of an overall assessment of their ability. They stay in their band for most of their lessons.

- *Setting*: this is when students are grouped according to their ability in a particular subject. They might be in different higher or lower sets for each subject.
- *Mixed-ability grouping*: this occurs when students are placed in groups which reflect the full ability range of that specific year group within the school.

Kutnick et al.'s 2006 report on *Student Grouping Strategies and Practices at Key Stage 2 and 3* and the journal article 'Secondary school students' preferences for different types of structured grouping practices' by Hallam and Ireson (2006) will both help you to explore the issue of ability grouping further. Kutnick et al.'s research focused on 24 case studies. It underlines how difficult it is to prove whether use of mixed ability or setting leads to higher attainment. The report also raises issues about progression from primary to secondary level. In Hallam and Ireson's paper, 62 per cent of the students they questioned expressed a preference for setting over mixed-ability teaching. The reasons for student preference are interesting to consider.

Activity 3.1   Grouping by ability

Part (a) of this activity can be completed on your own. Parts (b) and (c) require paired work, for example, with another beginning teacher.

a) Think about your own education. Which of the types of groupings outlined in this section have you experienced? How aware were you of the ability range within each of your classes? How did you feel about being assigned to a particular group? What impact do you think the nature of the groups you were in had on your learning?

b) Read the following statements about grouping and think about them from a teacher's perspective. Discuss your responses with another beginning teacher. Which do you agree or disagree with? Which are not so clear cut? Why?

1) In streamed classes all students are working at the same level which makes the teaching easier.

2) Mixed-ability classes prepare students better for the real world beyond the classroom.

3) Setted groups enable teachers to support students in a more carefully targeted way.

4) Mixed-ability classes enable lower-ability students to make faster progress than if they were in a low-ability group.

5) Streaming means labelling students at an early age which can stigmatize them for life.

(Continued)

(Continued)

6) Banded grouping has no educational value: it is just a device to make school timetabling easier.

7) Setted groups are motivating for learners.

8) Mixed-ability classes are more enjoyable to teach than the other types.

9) Most able students are not stretched sufficiently in mixed-ability groups.

10) Streaming allows for better whole school sharing of information about student progress.

11) Mixed-ability groupings develop students' social skills rather than raise their attainment.

12) Late developers will have the best chance of succeeding if they are placed in a mixed-ability group.

13) Mixed-ability teaching requires considerably more preparation than the other types.

14) Setted groups ensure that a student's capabilities in each subject area can be recognized and encouraged.

15) Very able students can learn to work independently in mixed-ability groupings.

16) At primary school, students are used to being grouped by ability for literacy, numeracy and some other subjects. If they are to continue to make progress in secondary school then a system of setting must be adopted.

17) Mixed-ability classes are less disruptive than other types.

18) Streaming enforces a competitive streak to learning.

19) Most students' learning occurs autonomously without the direct teacher intervention so it should not matter how students are grouped.

20) All classes are mixed ability.

21) Mixed-ability classes provide teachers with more opportunities to work with lower-ability students.

22) The choice of grouping arrangements should depend on the subject being taught as setting is more appropriate for some subject areas and mixed ability for others.

c) Read the executive summary (or the full report if you have time) by Kutnick et al. (2006) on *Pupil Grouping Strategies and Practices at Key Stage 2 and 3* and the journal article 'Secondary school pupils' preferences for different types of structured grouping practices' (Hallam and Ireson, 2006). Summarize (either as a list of statements or a mind map®) what the implications of the findings presented in the report and the article might be *for your own developing practice*. Share your summary with another beginning teacher.

Every Child Matters

The *Every Child Matters* (ECM) policy initiative came into force in England with the passing of the Children Act 2004 and, following subsequent related legislation, should be fully implemented by 2010. It stipulates an integrated multi-agency approach to supporting the well-being of children and young people from birth to age 19. This involves all those organizations which are responsible for providing services for children (including health, education, police and voluntary groups) in working together to protect, nurture and enable young people to achieve their full potential. It is perceived that this collaborative approach represents a challenge to all concerned, including teachers who now need to look beyond their narrower or more traditional roles and learn to work together for the good of the community (Brindle, 2006). The intention of ECM is that children and young people will also have a greater voice in commenting on issues which will affect them both individually and collectively. Every child, whatever their background or personal circumstances, should have the support they need to:

- be healthy
- stay safe
- enjoy and achieve
- make a positive contribution
- achieve economic well-being.

These five *outcomes*, as they have been called, permeate all aspects of current education policy, including new curriculum developments, and are referred to throughout this book (especially in Chapters 6 and 7). For discussion of the implications of the ECM agenda, and video clips which show how it has been implemented in two different schools, you can refer to www.teachers.tv/everychildmatters. In addition you could refer to extracts from two special supplements on how ECM is working at www.guardian.co.uk/everychildmatters.

In other countries in the UK similar legislation to ECM exists to support an integrated approach. For example, in Scotland, *Getting It Right for Every Child* (GIRFEC), which came in to force in 2005 has paved the way for implementation of new Children's Services legislation. For further information go to www.scotland.gov.uk/Topics/People/YoungPeople/childrensservices/girfec/Background.

Inclusion

Inclusion of children with special educational needs is the priority for twenty- first century schooling and is underpinned by the ECM legislation outlined in the last section. The policies and practices of an inclusive school involve everyone and ensure that all are involved and valued. The emphasis on an inclusive approach to learning has replaced a previous focus on integration (where a student was physically integrated into an educational setting amongst their peers without a requirement for the setting to change its environment or learning processes to accommodate the student). With integration the focus was on *place* and learning through *assimilation into the mainstream,* whereas inclusion is about *acceptance* and *supporting all learners* to achieve their maximum potential within a context where they are equally valued and their individual rights and freedoms are respected. The term *learners* includes those learners:

- at all levels of attainment
- of all ages
- of whichever gender, culture or social group
- from ethnic minority groups
- with disabilities, sensory impairments or ill health
- with communication, language or literacy difficulties.

Schools have a responsibility to provide a broad and balanced curriculum for all learners which caters for the specific needs of individuals and groups of students. They are also encouraged to provide other curricular opportunities outside the National Curriculum to meet individual needs. These might include speech, language or physical therapy. Teachers are able to modify, as necessary, the National Curriculum programmes of study to ensure that all students are engaged in relevant and appropriately challenging work. The Qualifications and Curriculum Authority (**QCA**) sets out three essential principles for developing a more inclusive curriculum, namely:

1) Setting suitable learning challenges;
2) Responding to students' diverse learning needs;

3) Overcoming potential barriers to learning and assessment for individuals and groups of students. (www.qca.org.uk/qca_1986.aspx, accessed 10 February 2008.)

If these principles are applied then the need for **dis-application** of aspects of the National Curriculum should theoretically be minimized. For more detailed information about these principles you should refer to www.nc.uk.net/inclusion.html.

In thinking through the practicalities of what inclusion means for your own planning and teaching, you could download a copy of the poster *Including All Learners* (available on the QCA website at www.qca.org.uk/qca_12632.aspx).

This provides useful definitions of terminology together with questions you will want to ask yourself as you begin to reflect on how you will tailor your planning and classroom delivery to meet the needs of individuals.

Learning difficulties and the *Special Educational Needs Code of Practice*

The *Special Educational Needs Code of Practice* (DfES, 2001), which came into effect in January 2002, provides guidance on policies and procedures enabling learners with special educational needs (SEN) to reach their full potential, be included fully in their school communities and make a successful transition into adult life. It stipulates that all mainstream secondary schools will admit students who have already been identified as having special educational needs while at primary school as well as those in Year 7 who may have as yet unidentified special educational needs. In addition, they should recognize that children's needs span a continuum and may also change over time. The result of this is that the transition to a new school might present particular challenges for students with special educational needs. The provision for students with special educational needs is the responsibility of the whole school. The Department for Education and Skills (DfES) code clearly states: 'All teachers are teachers of pupils with special educational needs' (2001: 59). If you would like to refer to the code, it can be downloaded or listened to at www.teachernet. gov.uk/docbank/index. cfm?id=3724. It is lengthy so you could refer to chapters 1 and 6 in that document to begin with. These pages will provide you with further background about principles and processes.

Children are deemed to have special educational needs if they have a *learning difficulty* which requires *special educational provision* to be made for them. The DfES code defines children as having *a learning difficulty* if they:

a) have a significantly greater difficulty in learning than the majority of children of the same age;

b) have a disability which prevents or hinders them from making use of educational facilities of a kind generally provided for children of the same age in schools within the area of the local education authority; or

c) are under compulsory school age and fall within the definition at (a) or (b) above or would so do if special educational provision was not made for them.

Children must not be regarded as having a learning difficulty solely because the language or form of language of their home is different from the language in which they will be taught.

Special educational provision means:

(a) for children of two or over, educational provision which is additional to, or otherwise different from, the educational provision made generally for children of their age in schools maintained by the LA [local authority], other than special schools, in the area;

(b) for children under two, educational provision of any kind. (2001: 6, 1.3)

The Special Educational Needs Co-ordinator (SENCO) in each school or college, together with the head teacher and other staff have particular responsibilities for the way the code is operated in the school. For information about the key responsibilities of the SENCO refer to page 65, section 6.5, in the DfES code. Most schools have a small special educational needs or learning support department whose staff support students both in withdrawal groups or in situ alongside the subject teacher in their classroom. Also, and increasingly as a result of work force remodelling (see Chapter 7) many schools offer additional types of support both in the classroom and beyond.

You will observe and work with some students with special educational needs who have been *statemented*. This means that a statutory assessment of their learning difficulties will have been carried out by the local authority and a statement of their learning difficulty will have been produced. Not all students who are assessed will be given statements. The code requires that those students with statements should have short-term targets set. The targets and strategies for achieving these targets are usually arrived at after discussions with the student concerned, parents/carers and teaching/support staff. The agreed strategies are then set out in an Individual Education Plan (**IEP**). The IEP only records provision which is additional to or different from the school's normal differentiated curriculum provision. Each student's IEP is reviewed annually and new targets set. There are also special arrangements for review at key transition stages such at the end of Year 6 and Year 9. If you are given any IEPs to read or are asked to participate in review processes, you should be aware that IEPs are confidential documents and you must handle them with great professional care.

Activity 3.2   Finding out more about whole-school approaches to Special Educational Needs students

Parts (a) and (d) require you to work closely with a more experienced teacher. For parts (b) and (c) you should work with a small group of beginning teachers in the same school.

a) Read through chapters 1 and 6 of the SEN Code of Practice (DfES, 2001). Then ask your mentor or special educational needs co-ordinator (SENCO) to allow you to read the school or college's own guidelines relating to children with special educational needs. Discuss with this person how the school implements and monitors these guidelines. Ask for examples of how this is done.

b) Working in a small group of beginning teachers consider a selection of IEPs used in your school or college. Discuss the range of special needs which have been identified and explore how as subject teachers each of you might start to develop some practical strategies to teach these students.

c) For each IEP select one target from the box headed IEP TARGETS and write down some practical strategies you could use to enable the student to reach their target. For example:

IEP Target: 'Increase self-esteem'
Strategy 1: give appropriate praise when student behaves as agreed.
Strategy 2: select student to carry out responsible task.

Discuss your ideas with the SENCO or other suitably experienced teacher, reflect on their advice and refine your ideas further as necessary.

d) Ask your mentor or the SENCO to explain the roles and responsibilities of *others* who support students' learning and to suggest ways in which teachers can effectively manage 'other adults' to improve their students' learning. Make a list of key suggestions to help you to liaise and work effectively with others in this learning team.

Differentiation

The materials you use with all groups of learners will need to be differentiated to suit the learning needs and prior learning of your students and to ensure that all are engaged in activities which challenge them appropriately. **Differentiation** can be planned for in many different ways, for example as follows.

By task

Different tasks or versions of the same task are provided for different students – some versions, tasks may be *scaffolded* using *a writing frame* whereas other versions may rely on the student to start the task without support.

By resource

The same task is provided but with a range of easier or more demanding resources.

By support

Some students in the group may work with a support teacher or learning assistant to complete the activity according to need.

By outcome

The same task is provided but it is open-ended so that different responses can be made by different students.

By grading

A task is provided with many parts. Some parts are more demanding and not all students will cover these.

You will need to choose the methods which are most appropriate for the individuals in your class. Learning how to *plan* for differentiation and how to introduce differentiated materials or tasks sensitively to students *without drawing undue attention to their differences* are both challenging aspects of your developing practice. As you become increasingly familiar with the students in your classes you will begin to develop your skills in this area. The reflective cycle of lesson planning and evaluation together with lesson observations and conversations with your mentor will all help you to identify specific support needs and appropriate strategies to use. We return to the issue of differentiation in Chapter 4.

There are several websites which you might want to refer to when exploring the different learning needs of your students and effective strategies to support them.

Multiverse

www.multiverse.ac.uk/ This website includes a comprehensive range of resources that focus on the educational achievement of students from diverse backgrounds.

Behaviour 4 Learning

www.behaviour4learning.ac.uk This website aims to provide high-quality and relevant resources that will enable you to engage with the principles of behaviour for learning to improve the management of classroom behaviour, enable achievement and foster the emotional well-being of learners.

Activity 3.3   Planning for differentiation

This activity can be completed individually and in conjunction with your mentor.

Look at the differentiation strategies listed in this section and, either on your own, or with your mentor, discuss which strategies have you observed or used in a classroom. What problems have you noticed or encountered? Which strategies appeared to be the most successful? Why do you think this was? What other strategies have you seen? Which would you want to try out?

Now plan with your mentor how you will incorporate one of the strategies into your own teaching.

Gifted and talented learners

There are many definitions of the diverse group of *gifted and talented* learners you will teach. The term was first used in the *Excellence in Cities* initiative with the aim of identifying the 5 to 10 per cent of students within each school who were eligible for a particular teaching programme which would meet their educational needs (QCA, 2007a). This QCA guidance on how to define these students identifies:

- *gifted* learners as those who have abilities in one or more subjects in the statutory school curriculum other than art and design, music and PE
- *talented* learners as those who have abilities in art and design, music, PE, or performing arts such as dance and drama.

Being gifted and talented is not only about attaining high test scores. It can also include those who might demonstrate leadership qualities, high-level practical skills or creative thinking. Furthermore, the skills of some of the gifted and talented students you teach might not be apparent to you. Some learners are underachievers with learning difficulties, while some may lack motivation or have low self-esteem. Other students could be suffering as a result of low teacher or parental expectations which means they might not be sufficiently challenged or stimulated by their learning. Boredom and frustration in high-ability children can be expressed in disruptive behaviour, with the result that they may be treated as if of low ability. These are just some of the reasons why adopting an inclusive approach to planning for learning is so important. Such reasoning is based on an understanding that the terms *achievement* and *attainment* are not interchangeable, and that care and attention is needed in the way in which teachers attach labels such as *low attainer* or *low ability* to particular students in their care.

There have been many attempts to define the characteristics of gifted and talented learners. The following list extends some earlier lists which were developed as a means of identifying those students of exceptional ability (see, for example, George, 1992). Gifted and talented students as a more diverse group of able learners can show some of the following characteristics. They:

- can think quickly and accurately
- work systematically
- generate creative working solutions
- work flexibly, processing unfamiliar information and applying knowledge, experience and insight to unfamiliar situations
- communicate their thoughts and ideas well
- are determined, diligent and interested in uncovering patterns
- achieve, or show potential, in a wide range of contexts
- might be particularly creative
- show great sensitivity or empathy
- demonstrate particular physical dexterity or skill
- make sound judgements
- could be outstanding leaders or team members
- are fascinated by, or passionate about, a particular subject or aspect of the curriculum
- demonstrate high levels of attainment across a range of subjects within a particular subject, or aspects of work. (www.nc.uk.net/gt/general/01_characteristics.htm)

You need to treat lists like this with caution as they cannot fully describe the nature of individual learners, each of whom may exhibit different characteristics from each other. However, they do provide a starting point for further reflection. There are a number of websites which contain a wealth of information, guidance and resources in relation to working with gifted and talented students, including:

- the QCA site at www.nc.uk.net/gt/index.htm
- National Association for Able Children in Education (NACE) website at www.nace.co.uk
- National Association for Gifted Children at www.nagcbritain.org.uk.

Activity 3.4   Gifted and Talented learners

The first two parts are paired activities, part (a) involving another beginning teacher and (part b) your mentor. Part (c) can be built into your planning, teaching and evaluation processes during school practice.

a) After reading the section in Chapter 3 on gifted and talented students and referring to the suggested website links, discuss the following with another beginning teacher:

   i) Clarify your views on the use of the term 'gifted and talented' and the definitions provided in the list of characteristics.

   ii) Indicate whether you have encountered (either in your own education, in your classroom observations or teaching so far) students who may be considered 'gifted and talented'. How were their gifts or talents evident? How were these qualities accommodated and or encouraged within the systems provided by that school or college?

Examples might include: the Fast Thinkers' club; a residential course for Year 9 to consider the demands of Key Stage 4 and courses/choices beyond that stage; quizzes and competitions such as entering the BA CREST (CREativity in Science and Technology) awards, or even the prestigious AstraZeneca Young Scientist of the Year.

b) Ask your mentor about how the youngest gifted and talented students might be identified and supported early on within your own subject area and across the curriculum. Make a list of the implications that these processes might have for your own approaches to planning and monitoring students' progress.

c) Plan a lesson that involves you in using one or more differentiated learning strategies (see Acitivity 3.3) for the more able students in your class. Review your lesson using the following questions:

   i)   How did you make judgements about these students' abilities?

   ii) How did you make judgements about the level of difficulty or challenge of the work?

   iii) Did you choose to give the more able students more work to do (in terms of quantity) or more difficult work?

   iv) Did these students appear to enjoy their given work/tasks? How well did they get on? What kinds of interest (or questions) did they reveal to you?

Finally consider the advantages and disadvantages of each differentiated strategy that is available. Discuss these with your mentor.

English as an additional language (EAL)

It is estimated that approximately 273 languages are now spoken by children in British schools and around 9 per cent of secondary school children speak a language other than English at home (CILT, 2005). The number for whom English is an additional language (**EAL**) has risen by 50 per cent since 1997 (NALDIC, 2007). Students for whom English is an additional language are those for whom English is not the language usually spoken in their home (their mother tongue). They have diverse needs in terms of support they require to develop their English language learning. Some students may arrive in your classroom already being able to speak two or more languages other than English. They may be refugees or asylum seekers still recovering from the trauma of what they have left behind. They may have moved with their parents to the UK for employment reason or may already be fluent in English and without need of language support. Cummins (1981) makes the important point that EAL students can become conversationally fluent within approximately two years of their initial exposure to English, but they will require five to seven years to catch up with native English speakers in terms of their academic language proficiency. Planning of appropriate and inclusive support strategies for these students must take into account factors such as: their age; the length of time they have been in the UK; their previous educational experiences; and their skills in other languages (DfEE and QCA, 1999).

Some schools make additional provision for EAL learners and will use Ethnic Minority Achievement Grant (EMAG) funding to finance additional specialist teachers and support staff. These might include EAL and EMA teachers or co-ordinators, bilingual teaching assistants (BTAs) and higher level teaching assistants (HLTAs) (see Chapters 6 and 7). However specialist staffing is usually limited to schools/colleges with significant numbers of bilingual or ethnic minority learners. In mainly monolingual areas, specialist staff are likely to be employed by the local authority (**LA**) rather than a school. They may undertake only advisory visits, short-term placements or offer peripatetic support to schools (Rankine and Thompson, 2007).

In planning and teaching your own lessons, you will need to think carefully about the subject terminology you are using and your own idiomatic use of language. When giving instructions, explaining concepts or asking questions ensure that you express yourself clearly and unambiguously. When students first arrive in your classroom and begin to try to make sense of their new linguistic context, they may appear to be very quiet but this does not mean they are not listening. Their confidence can be boosted at an early stage if they are given opportunities to use their mother tongue and to be involved in some way in speaking and listening activities. Here are some further suggestions for good practice which are just as useful for all other learners too. Think about why each of them might be helpful:

- Using pictures, photographs and other visual aids to support written text.
- Distinguishing between reading and talking.
- Organizing tasks into groups where collaboration must take place.

- Using alternative ways of recording information other than writing.
- Giving students opportunities to talk ideas through before discussing them in front of class.
- Using mind maps® to organize ways of thinking before writing.
- Allowing students to work in a language other than English.
- Using bilingual skills as part of the learning process.
- Organizing reading tasks in pairs where one stronger reader supports a weaker reader.
- Offering lots of opportunities for students to talk about what they are learning.

Refer to the separate subject support booklets entitled *Access and Engagement in …* (followed by the name of the National Curriculum subject name) which are available at www.standards.dfes.gov.uk/secondary/keystage3/all/respub. These will provide you with a range of practical strategies to support your students' EAL learning. You should also visit the National Association for Language Development in the Curriculum (NALDIC) website www.naldic.org. uk/ITTSEAL2/teaching/knowledge.cfm which includes a bank of portraits of EAL students, annotated reading lists and a wide variety of other materials designed for teachers in the initial stage of their training.

Bilingualism is an asset and research has shown that children who are bilingual can draw on their linguistic abilities in other learning processes. It is every teacher's responsibility to utilize and celebrate the diversity of language and culture within their own classrooms in order to ensure that all students are fully involved in their learning.

Activity 3.5   EAL fact finding

In your placement school or college try to find some answers to the following questions:

- How many different languages are spoken by students in the school?

- Are students given the chance to speak languages other than English at the school? If they are, where does this occur?

- Is written language (other than English) used around the school and, if so, where and why?

- What provision is made for specialist EAL support?

- How many students are there with EAL needs and what is known about their ethnicity?

(Continued)

(Continued)

- How are their English language learning needs identified, monitored and supported?

- How are their levels of literacy in their home languages assessed?

- What sort of cognitive testing is available to assess non language based skills (for example, memory, sequencing, and so on) and who does this?

- If your school does not have any EAL students, try to find out what would happen if a new EAL student were to start today. What support or provision is made available for this possibility?

Compare your findings with those of a beginning teacher working in a different location.

Personalized learning

In the twenty-first century there is an increasing emphasis on personalized learning in which curriculum and teaching methods are tailored to meet every individual's needs, interests and aptitudes to ensure they receive equality of opportunity (in terms of support) as they strive to achieve the highest standards possible in their subject-based learning (wherever they are placed on the ability spectrum) and to develop their *personal learning and thinking skills* (**PLT**s). Within the various ability grouping arrangements already explored, the particular needs of the individual learner must be a priority. It is an admirable aim but is also one which can present significant challenges for teachers. The implications of personalized learning and how this is embedded in assessment for learning are explored in Chapters 4 and 5. For further information on the latest thinking about personalized learning, refer to the introductory booklet which can be downloaded from: www.standards.dfes.gov.uk/personalisedlearning/about/.

Learning in out-of-school contexts

Learning does not just take place within a school building, nor does it end when students leave compulsory schooling behind. As we shall see in Chapter 4, e-learning can facilitate learning (including feedback dialogue) in the home and elsewhere. The National Curriculum emphasizes the importance of learning in out-of-school contexts such as fieldwork, theatre and museum visits and employment-related settings, and in taking opportunities for cross-curricular work in these situations (QCA, 2007b). The amount of time devoted to learning outside the classroom could vary significantly, depending on the schools and teacher training institutions in which you are working and their own priorities (Kendall et al., 2006). There is evidence of a decline in education outside the classroom in recent years which could be due to teachers' concerns about health, safety and litigation, issues of subject knowledge, their lack of confidence in teaching outdoors, and curriculum requirements which limit opportunities for learning in out of school contexts (Ofsted, 2004; Rickinson et al., 2004). Although it is not compulsory for beginning teachers to teach in out-of-school contexts, you should be able (with support from experienced staff) to plan opportunities for purposeful learning outside of the classroom in a safe environment. You will be able to reflect further on how to plan for such learning and its health and safety and legal implications in Chapter 7.

USEFUL WEBSITES:

Live links to these sites can be found on the companion website.

Education Outside the Classroom (the UK government manifesto) can be accessed at www.teachernet.gov.uk/teachingandlearning/resourcematerials/outsideclassroom. For outdoor classroom resources see also www.field-studies-council.org/resources.

How do national initiatives shape the learning experience?

Those of you who are beginning to teach within the English state educational system will find you are located within a heavily prescriptive and centralized system, dominated by a set of curriculum initiatives and a 'high stakes' testing agenda which undoubtedly exert an influence on your emerging classroom practice. Clearly it is important that you learn about what is required and expected of you within any classroom context and, indeed, national initiatives will inform aspects of your initial teacher education. However, to become a critically reflective practitioner, it is also vitally important that you take the opportunity to develop independent, critical judgements about initiatives and overarching curriculum structures within whichever system you are working. In this way you will be able to serve the interests of the specific learners you are teaching and be better placed to both challenge and contribute to debates about the future shape and content of teaching and learning.

The National Curriculum underpins teaching and learning from 5–16 in England and Wales in all core (English, Maths, Science and ICT) and foundation subjects. Its programmes of study are statutory. Since its inception in 1990, it has gone through a number of revisions. The latest version, launched in schools in

September 2007 following a period of review and public consultation, was due to become statute in September 2008 (as this book went to press). The National Curriculum is based on a statement of values which include valuing ourselves, our relationships with others, and the society and environment in which we live. Its aims, which have been shaped by the *Every Child Matters* (**ECM**) agenda and are included in the new programmes of study for every National Curriculum subject, are :

> The curriculum should enable all young people to become:
>
> - successful learners who enjoy learning, make progress and achieve;
> - confident individuals who are able to live safe, healthy and fulfilling lives;
> - responsible citizens who make a positive contribution to society. (QCA, 2007b: 5)

The 2008 National Curriculum includes a series of dimensions: global, enterprise, creativity, cultural understanding and diversity. These are intended to provide a context and focus for work within and between subjects and across the whole curriculum. They should give students opportunities for engaging with ideas and issues that affect their lives and the world beyond school (QCA, 2007b). You will need explore how each term is being interpreted and exemplified within your own subject area online and across the curriculum as a whole. For updates and new documentation on this topic and other aspects of the new national curriculum you should regularly refer to www.qca.org.uk/curriculum.

In the past 10 years, approaches to teaching and learning in England and Wales have been heavily influenced by the introduction of the non-statutory, but widely implemented *National Primary and Secondary Strategies*. These first arrived in all schools in 1998 and 2001 respectively and have been developed significantly since then. In many schools, in the core subjects of English, mathematics and science at least, it would appear that Key Stage 3 Strategy documents have superseded National Curriculum documentation. Together with GCSE and A level specifications, these are the most regularly referred to by departments to inform their schemes of work and day-to-day planning. As the latest version of the new National Curriculum takes shape in England and Wales it is inevitably accompanied by revisions to Strategy documentation. A revised Primary Strategy was published in November 2006 but it is too early to be certain of what will follow at secondary level or what the relationship between the documents might be.

14–19 Curriculum

A government White Paper in 2005 set out proposals for reforming 14–19 education in England and Wales, with the aim of equipping young people

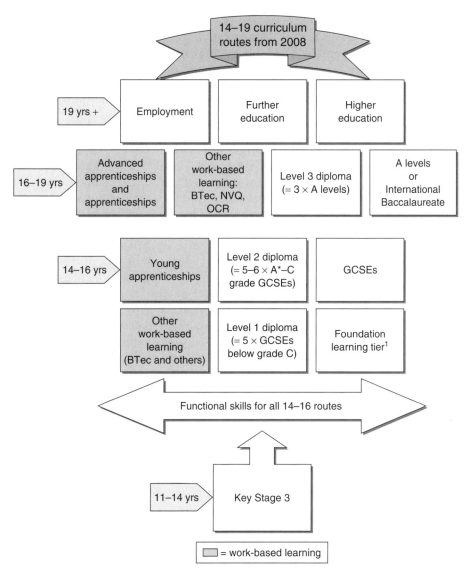

Figure 3.1 New curriculum routes for 14-19 year olds (adapted from Jewell, 2007)

with the skills and knowledge they will need for adult life. The proposals give vocational qualifications (such as levels 2 and 3 diploma courses as shown in Figure 3.1) parity in terms of esteem with academic GCSE and

A level courses and provide alternative pathways into higher or further education. Students in the 14–16 age range will also have greater opportunities to participate in work-based learning and courses in further education colleges than previously. Provision of the increasingly popular International Baccalaureate (IB) post-16 multidisciplinary diploma courses will be doubled by 2010 (for further information on the IB refer to the website at the end of this section). Reaction to the proposals in the 2005 White Paper has been mixed. Some have expressed disappointment that the radical proposals for change previously made by the Tomlinson Working Group on 14–19 in their final report (DfES, 2004) had been sidelined while opportunities had also been missed to close the divide between GCSE and post-16 qualification routes which remain very separate within the new proposals. Some critics have questioned a perceived lack of challenge for the most able students at A level standard (Mansell and Lee, 2005). One outcome of this is that the Cambridge Information Examination Board is working with some independent schools to develop a *Pre-U diploma* for candidates applying for undergraduate courses. This entrance examination will exist outside of the national framework described here. However, from September 2008, A level teachers in all subject areas begin preparing their students to sit new examinations: each A level specification contains four modules of assessment (two in AS and two in A2). The new A2 units have been designed to offer a greater degree of *stretch and challenge* than those on offer previously through use of a range of assessment strategies. Overall, the curriculum choices available from 2008 to the overwhelming majority of students at all levels will begin to have a different shape. Figure 3.1 provides an outline of the structure

For further information on the different routes and subject specific details you should also refer to the DfES, QCA and examination board websites at:

www.dfes.gov.uk/14-19/	Department for Education and Skills 14 –19 site
www.qca.org.uk/15.html	Qualifications and Curriculum Authority
www.aqa.org.uk	Assessment and Qualification Alliance examination board
www.edexcel.org.uk	Edexcel examination board
www.ibo.org/	International Baccalaureate Organization
www.wjec.co.uk	Welsh Joint Examination Council
www.ocr.org.uk	OCR examination board
www.pre-u.co.uk/	'Independent advice and support' for Pre-U.

Activity 3.6   Curriculum routes for 14–19 year olds

A small group activity (working in a small group with other beginning teachers who are all in different placement schools or colleges with 14–19-year-olds).

Those of you in the group who have suitable access should try to interview the curriculum co-ordinator in your placement school or college about the 14–19 curriculum routes. Find out:

- how the institution has already implemented/is planning to implement the different routes within its curriculum structures from 2008;

- the curriculum co-ordinator's views on the national qualifications framework (and also, if relevant, the Pre-U diploma).

Then summarize what kind of guidance is being offered to students at 14, 16 and 18 about which route(s) they should consider taking.

Share your individual findings with the rest of the group. What conclusions can you arrive at (as a group) about the choices and the guidance on offer in these different institutions? Write up these conclusions. Ensure you consider:

- How are vocational qualifications perceived generally, and how are they perceived within particular curriculum areas?

- What are the common features of provision and what are the areas of contrast?

- What particular concerns have these co-ordinators expressed?

Key skills and functional skills

Key skills are currently embedded within the assessment frameworks at all levels of the curriculum. There are six designated key skill areas. These consist of three *core* skills – communication, application of number, ICT– and three *outer skills* – working with others, improving own learning and performance, problem-solving. Some schools and colleges have fully embraced key skills and integrated them in to their schemes of work. However, the implementation of key skills has been problematic in many contexts with concerns being raised both about available space on timetables and assessment overload for both teachers and students.

Functional skills are currently being developed at three levels with the intention of bringing together key skills, adult literacy and numeracy. The DfES (2007) describes functional skills as: 'core elements of English, Maths and ICT that provide an individual with the essential knowledge, skills and understanding that will enable them to operate confidently, effectively and independently in life and at work'. Their introduction comes during a period when employers and the Confederation of British Industry (CBI) have argued that poor basic skills cause lost productivity (Edexcel, 2007). Embedded within the 2008 National Curriculum programmes of study for English, Mathematics and ICT at Key Stages 3 and 4 are the functional skills to be attained by students at levels 1 and 2 (see Figure 3.1). The implementation of functional skills testing in English, mathematics and ICT at GCSE level is scheduled to begin in 2009 (for English and ICT) and 2010 for mathematics. At the time of writing it is unclear what the arrangements will be for post-compulsory education or whether there is an intention to make direct links between the assessment of functional and key skills. Concerns have already been raised about the nature of the functional skills tests and their relationship to the subjects within they will be assessed. For example the National Association for the Teaching of English (NATE) fears that functionality will be taught and tested in a de-contextualised way (NATE, 2006). Functional skills work also needs to acknowledge education is a lifelong experience and that employers have a responsibility to support employers through work-based training. You are advised to keep up to date with developments in this area by consulting the QCA and examination board websites (listed earlier in this section) for details.

Activity 3.7   Finding out more about functional skills

You can complete part (a) individually and the remaining parts in conjunction with beginning teachers, teachers and students in different areas of the curriculum in one school.

a) What are your personal views about the teaching and the testing of functional skills? How do your views compare with those of a beginning teacher in another subject area? If you are training to be an English, ICT or Mathematics teacher you may find that you have very different thoughts on this from a teacher in another curriculum area.

b) Now investigate the views of some experienced teachers in different curriculum areas and students learning about functional skills. Do their various perspectives change or confirm your own earlier impressions?

c) Find out how your placement school is embedding the teaching of functional skills within the whole curriculum. You could focus on one specific skills area and investigate its implementation and teaching together with the way this is being monitored at a whole-school level.

Literacy

Use of the term *literacy* is widespread in primary schools and has even begun to be seen as a discrete element of the timetable in some secondary schools. But what does *literacy* mean and why should it be of concern to beginning teachers from *all* subject areas? Prior to the late twentieth century, literacy was deemed to be concerned largely with *reading* and *writing*. In the twenty-first century, *speaking* and *listening* are more readily accepted as being key elements of literacy. Furthermore, in recent years terms such as *media literacy*, *visual literacy*, *emotional literacy* and *scientific literacy* have also become familiar. In Australia and New Zealand some of these terms have been more fully acknowledged within these nations' curriculum structures. If it is carefully integrated within the curriculum, literacy should be about learning to apply reading, writing and speaking skills and strategies in a range of different situations and should be about far more than form-filling, writing job applications and using functional English.

In England and Wales, *The National Literacy Strategy* was introduced by a government intent on pushing up standards and developing a more literate young workforce that would be equipped for entering 'a fulfilling adult life' (DfEE, 1998: 1). The Strategy's *Framework for Teaching English in Years 7, 8 and 9* (DfEE, 2001) was introduced to all schools, midway through a pilot project and before its evaluation was complete (Furlong et al., 2001). Although a non-statutory document, the 'policing of Key Stage Three teaching' (Fleming and Stevens, 2004: 19) through Ofsted and Strategy team consultants has ensured its widespread adoption in schools. Undoubtedly, it has had the most impact on English teaching. However, the Strategy also has a strong cross-curricular focus. Ensuring students become literate members of society is not just the remit of the English department: all teaching staff from every subject area have a responsibility to teach students to use language accurately and effectively to express themselves, as the rationale to the *Framework for Teaching English* states:

> Teachers have a genuine stake in strong language skills because language enables thought. Language goes beyond just 'writing up' what is learnt and 'looking up' information in a text; it is in acts of reading and writing that meanings are forged, refined and fixed. Finding the right words, giving shape to an idea, articulating what is meant: this is where language is synonymous with learning. (DfEE, 2001: 15)

To support their implementation of *Literacy across the Curriculum* all schools received training materials which include subject-specific folders. A member of staff will also have responsibility for co-ordinating the literacy policy and practice across the school. The National Curriculum statement on 'Use of language across the curriculum' (DfES and QCA, 1999: 40) underlines the common responsibilities of teachers of all subjects. In terms of your responsibilities, it will be important to ensure that:

1. you model accurate and appropriate use of written and spoken Standard English in your instructions, questioning, management of discussion, writing on the whiteboard, assessment feedback, teaching resources, displays, planning documents, reporting to parents and carers and so on;
2. your students are taught to use reading strategies to help them locate information, follow arguments and synthesize or summarize ideas;
3. your students are taught to organize their writing coherently and to use correct spelling and punctuation and follow grammatical conventions;
4. you give students opportunities to share and try out their initial ideas orally and to experiment with different forms of presentation which require little or no writing (such as drama activities involving role plays, tableaux and still pictures or storyboards, posters, diagrams, collages, debates and PowerPoint presentations);
5. you enable students to learn to use and spell correctly the technical and specialist vocabulary, expressions and other language structures associated with your particular subject(s).

Point 4 is particularly important as teachers can tend to ascertain their students' understanding via written responses. This emphasis on writing can not only devalue skills development in other methods of communication but also make it difficult for those English as an additional language learners (who have newly arrived in the country or have little English) to participate or demonstrate their understanding.

The following sections on reading, writing and spelling provide further specific details about these key processes.

Reading

Whatever your subject area, you will be faced with the challenge of enabling your students to read and engage with written and visual material when not all of those in your classes will be confident readers. It is important that you develop an understanding of the challenges students face when they read different types of texts such as reports, calculations, graphs, surveys, poems, instructions, scripts, historical artefacts and multi-modal texts (that is, texts that use more than one mode of communication such as films, gaming texts and web pages). You also need to be aware of the variety of strategies which readers can use so that you can support your own students' reading and learning.

The main types of reading are:

- continuous reading
- close reading (with attention to details and/or aspects of style)
- skimming
- scanning
- reading backwards and forwards (for example, to check for clues or evidence).

Through the work of Wray and Lewis (1997) on the *Nuffield Extending Literacy Project* (EXEL) the EXIT Extending Interactions with Texts model was developed (Lewis and Wray, 2000). This model is said to have had a major influence on aspects of the *Framework for English in Years 7, 8 and 9*, especially that concerned with writing non-fiction and *Literacy across the Curriculum* (Harrison, 2002). Lewis and Wray (2000: 17) identified 10 elements of the complex process that occurs during the reading of information texts:

1. Elicitation of previous knowledge.
2. Establishing purposes.
3. Locating information.
4. Adopting an appropriate strategy.
5. Interacting with text.
6. Monitoring understanding.
7. Making a record.
8. Evaluating information.
9. Assisting memory.
10. Communicating information.

A number of strategies for reading, writing or 'interacting with texts' (ibid.) link closely with the above 10 reading processes. The most well known and widely used of these are **DARTs** (Directed Activities Related to Texts) (see also Chapter 2). Lunzer and Gardner's development of DARTs stemmed from research which uncovered the limited interactions that took place during reading in school either between a reader and a text or between groups of readers in the classroom (Lunzer and Gardner, 1984). Consequently, DARTs are activities that create opportunities for shared exploration of texts, thus providing feedback which is especially needed by weaker readers if they are to develop their textual comprehension. Ultimately, the interaction and discussion which DARTs stimulate about a text or an issue should be of primary importance rather than the dogged pursuit of correct answers. DARTs include the following:

Reconstructive activities

Examples include:

- prediction (of next lines, chapters, events, endings)
- cloze (a type of prediction where words, phrases, line endings or rhymes are blanked out and readers use contextual clues to 'make' the text
- sequencing (of lines, sentences, paragraphs, stanzas, images, and so on).

Processing activities

Examples are:

- highlighting, underlining or text marking
- labelling
- card sorting and statement games
- drawing spider diagrams, mind maps® or graphs
- generating questions about a text.

Re-creative activities

These include:

- storyboarding
- rewriting the text in a different genre or from a different point of view.

DARTs are very prevalent in the teaching of English, humanities and science subjects and are also used to promote the development of thinking skills across the curriculum. Like any activity they need to be used sparingly and only where appropriate.

Activity 3.8   Embedding and supporting reading activities in your planning and teaching

This activity involves paired work with another teacher.

a) Take stock of the range of different reading which students will be required to undertake in your subject area and the purposes of this reading (refer to the list of text types in the first paragraph of this section). What particular challenges do you think each text type could present them with? In consultation with another beginning teacher or your mentor try to decide on what might be the most suitable activities you could use to make each of these different text types accessible to your students.

b) Take three short pieces of a text type on a related theme which are commonly used in your subject area with a particular year group. Submit them to a readability test such as SMOG (simplified measure of gobbledgook) available at www.literacytrust.org.uk/campaign/SMOG.html.

What issues does this test raise for you about the suitability of the texts you have chosen and of the readability test itself?

c) In your lesson observations look carefully at the different reading activities (such as DARTs) used with each teaching group. Which appear to be the most effective in engaging students and developing their understanding? Are any activities over-used or under-used? Make sure you follow up your reflections with your mentor and aim to try out some of the activities with your own classes.

Writing

As a beginning teacher you may well be someone who has previously been successful at writing. Therefore, you might find it hard to understand that some students will find writing to be a laborious and stressful activity. It is essential that you do not underestimate the skills needed for what might seem to be simple tasks such as jotting down homework information or making notes when watching a film clip or summarizing key points heard in a talk you have listened to. If students are to make progress with their writing you will need to ensure you build their confidence by:

- modelling and demonstrating the forms and styles of writing you wish them to create
- ensuring students understand the intended audience and purpose(s) for their writing
- providing opportunities to rehearse ideas orally and/or make rough drafts where appropriate
- allowing alternative forms of presentation (for example, storyboard, poster, diagram, PowerPoint, role play) which may have a limited writing requirement
- giving clear instructions about your expectations (in terms of length, structure, layout, headings, spelling, and so on) and the criteria you will use to assess the written work

- thinking carefully and seeking advice about how you will assess the writing (for example, what type of corrections, whether you will grade the work, how you will provide feedback to inform future written work)
- not using writing tasks as a means of control in your classroom.

One strategy which you might use to *scaffold* their writing is the *writing frame* (see Chapter 2). Originally advocated for use by primary school children as a way to initiate the writing of whole texts or to enable students to make links between sections of a text, writing frames are now widely used across many subject areas across all ages. Forests of worksheets have sprung up as a result. The frames are intended to support learners' interactions with texts and provide an integrated approach to their development of reading, writing, speaking and listening and social skills. Writing frames can be invaluable for less confident communicators in that they give them a structure for their ideas which can be withdrawn as the writer becomes more confident. The structure might include:

- sentence stems for completion (that is, 'I agree that …', 'In my view … ', 'In contrast, you could say … ')
- sentence shells with blanked out phrases (that is, 'The verbs … and … used in the line show the writer's … ' or ' When the … mixes with … solution, a … reaction occurs'.)
- paragraph openings
- paragraph endings
- word banks (that is, words connected with fire to support descriptive writing: *flame, alight, fiery, burst, smoulder, smoke, tinder, rage, billow, crackle, flicker, spark, blaze, scorch, incinerate, sweltering, ignite, molten, flare, draw, burn, kindle, fume, incandescent, conflagration, wildfire*).

Unless writing frames are used with care, they can become straitjackets which reduce both the level of challenge offered by a text and the opportunities for high-level individual responses to it. Furthermore, students could spend whole days using one writing frame after another in different subject areas. It will therefore be important for you to investigate the different writing strategies used in your placement school to ensure that you use a variety of approaches to engage learners.

If you are completing your training in England you will be required to pass skills tests in literacy, numeracy and ICT. If you are anxious about these tests, it is very important that you share your concerns with your course tutor as soon as possible so that you can be supported appropriately.

Activity 3.9   Literacy

An individual activity.

a) Look again at points 1–5 on page 92 concerning your responsibilities for literacy within your own teaching. What challenges do they present for you as a beginning teacher? Think honestly about your own spoken communication skills and the accuracy of your written expression. Can you identify aspects of your literacy skills that might need attention before you model them with a class? Make a list and share these with your mentor or an English teacher or your course tutor. Identify the strategies or resources you might need to adopt to build your own confidence.

b) Refer to Appendix 3 of the Framework for Teaching English in Years 7, 8 and 9. This can be accessed at www.standards.dfes.gov.uk/secondary/keystage3/respub/englishframework/section3appendices/spelling_lists/. It consists of general and subject spelling lists of words which represent common errors for this age range. These lists are not intended for blanket teaching but your own students may need to be helped to learn particular words they are uncertain about. Use these lists as the starting point for a number of on-going activities:

   i) Carry out a personal check on your own spelling and investigate strategies for learning words which you find difficult to spell. These include look–cover–say–write–check, rhymes, words within words and mnemonics (see Chapter 2). You could ask a beginning English teacher to help you get started with these strategies.

   ii) Develop one of the subject spelling lists further (or start one if your subject area is not listed) into a glossary of words and phrases you would want students aged 11–19 to use confidently in your subject.

   iii) Find out about the cross-curricular policy and strategies used in your placement schools to support spelling and vocabulary building by talking with your school's literacy co-ordinator.

Numeracy and mathematics

Numeracy skills are essential for adult life. Those learners who leave school without them have been shown to place themselves at a serious disadvantage (Bynner and Parsons, 1997). As with literacy and ICT, there is an expectation that teachers are numerate and able to use their skills effectively in the classroom. The term *numeracy* is sometimes used interchangeably with mathematics. It is concerned primarily with number and the way numbers operate. A numerate person is someone who is able to solve numerical problems such as those involving money or measurement. They will also be familiar with how numerical information can be stored, counted and presented. However, numeracy is but one element of the much broader subject of Mathematics, as is demonstrated below in the Key Stage 3 programme of study:

> Mathematical thinking is important for all members of a modern society as a habit of mind, for its use in the workplace, business and finance, and for both personal and public decision-making. Mathematics is fundamental to national prosperity in providing tools, for understanding of science, engineering and technology, and for participation in the knowledge economy. The language of mathematics is international. The subject transcends cultural boundaries and its importance is universally recognised.
>
> Mathematics equips pupils with uniquely powerful ways to describe, analyse and change the world. Pupils who are functional in mathematics and financially capable are able to think independently in applied and abstract ways, to reason, solve problems and assess risk.
>
> Mathematics is a creative discipline. It can stimulate moments of pleasure and wonder for all pupils when they solve a problem for the first time, discover a more elegant solution, or notice hidden connections. (QCA, 2007c)

The mathematics curriculum therefore aims to develop learners who are not only numerate but who are creative, have enquiring minds and are able to solve problems.

National policy in England and Wales has enforced the place of numeracy as a key skill within the curriculum across the 5–19 age range both within the *Primary Framework for Mathematics* (revised 2006 version) and the *Key Stage 3 Strategy for Mathematics*. Some critics have previously questioned whether the Strategy has a research basis (Brown et al., 1998; Costello, 2000) and the extent to which daily mathematics lessons have had an impact on learners' confidence and competence (Kyriacou and Goulding, 2004).

Associated developments in assessment and examinations are intended to support the development of aspects of numeracy for all learners through, for example, functional skills testing at Key Stage 3 and assessment of key skills. If you are completing your training in England, you will be required to pass a numeracy QTS skills test. This requires you to demonstrate you can:

- carry out mental calculations using time, fractions, percentages, measurements and conversions
- interpret and use statistical information accurately
- use and apply general arithmetic correctly.

For further information about these tests refer to www.tda.gov.uk/skillstests/ numeracy.aspx.

Many teachers have questions concerning the place and provision for numeracy within the curriculum. The following activities should help you to explore some of these.

Activity 3.10   Numeracy and mathematics

An individual activity.

a) What are the personal pleasures and challenges for you of numeracy and, more broadly, of mathematics? Reflect on your own mathematics education as well as your current numeracy skills. Build up a list of your strengths and areas for development. What do you need to do in order to contribute fully to numeracy within your taught programmes in school?

b) Select one of the following topics and investigate it either on your own or with another trainee from your subject area.

   i) What is the range of mathematical skills and mathematical language required in your subject area? Does there appear to be progression in these mathematical demands? To what extent do these demands correlate with programmes of study in mathematics?

   ii) In your placement school is there a whole-school policy for developing numeracy? If so, does the policy involve a numeracy co-ordinator? What is this person's remit? Does the policy refer to use of calculators across the curriculum? How, and how effectively, in your view is the policy being implemented in practice? To what extent is the potential for developing the use and application of mathematical skills in other subjects recognised, realised, and actively supported by the mathematics department?

   iii) What support does the special needs department in your placement school provide for students in coping with numeracy across the curriculum? How are mathematical weaknesses – knowledge gaps, errors or misunderstandings – managed across the curriculum as they arise in different subjects?

Information communications technology and e-learning

All beginning teachers are required to have a working knowledge of information communications technology (ICT) terminology, practical skills and a range of applications suitable to their subjects, as well as to take opportunities to use

ICT with their own students when and where appropriate in different learning situations. For those of you training in England, an ICT skills test must also be passed during your initial teacher training year. The test assesses your ability to fulfil the basic ICT tasks using software applications for word processing, spreadsheets and databases, presentations, email and browsing the web. For further information about test content you should consult www.tda.gov.uk/skillstests/ict/testcontent.aspx. If you are working with 11–14 year olds then these students will also take an ICT functional skills test at the end of Key Stage 3.

Kirschner and Paas define e-learning as: 'learning (and thus the creation of learning and learning arrangements) where the Internet plays an important role in the delivery, support, administration and assessment of learning' (2001: 350). This type of learning can take a number of forms, including the use of the Internet for research purposes or to find usable data. In whatever way it is used, the teacher needs to consider how the learning of the students will be structured. Will students be allowed to find websites by themselves (which could possibly lead to expenditure of a large amount of time to locate and utilize only small amounts of data)? Or will students be given a list of websites to visit? In addition, as the Internet has no medium for checking the truth of 'facts', how will the information retrieved be assessed for its validity? An obvious example is that of **Wikipedia**, where anyone can add information, possibly resulting in incorrect materials. (For more about wikis refer to Chapter 4.)

Opportunities for use of ICT and e-learning are increasingly embedded within subject schemes of work and whole-school policies. When used with care, ICT resources of all kinds can aid the development of students' speaking and listening and personal skills and enable them to work in pairs or small groups with considerable independence. Wireless devices such as wireless keyboards and mice can release teachers from the front of the classroom and facilitate greater student participation (Dymoke, 2005). Videoconferencing can give students access to a wider world, not only geographically but also to a world of experts and experiences that would be difficult to replicate in the classroom (Comber et al., 2004; Lawson and Comber, 2005). Interactive whiteboards (IWBs) can also aid engagement in learning (if all students in a group are encouraged to use the IWBs' tools) and enable greater access to web-based resources. However researchers are still divided on their impact on learning (for example Glover and Miller, 2001). For case studies and teachers' views on IWBs refer to www.virtual learning.org.uk/whiteboards/index.html. Caution is needed to ensure that IWBs do not simply become an expensive twenty-first century version of the blackboard and chalk.

New technologies also offer the potential to develop virtual learning environments and communities. Discussion boards within virtual learning environments (**VLEs**) or carefully monitored chat rooms can be very powerful tools for enabling previously separate groups (either within or across different types of learning communities) to think collaboratively and creatively and to experiment with new directions for teaching and learning (Leach, 2001). Lewis and Allen (2004) identify a number of reasons for the establishment of virtual learning communities within an organizational structure. They translate to a classroom environment as including:

- a response to an identified need for student development
- encouraging integrated responses to complex issues/questions
- enabling students to overcome geographical boundaries in time and space
- supporting continuous development
- bringing students together to share good practice
- providing new approaches to learning
- supporting learning programmes
- achieving project outputs.

As a result of these different aims, they identify three types of community: simple, managed and complex.

Simple virtual learning communities

These often come together spontaneously due to a shared interest. There might be a small core active group with a closed or open nature with respect to membership. Alternatively, a large initial membership may exist dependent on the dynamic of the situation. These communities can be exemplified by discussion boards on VLEs such as *Blackboard*.

Managed virtual learning communities

In a managed virtual learning community, there is more *formal* support from an organization than in a simple VLE (through a moderator or facilitator) and there is a flow of knowledge and skills between the community and the wider organization. For example, in a classroom context this might include a teacher involving other colleagues in responding to specific questions from students, or shared provision of resources/support from staff members.

Complex virtual learning community

These are communities which exist across a region, or across a complex organization. In the case of a school, this might be the community extending between schools, or a community within a school and across the whole curriculum. Hence, this might include such opportunities as collaborative projects, or student participation with students from other places.

Within a school context, the complexity of any virtual learning community will be determined, and perhaps limited, by the nature of the need(s), available technology and technical abilities of the staff involved. However, the development of free VLEs such as *Mamba* and *Moodle* (which work in similar ways to *Blackboard*) make such developments more realizable for school-based frameworks. Where such VLEs are not available, common software packages such as presentational, word processing, spreadsheet, and desktop publishing packages still offer a huge degree of flexibility and much potential in developing the ICT strand of learning.

Wherever they are trained, all beginning teachers need to develop both confidence and competence in ICT in order to know when its use will enhance or contribute in a distinctive way to the learning experience being planned. Think about the learning objectives and outcomes you will want to achieve and how the 'affordances' (Laurillard et al., 2000: 1) or potential benefits of the software or device(s) you are using will help you to achieve those objectives within the context in which you are working. It also important to remember that **affordances** are not open (Somekh, 2004) since they can be constrained by other factors such as school timetables, rooms, resource allocations and previous ICT experiences of students or the other staff you are working with. Therefore, if the ICT use is simply an add on rather than integral element of your teaching plan, then think again. Information and communications technology developments need to add value to what can already be achieved through use of previously established approaches (Hennessey et al., 2003). Allow yourself plenty of time for careful planning to ensure judicious and effective use of the available ICT resources. You can develop your thinking further about planning for ICT use in Chapter 4.

You will also find that many schools use ICT systems for administrative and data collection purposes such as registration, record-keeping, report-writing, student assessment and progress profiling. You should gain hands-on experience of some of these during your placements. You will learn more about ICT for assessment purposes in Chapter 5.

The range and quality of software applications, learning platforms, handheld devices and other hardware continues to grow. The main computer hardware and software applications of ICT that you should aim to be familiar with are listed below but the level of competency required will depend on the needs of your specific subject:

- word processing and desktop publishing
- communications (Internet, email, VLEs, web authoring, social software like Facebook, Flickr and Youtube)
- mind-mapping programs
- graphics and animation packages
- information systems (databases, CD-Rom, DVD)
- spreadsheets for processing numerical data
- data-logging for scientific measurement
- control technology (computers controlling machines)
- presentation software and hardware (such as PowerPoint and digital projectors)
- videoconferencing and web cams
- digital photography and film editing packages
- handheld and wireless devices including interactive voting systems, wireless mice, tablets, personal digital assistants (PDAs), iPods and MP3 players
- interactive whiteboards.

The variety of applications and software can seem challenging. To get started in the classroom it is best to concentrate on a small number of uses at first and gain confidence in them. Above all, you need to know how well the ICT serves the needs of students and enables them to engage and make progress with their learning. You may well find that many students are much more computer literate and confident than you are. Try not to be daunted by this but use it to your advantage and enable them to take the initiative as well as to support others in the classroom.

You should be able to develop your ICT skills further in at least some of the following ways:

1. by the research, preparation and presentation of your assignments, class resources, lesson plans and other teaching materials
2. by exploring potential applications in your classroom teaching and developing awareness of appropriate use. To get started with this investigate the BECTA (British

Educational Communications and Technology Agency) site at www.schools.becta. org.uk

3. by using your training institution's virtual learning environment and/or your school's intranet to communicate with other student teachers, your tutor and/or your school mentor, to share resources and to explore issues related to your own developing practice.

Activity 3.11   ICT Skills

An individual/group activity (parts a and c); individual (part b and part d – individual with mentor support).

a) Identifying and refining your ICT skills

   i) Refer to the list of ICT hardware and software applications listed on page 103. What are your current levels of familiarity and competence with each of these?

   ii) Check what ICT resources (including human resources) are available in your training institution and in your placement schools.

   iii) Find out from your tutor what level of competence you will be expected to have attained in order to achieve QTS or to improve your skills further (if you are already at QTS level) in both use of ICT in your classroom teaching and in other professional aspects of your work. Set yourself clearly defined and realistic half-termly or termly targets and log your progress with these.

   iv) Refer to points 1–3 of the guidance on ICT skills development above. Discuss with other beginning teachers in your own subject area how you can support each other in developing your skills. Agree a programme and put it in place.

b) Identifying your students' ICT skills. Find out about the existing and required skills of the students you will be teaching. What is their existing level of competence? How does it compare with yours? What are the minimum ICT requirements in your main teaching subject for students? How is ICT embedded within the curriculum? What are ICT policy and provision like in your placement school/college in terms of student access and teacher expertise/use?

c) Arrange to observe and evaluate one or two lessons taught by other experienced teachers in your subject area where ICT is in use. These may involve whole classes but not necessarily so. There are several issues which you need to look out for: the skills needed by students, teacher and support staff; the management of the equipment and resources; the context in which tasks are set. In evaluating the lessons focus on the learning outcomes expected from the activities. Does the use of ICT offer **affordances** to the intended learning or could the outcomes have been achieved more effectively through simpler, more conventional methods? What do the activities contribute to the development of students' ICT capability?

d) Teaching a lesson with ICT. Using ICT in the classroom may seem a daunting prospect at first but you should aim to become confident in using ICT wherever it is appropriate in your teaching. Ensure you prepare and teach at least one lesson (and preferably a sequence of lessons) in which teacher and student use of ICT is fully integrated into the learning.

With your mentor's support:

- Draw on your observation experiences and ensure that you have planned the lesson(s) carefully. Make sure you have a clear idea about what you want your students to achieve and how ICT will help them to learn.

- Book equipment/room access well in advance and give yourself plenty of time to practise using equipment and software while planning.

- Ask your mentor to observe your lesson and make sure you reflect on this observation and your own lesson evaluation with this person so that you can identify further developments needed.

CONCLUSION

In this chapter you have learned about the different ways in which learners can be managed, grouped and supported within inclusive education environments. You have gained insights into the impact of national policies which determine (to a greater or a lesser extent) lesson content, delivery and assessment of learning. You have begun to consider the implications of these contexts and policies for your own developing practice. In the next chapter, our lens zooms in from this wide angle to a much tighter focus on the teaching rooms themselves in order to explore how learning and teaching are managed within these often small but vital spaces.

REFERENCES

Bynner, J. and Parsons, S. (1997) *Does Numeracy Matter? Evidence from the National Child Development Study on the Impact of Poor Numeracy on Adult Life*. London: Basic Skills Agency.

Brindle, D. (2006) 'It's all about results: interview with Mark Friedman', *Society Guardian*. http://society.guardian.co.uk/children/story/0,,1935963,00.html (accessed 2 June 2007).

Brown, M., Askew, M., Baker, D., Denvir, H. and Millett, A. (1998) 'Is the National Numeracy Strategy research based?', *British Journal of Educational Studies*, 46(4): 362– 85.

CILT (National Centre for Languages) (2005) *Language Trends 2005 – Community languages: survey statistics*. www.cilt.org.uk/research/languagetrends/2005/community.htm (accessed 20 July 2007).

Comber, C., Lawson, T., Gage, J., Cullum-Hanshaw, A., Allen, T., Hingley, P. and Boggon, J. (2004) *Evaluation for the DfES Videoconferencing in the Classroom Project: Report for Schools*. London: DfES. www.becta.org.uk/research/research.cfm?section= 1&id=3503 (accessed 31 May 2007).

Costello, J. (2000) 'The National Numeracy Strategy: evidence from the research base of mathematics education', *Mathematics in School*, 29(2): 2–5.

Cummins, J. (1981) Age on arrival and immigrant second language learning in Canada. A reassessment, *Applied Linguistics*, 2: 132–49.

Department for Education and Employment (DfEE) (1998) *The National Literacy Strategy: Framework for Teaching*. London: DfEE Publications.

Department for Education and Employment and the Qualifications and Curriculum Authority (DfEE and QCA) (1999) *The National Curriculum for England*: *English*. London: DfEE and QCA.

Department for Education and Employment (DfEE) (2001) *Framework for Teaching English in Years 7, 8 and 9*. London: DfEE.

Department for Education and Skills (DfES) (2001) *Special Educational Needs Code of Practice*. London: DfES.

Department for Education and Skills (DfES) (2004) *14–19 Curriculum and Qualifications Reform: Final Report of the Working Group on 14–19 Reform*. London: DfES Crown Publication.

Department of Education and Skills (DfES) (2007) *Generic definition of functional skills*. www.dfes.gov.uk/14-19 (accessed 14 March 2007).

Dymoke, S. (2005) 'Wireless keyboards and mice: could they enhance teaching and learning in the secondary English classroom?', *English in Education*, 39(3): 62–77.

Edexcel (2007) *Functional Skills: Edxcel Thinks*. www.edexcel.org.uk/VirtualContent/ 103617/2007_5_8_March_Functional_Skills.pdf (accessed 15 March 2007).

Fleming, M. and Stevens, D. (2004) *English Teaching in the Secondary School*. 2nd edn. London: David Fulton. (1st edn 1998).

Furlong, T., Venkatakrishnan, H. and Brown, M. (2001) *Key Stage 3 National Strategy: An Evaluation of the Strategies for Literacy and Mathematics Interim Report*. London: ATL.

George, D. (1992) *The Challenge of the Able Child*. London: David Fulton.

Glover, D. and Miller, D.(2001) 'Running with Technology: the pedagogic impact of the large-scale introduction of interactive whiteboards in one secondary school', *Journal of Information Technology for Teacher Education*, 10(3): 257–76.

Hallam, S. and Ireson, J. (2006) 'Secondary school pupils' preferences for different types of structured grouping practices', *British Educational Research Journal*, 32(4): 583–601.

Harrison, C. (2002) *Key Stage 3 English: Roots and Research*. London: DfES.

Hennessey, S., Ruthven, K. and Brindley, S. (2003) 'Teacher perspectives on integrating ICT into subject teaching: commitment, constraints, caution and change', *Journal of Curriculum Studies*, 37(2): 155–92.

Jewell, S. (2007) 'Plan your route to work', *Guardian: 14–19 reforms Supplement*, 6 March: 2.

Kendall, S., Murfield, J., Dillon, J. and Wilkin, A. (2006) *Education Outside the Classroom: Research to Identify What Training is Offered by Initial Teacher Training Institutions*, National Foundation for Educational Research, Research Report RR802. London: DfES.

Kirschner, P. and Paas, F. (2001) 'Web enhanced higher education: "a tower of Babel"', *Computers in Human Behavior*, 17(4): 347–53.

Kutnick, P., Hodgkinson, S., Sebba, J., Humphreys, S., Galton, M., Steward, S., Blatchford, P. and Baines, E. (2006) *Pupil Grouping Strategies and Practices at Key Stage 2 and 3*, DfES Research Report 796. Brighton: University of Brighton.

Kyriacou, C. and Goulding, (2004) 'Have daily mathematics lessons enhanced student confidence and competence?'. *Proceedings of the British Society for Research into Learning Mathematics*, 24(2): 57–62.

Laurillard, D., Stratfold, M., Lucklin, R., Plowman, L. and Taylor, J. (2000) 'Affordances for learning in a non-linear narrative medium', *Journal of Interactive Media in Education* 2000(2). www-jime.open.ac.uk/00/2/laurillard-00-2-t.html (accessed 1 September 2006).

Lawson, T. and Comber, C. (2005) *Effective Videoconferencing in the Classroom: summary report from six case studies*. Coventry: Becta www.becta.org.uk/page_documents/research/vc_case_studies_summary_report.pdf (accessed 3 May 2007).

Leach, J. (2001) 'Teaching's long revolution: from ivory towers to networked communities of practice', in F. Banks and A. Shelton Mayes (eds), *Early Professional Development for Teachers*. London: David Fulton/Open University. pp. 379–94.

Lewis, M. and Wray, D. (2000) *Literacy in the secondary school*. London: David Fulton.

Lewis, D. and Allan, B. (2004) *Virtual Learning Communities*. Maidenhead: Open University Press McGraw-Hill.

Lunzer, E. and Gardner, K. (1984) *Learning from the Written Word*. Edinburgh: Oliver and Boyd.

Mansell, W. and Lee, J. (2005) 'Stillborn A level shake-up mourned', *Times Educational Supplement*, 25 February pp. 1.

National Association for the Teaching of English (NATE) (2006) *Statement on Functional English*, 14 April, www.nate.org.uk (accessed 15 March 2007).

National Association for Language Development in the Curriculum (NALDIC) (2007) *Teaching and Learning*. www.naldic.org/ITTSEAL2/teaching/index. cfm (accessed 20 October 2007).

Office for Standards in Education (Ofsted) (2004) *Outdoor Education: Aspects of Good Practice*. Document reference number: HMI 2151. London: Ofsted.

Qualifications and Curriculum Authority (QCA) (2007a) *Guidance on Teaching the Gifted and Talented.* www.nc.uk.net/gt/index.htm (accessed 20 June 2007).

Qualifications and Curriculum Authority (QCA) (2007b) *The New Secondary Curriculum: What Has Changed and Why?* www.qca.org.uk/qca_11740.aspx (accessed 30 July 2007).

Qualifications and Curriculum Authority (QCA) (2007c) *Programme of Study: Mathematics Key stage 3.* www.qca.org.uk/qca_12195.aspx (accessed 30 July 2007).

Rankine, J. and Thompson, A. (2007) *Working with EAL Specialists and Other Support Staff.* Naldic website. www.naldic.org.uk/ITTSEAL2/teaching/working. cfm (accessed 19 June 2007).

Rickinson, M., Dillon, J., Teamey, K., Morris, M., Choi, M., Sanders, D. and Benefield, P. (2004) *A Review of Research on Outdoor Learning.* Shrewsbury: Field Studies Council.

Somekh, B. (2004) 'New technologies in education symposium', *British Educational Research Association Conference,* University of Manchester Institute of Science and Technology, September.

Wray, D. and Lewis, M. (1997) *Extending Literacy: Children Reading and Writing Non-Fiction.* London: Routledge.

4 CLASSROOM MANAGEMENT
Phil Wood

By the end of this chapter you will have :

- been introduced to the importance of classroom management in developing as a reflective practitioner
- considered the need for both planning and evaluation of classroom practice
- been introduced to the dynamic nature of the classroom evironment.

INTRODUCTION

Classroom management is a central concern of beginning teachers, as they need to ensure that the classroom is a secure and positive place within which learning can take place. Classroom management itself covers many aspects of the day-to-day working of the learning environment. Here, classroom management is seen as a process which starts well before the students reach the classroom itself, involving careful preparation of both teaching and the room, alongside detailed planning. Once the lesson starts, it also involves behaviour management, the management of the physical space by the teacher, and the various pedagogical approaches the teacher intends to use. Perhaps the most central of these is the use of questioning and explanation, together with group work.

All teaching spaces are extremely complex environments requiring many different skills and approaches if they are to work efficiently and in a way which will allow for students to feel both secure and engaged.

PREPARATION

Careful preparation is essential to making early successes in the classroom. You need to anticipate what you believe the potential issues and problems are that you might face. The sooner you begin to confront any initial fears, the sooner you can start to plan in a way that minimizes these issues. One way in which you can begin to anticipate and plan for the classroom is by observing teachers and children. The more you can begin to identify and understand the various elements which make up a dynamic classroom environment, the more you can develop your own ideas and practices. Finally, being fully prepared for the classroom includes having a clear idea of what you yourself want to achieve once in the classroom. This requires the use of **lesson planning** so that you understand what it is each lesson will attempt to achieve and the medium through which this will be done. It should be highlighted here that classroom management is the most commonly cited concern of beginning teachers (McCormack, 1997), and therefore you should not feel that your own concerns in this area are anything but inevitable. It is how you prepare and develop from this starting point which counts.

Initial preparation

Before entering the classroom (or any other teaching space) to take a class, there is a need to understand the context of the classroom within the whole-school culture. Schools are complex places (Radford, 2006), and as a consequence they have different approaches and perspectives concerning issues such as expectations of uniform, behaviour, and so on. You need to understand these cultures and the policies which result from them as quickly as possible. Some schools may have a very rigid escalator of sanctions if students are badly behaved. In other schools these sanctions may be far less rigid and allow the individual teacher greater scope to develop their own behaviour strategies. Behaviour management is discussed in more depth later in the chapter, but it must be recognized that consistency is an important factor in behaviour management, and this often stems from the culture and policy of the school.

As well as understanding the 'formal' elements of the school culture and policy, you should begin to understand how classrooms operate as dynamic entities. The most effective way of doing this is through the use of observation (see Wragg, 1994). It is all too common for beginning teachers to feel as if they may be wasting their time when asked to observe lessons, but this is often because they have no focus for doing so. If we attempt to 'watch' a lesson with no particular purpose in mind, then there is too much happening for the experience to be meaningful. It is necessary to consider what elements of the classroom are of interest when carrying out a particular **observation**. Some ideas for particular foci are given in Table 4.1.

If different lessons are used to focus on different elements of the classroom and the people within it (perhaps focusing on one or two questions in each

Table 4.1   Examples of observation foci for beginning teachers when observing
a classroom

- How do students enter a room, and what are the 'rituals' they go through before starting to learn?
- What are the patterns of movement and body language of the teacher?
- How does the teacher communicate with students in different contexts?
- How does the physical layout of the room affect communication and learning, and how does it relate to the task undertaken by students?
- Where are the students seated and how does this impact on their learning?
- What are the strategies the teacher uses to ensure a positive climate within the classroom?
- How are resources introduced and used?
- What are the types of questions asked in the lesson and how does this impact on the quality of responses given?
- What is the last part of the lesson focused on?
- What rituals exist to ensure an orderly end to the lesson?

observation) a two day period of observation becomes quite short and time well spent.

When observing, it is useful for you to have a clear method of recording what has been observed. This can be a series of simple bullet pointed notes, or, in the case of an analysis of the teacher's movements and the students who are asked questions, an annotated plan of the room might be more appropriate. This shows that not only preparation for teaching, but preparation for observation is important. Without a clear purpose for observation and a clear decision on how the information is to be recorded, the experience may not reap the same degree of understanding. A final element of observation which should be undertaken is inclusion of a reflective element to the experience (as has been outlined in Chapter 1). Once the observation has been completed, if at all possible it is extremely useful to discuss the outcomes with the class teacher, as this may offer insights into the reasoning behind what has been seen, and will develop your understanding further. In your reflections on observations, become used to asking some basic reflective questions such as:

- What have you learnt?
- What observations did you make that were the same/different from those of the class teacher?
- What will you observe next?

Activity 4.1   Observation

Part a) of this activity can be completed individually and part b) with another beginning teacher or colleague

a) Draw an outline human figure in the middle of a sheet of paper. This is the teacher you are observing. As the lesson proceeds, annotate your diagram with anything that you notice which helps that teacher to teach effectively. You will probably find several things to note about eyes and voice, as well as some about hands, mouth, shoulders, legs and so on. Try to be aware of non-verbal communication or body language, and to look out for signals which convey confidence, self-assuredness, calmness, enthusiasm, and so on – all the things which you will want to emulate in your own physical presence. Be prepared to show the finished product to the teacher you have been observing and discuss your findings. Reflect on the important signals this gives you in considering your own practice in the classroom.

b) Once you have completed this exercise ask someone to produce the same diagram based on their observation of you.

Lesson planning: a framework for preparing the classroom

The key to good teaching lies in careful preparation and planning of lessons. It is often the case that poor teaching, classroom management and behaviour stem from a lack of explicit planning. As you start to teach, there are a large number of elements which you need to take into account if a lesson is to work. These include the focus of the lesson, the management of the learning as identified in this chapter, alongside considerations of **assessment** and **behaviour management**. If such a complex situation as a lesson is to be successfully managed, there needs to be a clear framework for the learning and its management. This framework is most usefully characterized as a lesson plan.

It is tempting for the beginning teacher to see experienced practitioners apparently not making use of written lesson plans, and to assume that the creation of lesson plans is not a necessary task. This is to misjudge the often acute skill that experienced teachers have gained through experience of being in the classroom. These practitioners will carry in their minds patterns of lessons and a clear understanding of the learning they are aiming for, which have been assembled through hard won experience and development of curricula over a long period of time. At the same time, even these teachers will produce lesson plans, particularly for formal observations or for **Ofsted** inspectors. On these occasions the lesson plans are not merely for personal use, but are for a 'wider

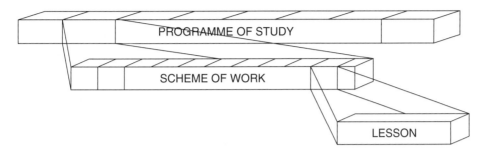

Figure 4.1   The links between lesson plans, schemes of work and a programme of study

professional audience', a situation that you, as a beginning teacher, are in all of the time.

Lessons should not be seen in isolation and are usually grouped to allow students to develop understanding and skills within an area of knowledge. As Figure 4.1 shows, a number of lessons are used to cover the elements of a scheme of work, and a number of *schemes of work* cover a *programme of study*.

A programme of study is an example of a long-term plan. A long-term plan outlines the learning to be covered over a lengthy period of time. In the case of a programme of study, it is a summary of all the work to be covered within a key stage. The format in which they are written can vary widely, from a very simple list of the topics to be covered, to a more detailed consideration of the content, skills and concepts to be developed and learned. Whatever the format, the development of long-term plans is central to the process of curriculum development. They determine the shape and nature of the learning which students will participate in.

There are a number of issues which need to be taken into account when developing programmes of study. First, there is the need to ensure that there are clear strands of progression. Students will find their learning more difficult if it does not follow a clear 'route'. The long-term plan will be broken down into a series of medium-term plans or schemes of work. These schemes, and the individual lessons within them, need to follow on from each other. If their focus constantly changes, and they do not relate to each other, the developing experiential basis of the learning embedded within them will be lost.

Second, there is the issue of resources. In some subject areas, there are not enough resources for all students to cover the same area of a programme of study at any one time. This is especially true of English, where there might not be enough books for all the students in a year group to read the same book at the same time. This leads to the need for the elements in a programme of study to still work well together, but at the same time allow for a great enough degree of flexibility for those elements to be completed in a variety of sequences.

Finally, there should be a consideration of the links between the elements, or schemes of work, which make up the programme of study. Students can begin to see each scheme of work as a hermetically-sealed element of learning if you are not careful to show links between them. However, this is crucial for developing a wider sense of the content and nature of a subject, and in helping students to grapple with the inherent complexity which is contained within all subjects.

Figure 4.1 strongly suggests that lesson planning should include a conscious element which considers the scheme of work so that the work to be covered is considered in relation to both previous learning and future directions.

One of the first problems with successful planning is to recognize that the process is both difficult and time-consuming, at least at first. Therefore you need to have a clear conceptualization of the process of planning. Butt (2006) suggests a series of questions that might be considered when starting to plan lessons:

- What is the scheme of work that the students are following?
- What has been taught and learnt in the previous lesson(s)?
- What do you want the students to learn in the lesson you are planning (and in future lessons)?
- How will your lesson plan facilitate learning?
- What resources will you need?
- What activities will the students undertake?

And post lesson:

- How will you know what the students have learnt (assessment)?
- How will you know how effective the lesson has been from your perspective as the teacher and the students' perspective as learners (evaluation)?
- What action will you need to take in future lessons to ensure that effective learning is taking place? (Butt, 2006: 8)

These questions demonstrate that the process of lesson planning requires a number of ideas to be taken into account. One common problem with lesson planning at the start of an individual's training is that they see the lesson as an 'event'. This can lead to each lesson being planned in isolation from those which go both before and after it. As a consequence, this can lead to a lack of progressional thinking. It is important to first understand how a suite of lessons will fit together, either as a part of a scheme of work, or the scheme of work in its entirety (see Figure 4.1). This will then allow you to consider the different approaches you wish to take, the different assessment opportunities you want to embed within the learning, and the main concepts and principles you want the students to understand and develop over the period of the lessons. Once this initial consideration has been made, and the broader picture of the lessons to be planned has been understood, it is then possible to develop each lesson in more detail.

Any lesson is centred upon the learning activities which will take place within it. In turn, these are developed from consideration of the learning objectives which the teacher decides will be the focus for the lesson.

Learning objectives are a central element of the planning process as they give the lesson a focus. When shared with students, they give a very clear signal about the nature of the lesson and what you expect your students to know and understand by the end. Teachers should remember that they are developing *learning* objectives, and not *teaching* objectives. Hence the objectives need to be carefully constructed so as to make the students central to the process. This can be achieved by using some of the following stems:

- *know that ...* (knowledge and factual information)
- *develop/be able to ...* (skills: using knowledge, applying techniques, and so on)
- *understand how/why ...* (understanding: concepts, reasons, effects, principles, processes, and so on)
- *develop/be aware of ...* (attitudes and values: empathy, caring, sensitivity towards social issues, feelings, moral issues, and so on) (DfES/QCA, 2002: 72).

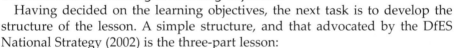 Weblink: Visit the companion website at www.sagepub.co.uk/secondary further consideration and reading on learning objectives

Having decided on the learning objectives, the next task is to develop the structure of the lesson. A simple structure, and that advocated by the DfES National Strategy (2002) is the three-part lesson:

Starter > Main learning activity > Plenary

This structure is intended to allow the teacher to introduce the lesson through some form of short activity which acts as a 'hook', that is, something which gains the interest of the students relating to what is to come. This should lead naturally on to the learning objectives for the lesson, which should clearly state to the students what the focus of the lesson is, what they should know, understand and be able to do by the end of the lesson, and how they will do this. This is then followed by the main activity/activities which should expand on the learning objectives and allow the students to develop their understanding and skills in the area of interest. The lesson finishes with a plenary which should enable the teacher to recap on the objectives and assess how much the students have learned and how well they have developed their understanding and skills. There should also be a clear link to the next lesson(s) in the sequence so that students can retain a clear understanding of their developing learning throughout a scheme of work.

Each of the planned activities should take account of the different needs of the learners in the group. Even where groups have been **setted** or **streamed** by ability, there will still be a range of abilities, strengths and weaknesses. Activity design must take account of this through the use of **differentiation**. This is the planned process of intervention in the classroom to maximize potential based on individual needs. It is a complex issue in its own right, and there are many different ways in which differentiation can be approached and utilized. However differentiation is used, it should be made clear in any lesson plan. This may include reference to the use of other adults during the lesson, in terms of who they should aid, and in what manner. (For more information on teaching assistants refer to page 139.)

Weblink: consideration and reading on differentiation

The lesson structure described is a simplification, as it is often not the case that only one main activity will occur in a lesson. There might be a number of activities, some or all of which might be punctuated with a short plenary to gauge understanding. The number of activities used will depend on factors such as: the ability range of the group; the particular concepts or subject content being covered; the approaches being taken; the length of the lesson. To add to this complexity, it must also be remembered that, however they have been constituted, any group of students will have a mix of ability. Therefore, conscious use of differentiation (both in the process of planning and the final lesson plan document itself) must clearly indicate how the planned activities will take account of this.

Activity 4.2   Lesson plan formats (1)

Part a) should be completed in discussion with other teachers and part b) can be completed individually.

a) The model of lesson format which is outlined in this section is that proposed by government agencies. However, what evidence is there that this format promotes learning in its most positive way? Discuss with teachers in your placement school the extent to which they use the three-part lesson, and what they believe the advantages and disadvantages of the format are. In their view, is it always the most appropriate format?

b) Try to envisage some learning activities which might best fit into the three-part lesson. Why might this be the case, and what format would you substitute instead?

How these ideas are actually written down as a lesson plan are partly the result of subject conventions and personal preferences. A number of different possible

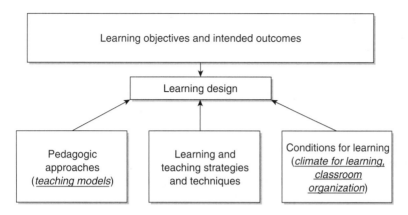

Figure 4.2 A framework for lesson planning (DfES, 2004)

templates are provided by the DfES (2002) as part of the *Key Stage 3 National Strategy (Training Materials for the Foundation Subjects: Module 3. Lesson Planning)* and are a useful starting point for considering useful formats for lesson plans.

In summary, the process of lesson planning can be seen (Figure 4.2) as a fusion of learning objectives, pedagogic approaches (approaches to teaching), learning and teaching strategies, and the contexts for learning.

You should see lesson plans not only as a framework for the lesson to be taught, but also as the starting point for evaluation and reflection. If practice is to improve, you need to give consideration to what has gone well and what has not within all lessons. This will require you to reflect on the experience of the lesson. One way in which this reflection can be structured is by using the lesson plan as a 'cognitive artefact' (that is, a physical record of the thought process and resultant learning sequence) of the lesson which has been taught. By doing this, the lesson plan can be directly utilized to help you understand how to improve your practice.

Lesson evaluation

In developing your role as a reflective practitioner, the creation of a lesson plan and its subsequent execution within the classroom should naturally lead to the completion of a lesson evaluation. It is often the case that the immediate impression gained in a lesson is both subjective and inaccurate. More considered and developed reflection can begin to put emerging issues into perspective (refer to the advantages of reflective practice outlined in Chapter 1). A reflective approach ensures that successful aspects of the lesson and an objective consideration of those areas requiring improvement can both be highlighted in a critical but supportive environment.

Suggested areas for evaluation and reflection might include:

1. Summary – a brief overview of the lesson.
2. Were the learning outcomes achieved? How do you know?
3. Did the class respond to your lesson? If not, why not? Were any parts of the lesson particularly successful? If so, why?
4. What special difficulties did the students have with any practical, group or individual work? What were the causes of the difficulties? Consider ways in which you differentiated the learning and deployed other adults in the classroom.
5. How long did the activities take? Was the time allotted adequate?
6. Would you use a similar approach again when teaching this topic? How might you modify it?
7. In reflecting on this lesson, what issues have emerged about your developing classroom practice?

Activity 4.3   Lesson plan formats (2)

This activity can be completed individually.

Use the *Secondary Strategy* materials to obtain several formats of lesson plans. Analyse the formats for what you perceive to be the advantages and disadvantages in their layout and content. Use this critique to help you to design your own format of lesson plan.

THE PHYSICAL CLASSROOM ENVIRONMENT

Part of successful classroom management concerns the way in which you manage the physical environment in which you will teach. This is very important as the pattern in which the furniture is arranged, the location of resources, and the general physical appearance of the room in which you teach all have a potential impact on the way students will respond to you and the environment. As a consequence of this, there will be a knock-on impact on the level of learning and behaviour. The use of physical space is part of the need to develop and sustain a positive and conducive climate for learning.

Organizing the physical environment

All classrooms need space for learning, teaching and storage. Thought should be given to the needs of learners, and how the physical layout of a classroom

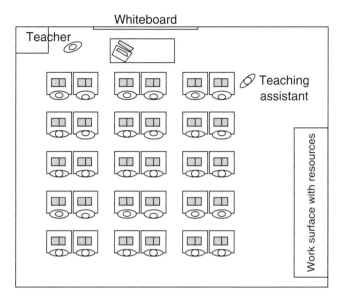

Figure 4.3 Desks in rows

will best serve the needs of the activities which will make up the learning experience.

There are a number of different ways in which a classroom can be set out, and each way has both advantages and disadvantages.

Desks in rows

This is the traditional and most-frequently seen layout of the classroom in many schools (Figure 4.3). Students are paired, and everyone faces the 'front' of the classroom, with the focal points being the teacher and the whiteboard.

Seminar layout

This type of layout is more often seen in post-16 teaching rooms (Figure 4.4). It is essentially a large horseshoe which allows for the students in the class to face each other and is especially good for whole-class discussion.

Groups layout

Within the groups layout there could be less focus on the teacher at the front of the room for large parts of the lesson and more focus on working with other students in pairs or small groups (Figure 4.5).

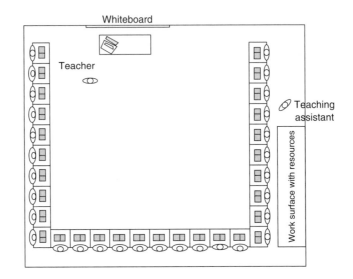

Figure 4.4 Seminar layout

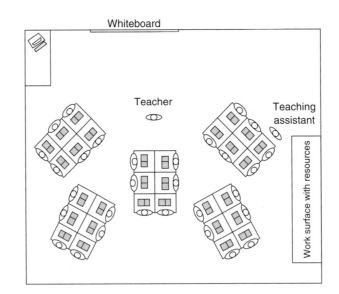

Figure 4.5 Groups layout

Some classrooms are very different in nature to this typical layout. For example, science teachers will often work within laboratories or rooms where the pattern of desks, and the extent to which they can alter that pattern, are severely restricted.

Here, there is a much greater emphasis on a safe environment, where management of students, their movement in the classroom, and the safe storage of their belongings are of primary concern (refer to CLEAPSS, 2007 and Association for Science Education, 2004). Similar issues will be important in design and technology classrooms where health and safety is again a central concern for the management of the physical space.

In some classrooms, such as drama studios and sports halls, there is yet another form of teaching environment, where there is little, or no, use of desks. In these cases there will be a greater emphasis on the management of students within a large space, and the need to ensure that students are able to interact positively at particular points in a lesson. While the space itself may present far fewer physical issues and barriers, the management of students within that space may be more problematic and will need to be considered fully in the development of classroom management skills.

Activity 4.4   Layout of teaching spaces

This activity can be completed individually and then shared with your mentor.

Using the diagrams in figures 4.2–4.5, your own experiences in school, and any observational experience you might have had to date, list what you think the advantages and disadvantages are concerning the types of layouts illustrated here. Also, make a point of observing in different spaces such as drama studios, science laboratories and sports halls. How does the management of these spaces differ? Share your developing perceptions with your mentor or another teacher.

Where possible, you should not consider classrooms as static spaces. In many classrooms, desks are rarely moved, and the activities which are used in the classroom are often the result of the layout which exists. Betoret and Artiga (2004) completed a questionnaire with over 130 beginning teachers, and found some simple patterns in their responses. Those who saw learning and teaching as a teacher-led exercise (with the outcomes of the activities being the reference for success) tended to prefer the 'desks in rows' style layout. Those who saw learning and teaching as being student-led, with the process as opposed to the outcome of the activities being the main criterion for success preferred the 'groups layout'. Perhaps this indicates that the way in which the learning process is conceptualized by the teacher has a fundamental effect on the physical layout of the room, and as a consequence, perhaps even the types of activity the students will be involved in.

One interesting perspective to note is that many primary school classrooms are considerably more dynamic in terms of physical layout. Students are often capable of altering the layout of a classroom in one or two minutes in response to the medium and focus of the activity to be undertaken. There is little standing in the way of secondary teachers using their classrooms in dynamic ways, other than a perceived and accepted culture.

In planning for the physical environment, it is important for you to consider other aspects as well as layout. How will the layout relate to your use, and need, for resources? Are students to be given heavily-managed, or very free, access to the resources that they will need for a lesson? These questions will have a significant impact on the way in which you locate resources within the room, and also the way in which students will be managed in their use.

It should be remembered that beginning teachers are often 'inhabiting' the space of another teacher, and you will need to take this into consideration when planning for the use of space. More experienced teachers often feel a sense of ownership of their classrooms, not only in terms of layout, but in how resources are stored and used, and how displays are managed. Tact and diplomacy in negotiating the use and alteration of space is therefore important.

Finally, over longer periods of time, there is also the need to manage the appearance of the classroom. This is particularly the case in terms of classroom displays. You should carefully consider the types of display produced and how they will relate to the learning which is taking place in the classroom; displays should not be static but should act as an active element in the learning environment itself. Haynes et al. (1992) believe that the learning environment is enhanced by displays and especially by exhibitions of student work. They argue that the use of creative displays stimulates the minds of students, whilst the individual display of student work inspires students to do better. However, if such displays are left on the walls of a classroom for a long period of time, their impact will lessen as the students become used to them, and as the content of the displays becomes detached from the work being undertaken by the students themselves.

This section has shown that classroom management starts before the lesson itself, through careful consideration of the classroom environment. This encompasses what you choose to display on the walls and the layout which is felt to be the most appropriate for the activities to be undertaken. It must not be forgotten that the physical environment of the classroom is complex in its own right, and only through careful anticipation, planning, reflection, and ultimately, experience will this important element of classroom management be successful.

Managing the physical environment

Once organized, the physical environment then needs to be managed. You need to develop the confidence with which you use your teaching space. It can be tempting to stay in certain parts of the room, especially at the front of a class; behind the teacher's desk, or next to the whiteboard. However, experienced teachers move around the room to ensure that there are no 'no-go' areas. This is especially true for science teachers who need fast access to all parts of a classroom for health and safety reasons. Some students may gravitate towards certain areas of the room if they know that you will not go there. This can then lead to behavioural issues. There are some important ideas relating to the management of physical space:

- *Use of proximity.* If the teacher moves closer to students there is a natural tendency on their part to focus on the teacher. This can be useful where very low level disruption or off-task behaviour is beginning to occur (Marlowe et al., 2004).
- *Movement.* When students are working, teachers should move around the room to check on progress and use their proximity to help keep students on task.
- *Positioning when speaking to individual students.* When speaking to individual students the teacher should try to get down to the same physical level of the student so that the communication can happen face-to-face. However this can make it easy for 'blind spots' to develop and therefore the teacher should position themselves in such a way as to allow them to scan the room whilst talking to the individual.
- *Using names.* To manage students and the physical space effectively, the use of student names is essential. This makes it much easier to control a group as any comment can be effectively focused on a particular student.
- *Developing rituals.* Early in the lifecycle of a group, it is important to establish rituals that they can follow, especially on entering and exiting a classroom. This might include expectations about taking off coats, sitting down or whether students must line up outside a classroom or come into it as they arrive. Again, the crucial factor of laboratory safety must be considered by those teaching in the sciences. As with the organization of the classroom furniture, you may need to accept that well-defined rituals, developed by experienced colleagues with their groups, might be in place already. These will need to be adhered to at least in the first instance.
- *Seating plans.* A crucial decision to be made in managing the physical environment is where individual students will sit. There are many different approaches to this but there should be a conscious decision taken as a group arrives for the first encounter with a teacher. More experienced teachers who have taught the students over a period of time are an excellent source of information when you make seating decisions: they know the students well and often have a clear idea of the permutations which will work and those that will not.

Activity 4.5 Managing physical space

This activity can be completed individually and then shared with a colleague.

Using the categories for the management of physical space listed in this section, observe a colleague and note the techniques used to manage the physical space of the classroom. At the end of the lesson discuss your observations with the colleague. From this, note three foci you would like to focus on in developing your own practice in the classroom.

BEHAVIOUR MANAGEMENT

The issue of behaviour management is possibly one of the most common concerns of beginning teachers, and will often be the element of the job which will continue to concern you well into your career. However, there are a number of perspectives which you can draw on to help you think about and develop your approaches to the behaviour of students. It is true, however, that behaviour can sometimes be less than positive through no initial fault of the teacher. Nevertheless, it is certainly their responsibility to take on the challenge and improve the behaviour of the students for whom they are responsible. As Paul Blum notes when considering experiences in difficult classrooms:

> Contrary to increasing voiced school-improvement theory and Ofsted myth, good teachers and good teaching materials will not extinguish bad behaviour ... Bad behaviour is not simply a by-product of bad teaching which lacks pace and rigour. You must not allow these much-voiced doctrines to grind down your self-esteem as a teacher in a difficult school ... You will survive and succeed in a difficult school if you are steadfastly enthusiastic, plan carefully and communicate colourfully when you get the chance. You must stay calm in the face of constant provocation and confrontation. In lessons, you must pursue positive behaviour management strategies energetically ... (Blum, 1998: 15-16)

The student perspective

Perhaps one way in which behaviour can be considered is to start from the perceptions of the students themselves. Supaporn (2000) suggests that students are clearly able to identify both the appropriateness of certain types of behaviour within the classroom and the reasons for the appearance of misbehaviour. There is also evidence that the perceptions of classroom management differ between students and teacher (Zeidner, 1988) which can lead to a misinterpretation of actions in both directions.

A study by Cothran et al. (2003) gives us a very useful framework for student perspectives of classroom and behaviour management. This study was conducted through the use of interviews with 182 students in 14 US secondary schools across ethnic and socio-economic backgrounds and in a spectrum of rural to urban settings. Although such a widespread number of settings were used, there were consistent views concerning teacher behaviours which impeded or aided classroom management. The main elements which students picked out were:

- *Early, clear expectations and consequences.* Students identified clear expectations as important and believed they should be clear from the start. They also stated that if expectations were not clear, and rules were fitted in later, students would not pay attention to them. Additionally, students suggested that their teachers should expect to be tested as students explore the boundaries of what is permissible. They expressed a strong preference for teachers who were clear and consistent in their classroom management. When students test the boundaries they want a teacher who has clear and consistent consequences in place. Those teachers who only threaten consequences but do not carry them through are seen as far less effective.
- When asked why they thought some teachers were less effective, they gave two reasons, the first being that some teachers wanted to be liked and were therefore less willing to carry through consequences, and some had no confidence or knowledge concerning the control of a group. However, while being too 'nice' can be seen as a problem, the students also felt that overly strict teachers were just as poor. They often took the fun out of lessons and students therefore played to this to create their own fun. Strict teachers were perceived as good as long as they attended to building positive relationships with students.
- *Relationships.* Students saw the development of positive relationships as being of great importance, as this was the central way in which trust on both sides could be built. If the relationship with a teacher was negative, this led to a lack of trust, and the associated poor behaviour which followed.
- *Care.* Students wanted teachers who showed that they genuinely cared about the students as people and also with regards to their learning, both inside and outside of the classroom. Conversely, if the teacher demonstrates that there is no care involved, and as a consequence that they are not really concerned about the students, then the effort level on the part of the students declined. The ability of teachers to let the students know a little bit about themselves (but not too much) was deemed important so that they could see them as real people.
- *Respect.* Students highlighted the fact that they do not automatically respect teachers due to the sole fact that they are teachers. Students wanted to be treated like adults, and that meant that there had to be a building of respect in both directions. This meant that students' views should be heard and respected, and that decisions should sometimes involve the students, rather than the teacher merely stating how things would happen.

This study seems to give some very clear indications of the important factors to be considered when developing a positive learning environment and minimizing the chance of negative behaviour developing.

Considering models of behaviour management

There is a large body of literature which covers the issue of behaviour in classrooms. The issue can be framed in different ways with the result that there are a number of theories and frameworks for dealing with behaviours which are deemed to be unacceptable.

Rogers (1997; 1998) divides behavioural difficulties seen in classrooms into two types: *primary* and *secondary*. Primary behaviours are subdivided into three main types:

- *Excesses.* When a certain behaviour occurs more often than it should, or when it lasts beyond the normal expected development stage of the individual. An example of this might be overt aggression in a student. At a very young age, children might display aggression as they have not learned at that point to control their moods. However, if this was still seen in a 13-year-old, there would be an expectation that they had reached a development level where they would be able to control such behaviours.
- *Combinations.* When a number of small behaviours begin to accumulate to become an obvious disruption. Each by themselves is not an issue within the classroom, but when they accumulate, this causes explicit disruption to the class. One group of students which might demonstrate this type of behaviour might be those with **attention deficit hyperactivity disorder** (ADHD) where a number of small behaviours, such as pen-tapping, calling out, making funny noises, might, if isolated incidents, be easy to deal with, or even tactically to ignore. However, when the behaviours come together, there is a potentially acute behaviour which has to be challenged.
- *Mistimed.* There are times when certain behaviours are not perceived as inappropriate, for example students talking in tutor time, or moving freely around a room during break-time. However, within the bounds of a lesson, these behaviours may be seen as wholly inappropriate and therefore mistimed if undertaken by a student.

Identified negative behaviours need to be challenged so that the learning environment is not disrupted, and it is the role of the teacher to ensure that they are dealt with positively, and in a way that neither disrupts the learning of others further, nor leads to further negative reactions from the student being challenged. This is of particular relevance in those settings, as already identified, where there are clear health and safety issues, such as in laboratories, or where students have a greater freedom in a large open space, such as in a sports hall or on a pitch outdoors.

The way in which a student reacts to being challenged about their behaviour is the *secondary* behaviour. This will range from being defensive and answering back to arguing with the teacher. It is important to consider how to respond to this type of behaviour. If a student merely responds in a negative tone, it may be judged best to *tactically ignore* their tone so as to dissipate the situation. However, if the response is very negative and public, it is necessary to ensure a positive and measured response. Again, the teacher's response also needs to be set within the cultural context of the school. If there is a clear behavioural policy with regards to student communication, it needs to be followed. For example, if the secondary behaviour of the student includes swearing at the teacher, it may be the case that the school behaviour policy treats this as a serious breach of code and results in an automatic meeting with a senior member of staff. This should therefore be the basis of the response from the classroom teacher.

There are many approaches which teachers take in the classroom concerning student behaviour, and it is important that you realize that there is more than a single way to develop a positive culture within the classroom. Porter (2000) gives a detailed overview of the various behavioural theories which inform behaviour management within schools. Whilst there is not space here to detail all these theories, perhaps one of the main ways in which the theories can be illustrated is by positioning them on a graph, linked to the relative power given to students and teachers (see Figure 4.6).

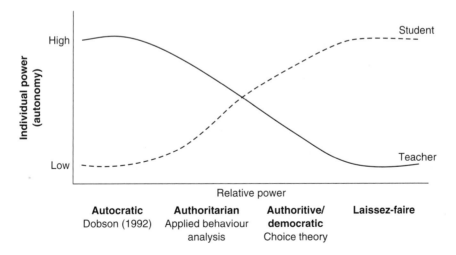

Figure 4.6 The balance of power between teacher and student in the classroom and its relation to different theories of behaviour [simplified from Porter (2000: 11)]

At one end of the spectrum is the autocratic view of behavioural theories, where teachers are believed to need complete control over students. Dobson (1992) proposes that we must punish children to ensure that they develop a moral framework. However, this is based on Biblical or philosophical beliefs and not on social theory. Equally extreme is the notion of laissez-faire behavioural approaches where students are given only minimal, or even no, behavioural guidance, and are therefore allowed to do whatever they choose. Neither of these extreme points are considered appropriate in modern school settings.

However, between these extremes are other theories which can act as the basis for behaviour management in classrooms. Two examples from different parts of the spectrum are:

- *Applied behaviour analysis.* This theory relies on the idea that behaviour is moderated by the response it receives. Hence, if the response to behaviour is positive, that behaviour will become more dominant, while if the reaction to a behaviour is negative, it will diminish. This theory therefore proposes that if we see behaviour in students which we want to encourage, we must follow its demonstration with a positive consequence. An example of this is the use of praise if a student has done something well, or the use of sweets with younger children if they have carried out a task or ritual which we are attempting to encourage. Conversely, if a student does something which we are aiming to discourage, their behaviour should be followed by a negative intervention, such as an appropriate punishment (see reference to behaviourism in Chapter 2).
- *Choice theory.* This theory focuses on the student as an active decision-maker. In other words, students act as they do out of choice. Therefore, the behaviours they demonstrate occur as they believe these will meet their needs. This then highlights the need for the teacher to act as a form of 'mentor' whose job is to help students make better choices, which still meet their needs but also do not impinge on the rights of others in the class. For example, if a student misbehaves, the teacher might give them a chance to defuse the situation by giving them a choice between two potential reactions; one which will lead to a worse result for the student if they wish to pursue it, or an alternative which will lead to the student perhaps apologizing or accepting they have done something wrong, but which leads to a conclusion of the situation. In this way the student has room to back down without losing self-esteem, and the teacher helps model good choice-making.

Activity 4.6   Behaviour Management

This activity can be completed individually.

When you have the opportunity to observe lessons (perhaps at the start of a school placement) focus on the behaviour of students and the way in which the teacher manages their behaviour. Compare their management techniques with the theories described in this section. Which techniques seem to be most successful?

After observing some lessons also reflect on the link between the different theories and the views of students on behaviour and classroom management. Does a pattern begin to emerge from the theories, student perspectives, and your own experiences?

Weblink: Visit the companion website for further reading on behaviour management

Transactional analysis: an alternative approach to behaviour management

Behaviour management can often be seen as a clear case of the teacher playing a neutral role in changing and enhancing student behaviour. However, transactional analysis changes the dynamic of behaviour management by highlighting the role that you as the teacher can have in causing behavioural problems in the classroom. Transactional analysis was developed as a psychological theory by Eric Berne (1966), who argued that all individuals have three ego-states (see Newell and Jeffery, 2002):

- *Parent*: behaviours copied from parents or parental figures.
- *Adult*: behaviours which are a direct response to the here and now, and tend to be wholly rational in character.
- *Child*: behaviours replayed from childhood.

Importantly, all individuals regardless of age are able to exhibit these behaviours, and can switch between them very quickly. For example, if two adults are arguing, it is often easy to hear one adult talking like a parent, trying to control the situation, while the other reverts to a child-like state and reacts very emotionally.

Berne (1966) further splits two of the ego-states into two subdivisions. Parents can be seen as either *controlling* parents, who try to control and discipline others (either positively in setting sensible rules, or negatively in constantly criticizing things), while *nurturing* parents attempt to look after others (either positively in watching over children empathetically, or negatively, by stifling children so that they have no opportunity to develop independence). The child ego-state can also be split into the *free* child who is spontaneous (either positively in being creative and having fun, or negatively in acting in energetic and inappropriate ways) and the *adapted* child who is constantly adapting their behaviour to gain approval from others (either positively by fitting into the dominant culture of the classroom, or negatively by following stronger characters unthinkingly).

These ego-states are the basis for the transactions which people carry out between each other, the most obvious being various forms of conversation. There are four basic transactional types (see also Burton and Dimbleby, 1995) which can occur between two people (Figure 4.7).

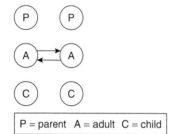

Complementary

A transaction where the ego-states complement each other, resulting in a positive exchange. This might include two teachers discussing some assessment data in order to solve a problem where they are both inhabiting the adult ego-state.

P = parent A = adult C = child

Angular

Here, the stimulation appears to be aimed at one ego-state, but covertly is actually aimed at another, such as the use of sarcasm. This may then lead to a different ego-state response from that which might be expected.

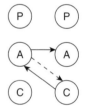

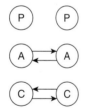

Duplex

This is a transaction that can appear simple, but entails two levels of communication, one often implicit. At a social level, the transaction might be adult to adult, but at a psychological level it might be child to child as a hidden competitive communication.

Crossed

Here, the parent acts as a controlling parent, but in aiming the stimulus at the child ego-state, a response from the adult ego-state, although perhaps perfectly reasonable but unexpected, brings conflict.

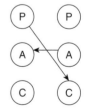

Figure 4.7 Complementary, angular and crossed models of transactional analysis

Using these four transactional types as a starting point, it becomes obvious that it is the crossed-transactions which can cause a problem within a classroom context. Within any classroom there is a constant, dynamic transaction going on between both teacher and students and between students. The management of this dynamic system can have important ramifications for both long-term and short-term relationships.

Some teachers assume that the transaction which they adopt with students should be a parent–child transaction. However, as teenagers begin to assert their independence and mature, they may well feel it appropriate to respond within a transaction in an adult-to-adult manner. If it is also accepted that teenagers have been identified as having problems with identifying emotions in others as a consequence of rapid growth of synapses in the neo-cortex (Morgan, 2005) the chances of a crossed-transaction is increased.

Activity 4.7   Behaviour and transactional analysis

This activity can be completed individually.

a) Reflect on an early experience in the classroom where there was a particular issue concerning a student's behaviour, such as arriving to a lesson late, or not putting down a pen when instructed. Note down three different ways in which you could react to this scenario, and three ways in which the student might respond.

b) Having completed (a), analyse your ideas using transactional analysis.

What would the likely outcomes be and why? What does this add to your thinking with regard to behaviour management?

A simple example is the order to put down a pen. If you order the students to 'put your pens down now' (a parent to child transaction), and a student replies, 'I am just finishing off my sentence before I forget it' (adult to adult transaction) there is the potential for a negative conversation to occur, although the statement by the student seems wholly rational. Indeed if a colleague were to say this in a staffroom, we would not deem it out of place in any way. A more adult-initiated start to the transaction might be to say, 'I would like to bring you back to focus on the summary points of the work we have been doing. As you reach a convenient point at which to stop, please redirect your attention to me' (followed by a minute's take-up time).

Therefore, transactional analysis, as a behaviour management framework changes the emphasis from the teacher as manager, to teacher as part of the dynamic which has to be managed. It shows that we have a responsibility to the students to ensure that we model and encourage positive transactions/ conversations in an attempt to develop positive climates within the classroom.

What the above discussion demonstrates is that behaviour management is a complex issue. It is only through careful planning, consideration through regular reflection and some understanding of the underpinning theory that you can begin to develop a behaviour management model that works with your various groups, and which allows you to help students learn in a safe and positive environment. However, this takes time and you should not expect that the practical skills which develop from a theoretical consideration will be mastered in a short space of time.

DEVELOPING COMMUNICATION: QUESTIONING AND EXPLAINING

Questioning and explaining are two skills which are of central importance to the development of learning in the classroom. If you are unable to explain concepts and ideas, you will struggle to help students learn. In the same way, questioning is vital for developing students' enquiry skills and for helping you assess how much they actually understand as you progress through a scheme of work. It should be stressed at the outset that skilled questioning takes time to develop as it is a complex art form. Your ability to explain and assess will also have a major impact on the extent to which students listen and take part in the lesson – poor explanations can actually lead to behavioural issues.

Explaining

What does it mean to explain something to someone? At a very simple level the answer to this question must be that explanations are the medium through which we help another person understand something. Kerry (2002) sees explanations as being the response to one of three implicit questions:

- What?
- How?
- Why?

In considering these questions, the explanation itself needs to take account of a number of issues and factors. First, key terms and concepts need to be defined so that, as the explanation procedes, the students can continue to understand what is being said. As a consequence, teachers must consider the form of language they are going to use in explaining something. For beginning teachers, this might be as part of the lesson planning process, but as experience and a widening repertoire develops, it might occur during the lesson itself. Beginning teachers often misjudge the degree of understanding of students and can pitch an explanation at too high or too low a level until they have experience of the prior learning and conceptual level that the students are working at. If the concept or idea is a difficult one for students to grasp, the explanation may need to have built-in repetition so that there are a number of occasions on which the student can be aided in understanding. However, there is a thin line between useful repetition and becoming over-repetitive and boring.

Where concepts are abstract to the students (for example if students are working on atomic structure or the erosive processes beneath glaciers) they may well find it difficult to understand what is being said. To help their understanding, concrete analogies which are couched in their own experience can help, for example by using different coloured snooker balls in talking about atoms, or using the way sandpaper scratches and smoothes wood in explaining the work done beneath glaciers. By giving examples that the students can relate to, there is a better chance that they will understand the concepts and ideas underlying the explanation. Another way of helping students to understand what is being said is to connect the content to other areas the students have already covered and which they understand. This helps them to locate the ideas in a wider sense, and also demonstrates that the subject being studied is part of a larger whole.

Activity 4.8   Explanations

This activity can be completed individually and then shared with a teacher.

a) Early in your first placement, observe an experienced teacher explaining a concept or skill to a group of students. What language is being used to help explain to the students clearly? Have everyday examples been used to help the student understand?

b) At the end of the lesson, discuss your observations with the teacher.

It is also the case that the explanation needs to be carefully paced to ensure that it is neither too quick, losing a number of the students along the way, nor too slow, in which case many of the students might lose interest. Another way of keeping the interest of students is to inject some humour into the explanation. This can make an explanation more memorable and aid memory, but has to be used carefully so that the focus of the students is still on the subject matter and not on your performance as the teacher.

Questioning

Questions are the backbone of communication between students and teachers in classrooms. They are an important medium for learning, used to develop ideas, challenge students, assess levels of understanding and to steer and ignite interest and thinking. You will need to ensure that questions are used in a considered way and to their greatest effect.

So why use questions? There are a number of reasons including (see Kerry, 2002):

- So that students talk.
- To show that we have an interest in students' thoughts and ideas.
- To stimulate interest and curiosity.
- To encourage a problem-solving approach to thinking.
- To help students externalize and verbalize knowledge.
- To help students learn from each other.
- To improve deep thinking.
- To promote independent learning.
- To monitor levels of learning.

Questions, when used well, can have a major impact on the level of learning of students, but to use them most effectively, it is important that the teacher understands the techniques and reasons for various approaches. Questioning can be simply classified in two ways which help us understand how we can better stretch students in their thinking.

Open and *closed*: closed questions which are posed, are those for which the teacher has a particular 'correct' response in mind; a question such as 'What is the capital city of France?' or 'Who wrote *To Kill a Mockingbird*'? In each case, there is only one correct response. Open questions, on the other hand, are those which can develop a range of responses, and give a greater opportunity for thinking by students, such as 'Was the invasion of Iraq an ethically sound decision?' or 'How might we analyse the development of habitats over time in this newly cleared piece of forest?' In these cases, there is much greater room for discussion by students as they begin to grapple with complex ideas and concepts.

In deciding which of these techniques is employed, you need to have a clear understanding of why the questions are being asked and the intended outcome of their use. If a short plenary is focused on gauging the amount of knowledge and information the students have taken in, then a series of closed questions will allow for a short, quickly paced review to occur. If the development of arguments and ideas is at the heart of the intention, then it is desirable to use more open questions which can lead to deeper, multifaceted ideas, concept development and opportunities for students to ask their own questions. This approach also allows you to facilitate greater development of reflection within the students.

In addition to open and closed questioning, it is also important that we challenge students in the level of thinking they engage in. One way of formalizing this is to use the levels of thinking suggested by Bloom (Bloom and Krathwohl 1956). (See Table 2.2).

This demonstrates that the questions we ask have a direct impact on the level of thinking required by students. Unfortunately, it is sometimes the case that questions are in the lower order area of Bloom's taxonomy leading to a lack of challenge in learning. This shows that it is crucial to plan for questioning in the early stages of developing your classroom pedagogy.

When planning lessons early in the period of training, it can be helpful for you to consider some of the key questions which students need to answer before the lesson itself. These can be written down on the lesson plan so that they are not forgotten and can help shape discussion within the classroom, developing good habits of questioning. You should also consider how questions will be posed. There are a number of approaches to targeting questions:

- *'Hands up'* where the question is asked and students raise their hands if they think they know the answer. This is the most frequently used method of 'choosing' a student to answer. However, it can lead to a small number of pupils dominating the session, and if only those who think they know the answer put their hands up, why do we choose them? Are we not equally interested in those who appear not to know the answer?
- *Enlisting* is a technique used by teachers where they choose those to answer and name them. This allows the teacher to focus on particular individuals to gauge understanding, and can be used very effectively in a number of ways. It can be used as a behaviour technique, to ensure that students stay on task as they may be chosen. It can also be used to praise students, especially those who might believe themselves to be weak in the subject. If the questions are chosen carefully so that the teacher knows the chosen student does know the answer, it then gives the opportunity for public praise. However, it is important that the teacher knows the students well to use this technique effectively.
- *Mini-whiteboards* can be used. These are small rectangular whiteboards. The teacher can ask a closed question and the students then write an answer on the board and hold it

up. This can give a quick general idea of the level of understanding and means that individual students are not put under pressure. Whiteboards can also be used very effectively in plenary sessions to ensure everyone gives an indication of what they have learned during a lesson.

When you ask questions, students in all parts of the room need to be actively engaged. It is a natural reaction that teachers will tend to engage with students in their direct line of sight, and those in the teacher's peripheral vision will be lost. This can then be a useful place to 'hide' for those who wish to play little part in the lesson, or for those who are unsure of their understanding (just the group we should be helping to develop their understanding).

Careful consideration must also be given to the sequencing and challenge of questions. As has already been stated, differentiated questioning will play a major role in the structure of learning and help to develop understanding. In some cases, a question may be posed at a level too high for a student, or group of students to understand. Here, the notion of scaffolding (see Chapter 2) becomes important as the question might need to be broken down into simpler questions which build back towards the original more complex question.

As confidence in questioning develops, it is possible for the teacher to take an increasingly small part in the process of questioning itself. If we wish students to become increasingly independent learners, we need to help them become effective questioners in their own right. Wood and Patterson (2004) suggest that classrooms are at least in part artificial social and cognitive environments as students are asked the questions by the individuals who know the answers, as a test of their own, most likely incomplete knowledge. In the vast majority of other social situations, the novice will ask the questions as they want to further their knowledge and understanding, using the expert as a starting point for their development. This is supported by evidence highlighted by Tizard and Hughes (1984) who found that 4-year-old children took part in 27 conversations per hour with their mothers on average, each having an average of 16 turns, with half the conversations being initiated by the children, asking an average of 26 questions per hour. As the children entered school, conversations fell to 10 per hour, and the vast majority were started and controlled by adults. Identified consequences included a fall in the amount of speaking, questioning, the number of requests for information, restricted language, and less active reflection and planning.

By giving students the opportunity to question you can begin to give them a level of independence and a greater contribution to the learning process. This can take a number of forms, from allowing them a specified period of a lesson to ask questions, or the use of a 'post-box' where they can write down and leave questions which can be answered at a predetermined time, perhaps once a week or every three lessons, for example. The students might even be given the opportunity to work as a class to develop their own foci for a scheme of work. In this case the concepts to be studied can be decided by snowballing questions from the individual pupil to the whole class before deciding on a list to be covered in lessons (see Wood and Patterson, 2004).

Activity 4.9   Questioning

This activity can be completed individually and then shared with a teacher.

During a lesson observation, focus on the following issues and write some notes on what you see:

1. What is the ritual for asking questions? Are hands put up or are students conscripted? What effect does this have on the proportion of students who are involved in the answering of questions?
2. To what degree are students encouraged to ask their own questions, either of themselves and their peers, or the teacher?
3. If a question is asked which does not bring a quick answer, how does the teacher approach the situation?
4. To what extent do closed and open questions lead to further enquiry and learning?

If you get the opportunity, discuss some of these issues with the teacher you have observed.

Weblink: access the DfES module and reading on questioning via the companion website

Group work

Questioning and explaining are both key skills for the beginning teacher to develop and refine. However, in both cases the focus of the learning is centred on the teacher. As your confidence grows, and basic classroom management is developed, it is a positive step to begin to help the students take a greater responsibility for their own learning. One way in which this can be done, is through the introduction of group work.

Blatchford et al. (2003) define group work as any activity where students are working together as a team, which can obviously cover a number of different types of activity. However, there are some common features which group work should entail. First, as the theory underpinning the use of group work relates to **social constructivism** students should have ownership of the process and work together to create and extend their own understanding of a topic. The extent to which students are given ownership of this process will depend on their age and their level of exposure to the techniques used. If students have had little experience of group work, it is unrealistic to expect them to work well in a completely independent fashion; this can only come with experience. The students should act as co-workers, with no single individual taking a role as the 'quasi-teacher', as this then dilutes or even prohibits the true social nature of the exercise. Finally, the activity itself should be a structured opportunity for learning, not a casual chance to discuss. It can be quite easy to allow a large degree of independence, which then descends into an opportunity for students to talk about anything but the activity being undertaken.

Group work is actually quite complex, and needs careful consideration. It often does not work very well due to a lack of careful planning. This is due to a lack of focus on how students will be trained in group work skills, or the constitution of the groupings. Group work skills can only be developed over a long period of time. The interpersonal traits required are not well developed in many students, and it is necessary to help them develop these.

Blatchford et al. (2003) focus on some basic dynamics which need to be carefully considered:

1. *Preparation:* there are a number of issues which need to be addressed before the lesson even begins if group work activities are to succeed. The layout of the tables needs to be considered; it needs to be flexible and appropriate. This may require the movement of tables from normal positions, whilst ensuring that there is room for students to move about easily and safely if needed. The size of the groups is context specific, for example, the type and extent of resources may be important in deciding group size, and, whatever the size, careful consideration should be given with regards to ability and sex make-up of the groups. Group work is easier when the teacher knows the students well as they understand better the behaviour dynamics and abilities within the student group, and can therefore create groupings which they know have a better chance of being successful. Finally, group stability needs to be considered; will they need to work over a number of lessons or will the groups be flexible and changed on a lesson to lesson basis?

2. *Interaction:* group skills are naturally imbued, and need to be developed. Teachers cannot expect students to be excellent communicators unless they are given the chance to use such skills and, as importantly, to discuss and debrief those skills once used. Hence a meta-level discourse needs to unfold, with time being given over to the discussion of the process itself, rather than the subject knowledge outcomes by themselves. Over the longer term, the focus of this reflection is on making the students ever more independent, and able to function as groups with little intervention from the teacher.

3. *Teacher's role*: teachers need to understand the underlying principles of social construc-
    tivism to ensure that they can support and develop the students' skills. The teacher is there
    to mentor and aid the work of students, and should attempt, as far as possible, not to
    become the focus of discussion. This is a role which should extend the zone of proximal
    development (see the section on Vygotsky in Chapter 2) by scaffolding student thinking,
    but not directing it. This can often be a difficult skill for teachers to develop as there is a
    degree to which they need to transfer some of their power as teacher to the students. This
    means that the teacher needs to have confidence in their own ability and the exercise they
    have developed to allow students the freedom to work without complete direction.
4. *Preparation of tasks*: as alluded to in point 3, group work is most positive when the task
    is well designed, not only taking account of the need to develop understanding and
    skills, but also of the particular make-up and dynamics of the group with which the task
    will be used. This is often not considered enough, and may be one of the factors in group
    work not being fully successful on occasion. All group members need to be fully
    involved, and this will mean a consideration of differentiation of resources, and even the
    task itself. It may also require the assigning of roles if the teacher believes that individ-
    uals may dominate discussion, or where students find it difficult to focus if meaning the
    resources on their own terms. The task should also have a clear element of meta-analysis
    within it (as mentioned earlier) so that the students are required to reflect on the nature
    and process of the activity as well as the outcomes.

Activity 4.10   Linking group work and learning

This activity can be completed individually and then shared with a teacher.

Referring back to Chapter 2, and using the ideas presented here, make some
notes on the elements of social constructivism you feel are crucial to develop
through group work. Use these to make a list of the essential features you would
need to include in setting any group work activity.

Weblink: extra reading on group work is available on the companion website

WORKING WITH OTHER ADULTS: THE ROLE OF THE TEACHING ASSISTANT

In developing good classroom management, the role of the teaching assistant
(or learning support assistant) should be both recognized and developed, to

create a more inclusive classroom not only for the students, but also for the staff involved. You will no doubt have teaching assistants in some of your lessons, and it is essential that you learn both how to integrate their skills into your teaching and how best to deploy them for the maximum impact on student learning.

Over the past five years the role of teaching assistants has become a major area for research. This has, in part, been the result of the increasing number of such professionals being employed within the English educational system (Cremin et al., 2005) but also has been due to major policy developments brought about by politicians. At the same time there has been a rapid change in the role of these professionals from the mundane 'housekeeping' role characterized by Duthie (1970) to higher-level teaching assistants of the twenty-first century who can take on some of the core responsibilities often reserved for teachers under a more traditional approach (Kerry, 2005). Kerry identifies 11 different titles from both the literature and practice which all relate to teaching assistant-style jobs, showing the difficulty in defining and even naming the role (Balshaw and Farrell, 2002). The resultant identified roles cover a spectrum. At one end, there is what is called the 'Dogsbody' where the tasks allocated are menial, such as filing, photocopying and so on, with little contact with students. Somewhere in the middle of the spectrum is the 'Behaviour manager' who works with students, but who provides support for an individual or for small groups. Here, there is obvious contact with students but it is limited to an emotional support role, the academic/content element of the lesson being of little concern. At the other end of the scale is the 'Mobile paraprofessional' often identified with high-level teaching assistants who takes on roles traditionally taken as being the preserve of the teacher, acting as an independent operator fulfilling a number of teaching and learning functions.

The role of the teaching assistant is variable, and is most likely determined, or negotiated, at individual school level. Moran and Abbott (2002) see the role of the teaching assistant as being multifaceted, with important characteristics including the need for a positive relationship with students, and as a consequence, often a motivator to students. Importantly, another central characteristic identified is the role of the teaching assistant in providing continuous feedback to the teacher as part of the ongoing planning and reflection process. In their study of teaching assistants in Northern Ireland, both in mainstream and special schools, they see the teaching assistant as a central element in the development of an inclusive classroom. A crucial process in allowing this to happen, however, is that the teacher realizes that a crucial ingredient of team success is in the clear definition of roles, classroom tasks and activities (see also Thomas, 1992).

Mansaray (2006) working in a primary context, found that the situation of teaching assistants within an organization is often ambiguous. In some classrooms there was a clear 'core'/'periphery' model in operation where the teacher was the core element of the teaching dynamic with the teaching assistant very much on the periphery. However, while there was clear evidence that students, even at a young age, were able to distinguish between teaching assistants and teachers, they also identified their roles as clearly overlapping. Students also often stated that the teaching assistants were more approachable and, because of this, they played crucial roles as 'connectors' within the classroom, bridging the gap between student and teacher, and also as 'mediators'.

Cremin et al. (2005) considered models of teaching assistant deployment within the classroom. They offer three potential models, all based on previous models within the literature, which were then piloted in a number of schools and analysed for **learning gain**:

1. *Room management*: this is a model based on the identification of teacher tasks and responsibilities which are then divided with specific roles and activities being given to the people working in the classroom. Hence, where specific focused interventions might be involved, individuals have a clear framework to use to ensure that all such activities are undertaken, but as distributed actions across the team involved.
2. *Zoning*: this is a model for allocating roles of those working in the classroom according to the classroom 'geography' and the groups that exist therein. Here, particular groups who exist within particular locations in the room with be focused on by a particular individual, thereby 'localizing' the interaction between adult and students. This model was first described by LeLaurin and Risley (1972).
3. *Reflective teamwork*: this is a model whereby staff working together discuss thoroughly, develop and advance the ways in which they work together as a team. This approach reflects the importance of team planning and the vital role of the teaching assistant as the link between students and teacher.

Within the context of the study, the room management model, appeared to give the greatest increase in engagement but required substantial planning and management time. The zone also showed positive results, but there was a greater degree of variability between individuals. Finally, the reflective teamwork model showed the weakest evidence for quantitative increase (although the groups selected proved to be anomalous), but was deemed the most popular with both staff and students. What all the models showed was the need for training and the development of teaching assistant skills if the interventions were to be successful.

> ### Activity 4.11   Deployment of teaching assistants
>
> This activity can be completed individually and then shared with the teachers you have observed.
>
> Using the model for teaching assistants outlined by Cremin et al. (2005), complete the following:
>
> 1. Observe two lessons which include the presence of teaching assistants. During the lesson, note down their activities and after the lesson, discuss with the teacher the extent to which they decide on the deployment of the teaching assistant, and their reasons for deploying them in that way.
>
> 2. Reflect on what you have experienced, and make some notes on what this has taught you about your deployment of teaching assistants which will inform your own future practice.

CHANGING PEDAGOGIES AND CLASSROOM MANAGEMENT

Introduction

Classrooms are beginning to change as new ideas and media are developed. Two of the most recent developments, both of which may play a major role in changing the nature of classrooms and the learning which occurs within them, are personalized learning and e-learning. In this section these developments are outlined. As you engage with these ideas, consider how you might need to change or develop your classroom management to take account of them.

Personalized learning

Personalized learning is a new and developing concept which is increasingly being seen as a central tenet of learning and teaching and hence classroom experiences. Having been introduced by both Tony Blair in 2003 and David Miliband in 2004 as a framework for improving the quality of students' education, it is not yet fully defined, let alone understood, and exists as a set of loosely-held principles. Even politicians themselves appear to have slightly different concepts of what the term means.

'In secondary education, future reform must have as a core objective a flexible curriculum providing a distinct and personal offer to every child' (Tony Blair, September 2003, quoted in Johnson, 2004: 224). Blair sees personalized learning as a school/authority level initiative, focused on curriculum and educational choice for the individual consumer. It should be seen as a critical element of New Labour's wider focus on personal choice in the public services.

David Miliband, however, had a more detailed and school/classroom level notion of what the term might mean. He highlights five areas of focus for the concept:

1. Knowing the strengths and weaknesses of individual students.
2. The building of personal confidence and competence by using teaching and learning strategies together with individual needs.
3. Individual curriculum choice.
4. Radical school organization in general, and more flexibility within the classroom.
5. Clearer and more dynamic links with external agencies.

Hargreaves (2004a; 2004b) has added further to the outline developed by David Miliband. Through work with the Specialist Schools Trust, he has developed the concept of the 'nine gateways' to personalized learning. These are seen as:

1. School design and organization.
2. Workforce development.
3. The use of new technologies.
4. Development of curriculum models.
5. Student voice.
6. Advice and guidance.
7. Coaching and mentoring.
8. Learning to learn.
9. Assessment for learning.

These 'gateways' demonstrate that the concept of personalized learning is focused not merely on school organization, but on ensuring that such structures allow for a more efficient, dynamic and motivating environment for teaching and learning within the classroom.

The main feature of these gateways is that they are all focused on the student, and the quality and experience of their education. Underlying this is a philosophy which demands that aspects such as school organization and links to other services need to be seen holistically as part of the educative process of the child, and not as some parallel managerial system.

Classroom elements of personalized learning

As set out by Hargreaves, some of the elements of personalized learning suggest the need to make the learning environment more dynamic and as a result, the

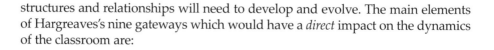

structures and relationships will need to develop and evolve. The main elements of Hargreaves's nine gateways which would have a *direct* impact on the dynamics of the classroom are:

1. The use of new technologies.
2. Development of curriculum models.
3. Learning to learn.
4. Assessment for learning.

The other elements will have an impact but are discounted at present here as being frameworks and structures which operate outside of the classroom and are therefore not variables which can be directly controlled by a subject team or individual teacher.

Assessment for learning

Much of the detail of this strand is covered elsewhere within this book (see Chapter 5). However, there is a clear link between the development of assessment for learning and personalized approaches to learning. With the potentially more fluid dynamics of personalized learning environments, it is of paramount importance that any feedback you give to students is relayed to them at a personal level, while ensuring more general pointers are given at a class level. In keeping with the mentoring approach, it should also be the case that assessment for learning is utilized to develop the autonomy of learners (Ecclestone, 2002), moving from procedural notions of autonomy (where students may be involved in pacing and evaluating their work) to personal and critical autonomies. In these latter forms of autonomy, students have become reflectors who are able to identify their level of understanding and can further develop through independent study (see Table 4.2 for an outline definition of each of these levels of autonomy), self-negotiated activities and self-evaluation. At this stage there is far less teacher-generated learning, their focus becoming more aligned to tutoring and mentoring.

Learning to learn

Over the past decade there has been a rise in the notion of dynamic interpretations of intelligence and learning. This has included principles such as multiple intelligences (Gardner, 1983) and the allied concept of learning styles (see Chapter 2). As the development of the notion of **meta-cognitive frameworks for learning** has developed, there has been an increasingly

Table 4.2 Levels of autonomy

Level of autonomy	Outline characteristics
Procedural	Some determination of pace, timing and evaluation of work, with the transmission of pre-determined content and outcomes
Personal	Development based on a knowledge of one's own strengths and weaknesses, therefore becoming more student-centred with negotiated outcomes and processes for achieving them
Critical	Independent, critical thinkers who are able to self-evaluate, and where formative assessment encourages critical reflection thereby questioning personal barriers to understanding

popular trend towards the development of 'Learning to Learn' frameworks and courses where such ideas are discussed and developed with students in an attempt to make them more efficient and critical reflective learners. Such courses and foci rely on the student identifying strengths and weaknesses in their learning and then using these to self-support improvement and continued development.

There is a ready appeal in using learning styles as a focus for learning. However, there is increasing discussion over the ways in which such principles are embedded within classrooms. Hattie (1999) shows that the **effect size** of following a learning styles/individualization approach is small in comparison to the effect of instructional quality. Hence, this begins to call into question some of the claims made concerning learning styles approaches. A further issue in relation to learning to learn programmes and approaches is the fact that there are a large number of contrasting theories concerning learning. Hall and Moseley (2005) highlight 13 different models which are all influential in providing frameworks for considering learning. The role of learning styles is empirically unproven at present, but it can be claimed that by concentrating on some of the positive elements of the approach, such as meta-cognition, it is possible to increase motivation and develop autonomy in students.

Hall and Moseley see the place of learning styles and learning to learn as: 'underpinning the strategic and reflective thinking element of an integrated framework for understanding thinking and learning' (2005: 253). Hence, teachers should focus on variety as opposed to strengths in students' learning: 'the outcome of engaging with style should be strategy. The goal of "personalised education" or "Learning to Learn" whether couched as learner agency or learner autonomy, is simply freedom, and descriptions of learning style should be tools "to break chains of habit and limitation" ' (Hall and Moseley, 2005: 254). This suggests that much of the recent development of learning to learn programmes has been based on dogma and unproven successes. However, if the core elements are extracted and used in a critical manner, they have much to offer in developing the learning of students by developing and planning for a rich and varied classroom experience.

Personalized learning: a complex system?

Many of the features which are discussed in the previous section are not new, and indeed some, such as use of ICT or assessment for learning, are already embedded within many classrooms. However, where personalized learning is potentially new and untested is in the relationships and links between the elements as opposed to the elements themselves. If personalized learning is to be truly realized at the classroom scale, each of the elements needs to be negotiated as a whole, with consideration of how they relate and merge to produce a definable, dynamic and efficient framework in which individuals can navigate their experience both individually and socially.

It is the dilemma of how to develop a positive learning environment which is the core of an emerging critique of personalized learning. This may lead to a number of tensions which need to be resolved:

- Computers are potentially defined as a 'teacher substitute', but where is the evidence that increased use of computers in an uncritical framework will actually help develop better and more capable learners?
- Do personal curricula make it difficult to blend the idea of choice with universal entitlement?
- Where is the social element of education within a personalized framework? Is it a continued movement to educational consumerism with a declining focus on the social/community based experience?

As with any emerging theory or pedagogical approach, there is an emergence of two parallel 'camps' who occupy bipolar extremes: those who see it as a panacea for correcting educational underachievement, and those who see it as vacuous political posturing. However, the reality of personalized learning is most likely somewhere between these two extremes, and that reality is only approachable from the development of the theoretical principles within the context of practice within classrooms.

Activity 4.12   **Personalized learning**

Personalized learning can be seen as part of a new philosophy, concerning some of the wider issues of schools such as organization and curriculum, but which might also have a fundamental impact on the classroom environment itself. Visit the Futurelab website (www.futurelab.org.uk), and spend some time understanding their beliefs concerning the learning environments and pedagogies of the future. How might the role of the teacher change?

This activity can be completed individually and then shared with another beginning teacher.

The use of information and communication technology

> In the 19th century the teacher was for most students the gatekeeper of knowledge, since learners had little or no independent, ready and inexpensive access to books. Some 150 years later, the teacher is no longer a gatekeeper, for the new technologies have made vast sources and quantities of information accessible to almost anyone, almost anywhere and at almost any time at the touch of a button. (Hargreaves, 2005: 22)

Information and communications technology is a major part of the lives of many young people, from use of games consoles to the use of mobile phones and the Internet. As such, it is no surprise that there is an increasing desire to use these technologies within an educational context. As such, they offer certain advantages in a classroom context (Hargreaves, 2005):

1. *Engagement and motivation*: students are generally motivated by the use of new technologies as they find them interesting and 'immediate' in their effect. With support and structuring they allow 'live' information into the classroom, and can be used to develop a more individualized level of resources and information.
2. *Independence, responsibility and control*: students can be helped to become increasingly able in accessing information and its subsequent critical use, and as such can be given more responsibility over their own learning. This develops independence and allows students to make greater use of the time available to them. However, the development of ICT skills is essential if this is to develop positively.
3. *Social skills*: where computer suites are developed with students in mind, they can offer a layout which allows pairs, or groups, of students to work collaboratively through the use of ICT.

4. *Participation*: by allowing work to be developed in different packages, there is a greater chance that students are able to produce varied formats of work, and a finished quality which is not too far removed from that which could be developed by a professional publisher. As such, this gives the opportunity for students' work to be publicly recognized and even to act as part of a school website, and so on.

Hence, there is a clear signal that ICT, and the development of ICT skills within students should be a central element of student development. It is therefore the responsibility of teachers to build in clear opportunities for students to use ICT in a variety of ways and in a variety of settings.

Weblink: DfES and QCA plus other resources on personalized learning/links can be accussed via the companian website.

E-learning

The use of some elements of ICT are discussed in Chapter 3 as they relate to learning. There is a perceived need for students to become 'digitally literate' and this has led to an ever increasing focus on the use of a number of technologies within and beyond the classroom.

Interactive whiteboards

Many schools now have interactive whiteboards as a standard element of the classroom environment. The essential feature of these is the projection of a computer screen image onto a large board, which is itself 'live'. Therefore, software packages or the Internet can be used, and navigated around as if it were a normal computer screen. This allows for you to use information interactively, as you and the students can browse for Internet information, play educational games or develop understanding through animated software, all directed from the board itself. This is the type of use that interactive whiteboards were designed for, although in some cases use is far more restricted, and a very technologically advanced piece of equipment becomes a normal whiteboard. Such restrictive use highlights the need for beginning teachers to spend time observing carefully and explicitly planned exemplar lessons which focus on the use of interactive whiteboards, and to ensure that use of the equipment is fully integrated into lessons where appropriate. However, it should always be the case that you have back-up resources for those lessons where the Internet might be used, as it is a fact of life that the school server can fail from time to time. If this happens, it can be very uncomfortable if an alternative exercise is not at hand.

Weblink: Examples of the use of interactive whiteboards are available via the companion website

Blogs

Blogs (short for weblogs) are a rapidly expanding form of Internet communication, their success perhaps due to the fact that they are essentially an easily created, easily updatable website. They allow individuals to publish instantaneously on the web from any Internet connection point. Early blogs were simple diary-like affairs which listed the sites an individual had been to, perhaps with a commentary on the content and perceived usefulness (Richardson, 2006). Soon, sites had developed sufficiently that collaborative comments from other users could be posted, thereby making them interactive, and allowing the capacity for discussion. As Richardson states: 'they are comprised of reflections and conversations that in many cases are updated every day (if not three or four times a day). Blogs engage readers with ideas and questions and links. They ask readers to think and to respond. They demand interaction' (2006: 18).

Eide and Eide (2005) believe that blogging has a huge potential for a positive impact on students. They argue that blogs can:

- promote critical and analytical thinking
- be a powerful promoter of creative, intuitive, and associational thinking
- promote analogical thinking
- be a powerful medium for increasing access and exposure to quality information
- combine the best of solitary reflection and social interaction.

Within the classroom context, Ray (2006) sees four main uses of blogs:

1. *Blogs to communicate*: developing an electronic bulletin board as a fast means to communicate with other interested parties, such as students, other colleagues and parents.
2. *Blogs as instructional resources*: developing ways in which homework can be further supported, through the publishing of tips, explanations, or samples of work. There might also be the development of hyperlink libraries to help structure the research of students.
3. *Blogs as collaborative tools*: students could set up blogs as groups so that they can work collaboratively on projects, such as field trips or enquiries/investigations. The blog allows the development of a meta-cognitive strand which allows for more explicit reflective opportunities for the students involved.
4. *Blogs as showcases for student projects*: a way of publishing student work to the Internet, which can be easily accessed by parents or other students.

However, there are potential problems with blogs. First, if core information and learning is to be transferred to the internet, the teacher needs to ensure that all students have equal access to the information. Second, given that blogs are intentionally written to allow for discussion on the Internet, there is a need to ensure that students are safe and are not exposed to online bullying, or predators. Finally, there is the issue of time. It is very easy to begin to use a blog as a medium for learning, and find that increasing amounts of time are used to write, update and police the resource. This is something which must be carefully considered before developing this technology too far.

Weblink: The companion website provides links to a variety of exemplar blog sites.

Wikis

Wiki is a shortened form of the Hawaiian word 'wiki-wiki', meaning 'quick'. First developed by Ward Cunningham in 1995, wikis were created to enable easy and quick publishing of information to the internet. An example of this rapid and easy publishing of information can be seen from the aftermath of the Indian Ocean Earthquake and tsunami. The event occurred just after midnight (GMT) on 26 December 2004. Within 24 hours of the event a wiki had been formed, had been edited 400 times and had expanded to a document of 3,000 words, supplemented with photographs, charts and other graphics. Within 48 hours, there were over 6,500 words, which had been edited 1,200 times (Richardson, 2006).

Wikis have therefore become a medium through which collaborative documents can be easily and quickly developed. This is the focus for potential uses in schools. It is very easy to set up free wikis on the internet, and some **VLEs** (see Chapter 3) are now incorporating them into their structures. A template is then developed which acts as the 'content page' for the wiki which students can then be asked to populate. This allows students to work collaboratively to produce a form of publication together. The teacher's role needs to be carefully considered, as it is important that the resultant document is accurate and useable. However, it is also an ideal opportunity for peer assessment (see Chapter 5) as students can be asked to edit elements of the publication written by others. *Wikipedia*, the online encyclopedia, can be used as a reference point when considering how a wiki might work in the classroom and the format that might be used.

Activity 4.13   Blogs

This activity can be completed individually but (b) should be discussed with your mentor.

a) There are a number of blogs which are run by enthusiastic teachers in most subjects. Using the Internet, identify three blogs which focus on your subject. What are they being used for? How successfully do you think they are being used? Complete an analysis of each of the blogs using the framework created by Ray (see p. 149 in this chapter). What does tell you about the way in which blogs are developed and used?

b) Once you have done this, try starting your own blog or wiki (there are a number of free providers which can be found through searching on the Internet). You might want to focus on a particular topic with a class. Be careful to consider both how you want the site to be used (that is, what you are trying to help the students gain from the experience) and discuss safety and access issues with your mentor *before* introducing the blog or wiki to your class.

c) Once you have tried using the blog/wiki for a period of time, reflect on whether the students have gained anything from using these media and what positive impacts it appears to have on their learning.

Podcasts

Podcasts are another, slightly more established, form of information capture for use in classrooms. They are recordings which are saved in an MP3 format, the file format used for digital music files, stored on MP3 players, mobile phones and PDAs (**personal digital assistant**). It is very easy to produce these files by downloading free software from the Internet, and then using a microphone to record files. In a classroom context, they are increasingly used to build up a library of topic summaries for revision purposes, or as part of explanations used in different settings. For example, a description and explanation of a particular point on a geography field trip can be recorded to allow students to move around a location without the need for the teacher to 'lead from the front'. The libraries of podcasts can be located on a school website, or a school server, thereby making them easy to download and use by the students.

In each of the above cases, the use of technology is allowing the classroom environment to extend beyond that of the physical walls of the school. While there are issues of equality of access, if these can be positively resolved, then e-learning developments such as these can make the learning environment both broader and more flexible. However, this also requires teachers to reconsider their role in students' learning as being less focused on the transmission of knowledge and more related to the aiding and mentoring of students to build their own learning capacities, very much in the spirit of social constructivist models.

Whichever the ICT medium used, there is no doubt that e-learning and the wider use of computers will play an increasingly central role in learning, both within and outside of the classroom. You will need to consider how you can best make use of these resources to serve purposes that you feel are important, rather than be carried along by technological experts who may not have an acute understanding of the needs and dynamics of the learning environment.

CONCLUSIONS

You enter a very complex and diverse situation when you first go into classrooms to teach. As suggested in the introduction to this chapter, you should not expect to find the experience easy, and you will only develop your ability as a teacher through careful planning and preparation, and through constant reflection on your experiences. However, by taking account of the issues raised here, you should be able to understand and develop your classroom practice. The last section of this chapter also demonstrates that classrooms are dynamic and open to change. Those of you who will become expert over time will be those who can critically assess the changes which you believe could enrich the experiences of your students, and act accordingly, rather than simply accepting national developments because the government states that they are the best approaches to take.

REFERENCES

Association for Science Education (2004) *Laboratory Design for Teaching and Learning*, Secondary CD-ROM, Hatfield Association for Science Education.

Balshaw, M. and Farrell, P. (2002) *Teaching Assistants: Practical Strategies for Effective Classroom Support*. London: David Fulton.

Berne, E. (1966) *Games People Play: The Psychology of Human Relationships*. London: Andre Deutsch.

Betoret, F.D. and Artiga, A.G. (2004) 'Trainee teachers' conceptions of teaching and learning, classroom layout and exam design', *Educational Studies*, 30(4): 355–72.

Blatchford, P., Kutnick, P., Baines, E. and Galton, M. (2003) 'Toward a social pedagogy of classroom group work', *International Journal of Education Research*, 39(1–2): 153–72.

Bloom, B.S. and Krathwohl, D.R. (1956) *Taxonomy of Educational Objectives. Handbook 1: Cognitive Domain*. New York: Longmans.

Blum, P. (1998) *Surviving and Succeeding in Difficult Classrooms*. London: Routledge Falmer.

Burton, G. and Dimbleby, R. (1995) *Between Ourselves – an Introduction to Interpersonal Communication*. 2nd edn. London: Arnold.

Butt, G. (2006) *Lesson Planning*. 2nd edn. London: Continuum.

Consortium of Local Education Authorities for the Provision of Social Services (CLEAPSS) (2007) *CLEAPSS Science Publications*, CD-ROM, Uxbridge: CLEAPSS.

Coffield, F., Moseley, D., Hall, E. and Ecclestone, K. (2005) *Should We Be Using Learning Styles? What Research Has to Say to Practice*. London: Learning and Skills Research Centre.

Cothran, D.J., Kulinna, P.H. and Garrahy, D.A. (2003) 'This is kind of giving a secret away …': students' perspectives on effective class management, *Teaching and Teacher Education*, 19(4): 435–44.

Cremin, H., Thomas, G. and Vincent, K. (2005) 'Working with teaching assistants: three models evaluated', *Research Papers in Education*, 20(4): 413–32.

Department for Education and Skills (DfES) (2004) *Pedagogy and Practice: Teaching and Learning in Secondary Schools. Unit 1: Structuring Learning Key Stage 3 National Strategy.* London: HMSO.

Department for Education and Skills and the Qualifications and Curriculum Authorities (DfES/QCA) (2002) *Training Materials for the Foundation Subjects: Module 3. Lesson Planning.* London: DfES.

Dobson, J. (1992) *The New Dare to Discipline.* Wheaton, IL: Tyndale House.

Duthie, J. (1970) *Primary School Survey: A Study of the Teacher's Day.* Edinburgh: HMSO.

Ecclestone, K. (2002) *Learning Autonomy in Post-16 Education.* London: RoutledgeFalmer.

Eide, F. and Eide, B. (2005) 'Brain of the blogger'. http://eideneurolearningblog.blogspot. com/2005/ 03/brain-of-blogger. html (accessed 18 July 2007).

Gardner, H. (1983) *Frames of Mind: The Theory of Multiple Intelligences.* New York: Basic Books.

Hall, E. and Moseley, D. (2005) 'Is there a role for learning styles in personalised education and training?', *International Journal of Lifelong Education*, 24(3): 243–55.

Hargreaves, D. (2004a) *Personalised Learning – Next Steps in Working Laterally.* London: Specialist Schools Trust.

Hargreaves, D. (2004b) *Personalised Learning – 2: Student Voice and Assessment for Learning.* London: Specialist Schools Trust.

Hargreaves, D. (2005) *Personalised Learning – 3: Learning to Learn and the New Technologies.* London: Specialist Schools Trust.

Hattie, J. (1999) 'Influences on student learning'; inaugural lecture: Professor of Education, University of Auckland, 2 August 1999.

Haynes, M., Bowen, S., Tuxford, J. and Ridley, S. (1992) 'Give your room a face-lift! (classroom displays)', *Instructor*, 101(7): 38.

Johnson, M. (2004) 'Personalised learning', *Public Policy Research*, 11(4): 224–8.

Kerry, T. (2002) *Explaining and Questioning.* Cheltenham: Nelson Thornes.

Kerry, T. (2005) 'Towards a typology for conceptualising the roles of teaching assistants', *Educational Review*, 57(3): 373–84.

LeLaurin, K. and Risley, T.R. (1972) 'The organisation of day care environments: "Zone V", "Man to man assignments"', *Journal of Applied Behaviour Analysis*, 5(3): 225–32.

Mansaray, A. (2006) 'Liminality and in/exclusion: exploring the work of teaching assistants', *Pedagogy, Culture and Society*, 14(2): 171–87.

Marlowe, M., Disney, G. and Wilson, K.J. (2004) 'Classroom management of children with emotional and behavioural disorders', *Emotional and Behavioural Difficulties*, 9(2): 99–114.

McCormack, A. (1997) 'Classroom management problems, strategies, and influences in physical education', *European Physical Education Review*, 3: 102–15.

Moran, A. and Abbott, L. (2002) 'Developing inclusive schools: the pivotal role of teaching assistants in promoting inclusion in special and mainstream schools in Northern Ireland', *European Journal of Special Needs Education*, 17(2): 161–73.

Morgan, N. (2005) *Blame my Brain.* London: Walker Books.

Newell, S. and Jeffery, D. (2002) *Behaviour Management in the Classroom: A Transactional Analysis Approach.* London: David Fulton.

Porter, L. (2000) *Behaviour in Schools: Theory and Practice for Teachers.* Buckingham: Open University Press.

Radford, M. (2006) 'Researching classrooms: complexity and chaos', *British Educational Research Journal,* 32(2): 177–90.

Ray, J. (2006) 'Welcome to the blogosphere: the educational use of blogs (aka edublogs)', *Kappa Delta Pi Record,* 42(4): 175–7.

Richardson, W. (2006) *Blogs, Wikis, Podcasts and Other Powerful Web Tools for Classrooms.* Thousand Oaks, CA: Corwin Press.

Rogers, B. (1997) *The Language of Discipline: A Practical Approach to Effective Classroom Management.* 2nd edn. Plymouth: Northcote House.

Rogers, B. (1998) *'You Know the Fair Rule' and Much More: Strategies for Making the Hard Job of Discipline and Behaviour Management in Schools Easier.* Melbourne: ACER.

Supaporn, S. (2000) 'High school students' perspectives about misbehaviour', *Physical Educator,* 57: 124–35.

Tizard, B. and Hughes, M. (1984) *Young Children Learning.* London: Fontana.

Thomas, G. (1992) *Effective Classroom Teamwork: Support or Intrusion.* London: Routledge.

Wood, P. and Patterson, C. (2004) 'Questions, questions, questions', *Teaching Expertise,* 5: 47–9.

Wragg, E.C. (1994) *An Introduction to Classroom Observation.* London: Routledge Falmer.

Zeidner, M. (1988) 'The relative severity of common classroom management strategies: the students' perspective', *British Journal of Educational Psychology,* 58: 69–77.

5 ASSESSING STUDENTS
Tony Lawson

> ### By the end of this chapter you will have:
> - been introduced to the key issues concerning monitoring, assessment, recording, reporting and accountability
> - begun to understand some of the theoretical background to assessment
> - learnt about the terminology associated with assessment
> - reflected on your initial experiences of assessing students.

INTRODUCTION

Assessment pervades schooling and the curriculum. Like it or not, one of the main functions of secondary schooling is to grade, sort and make judgements about the knowledge, skills and attitudes of individual students, and it is one of your main responsibilities to assist your students to achieve the best that they can in a system which continually judges them, both formally and informally. Assessment is therefore about power – an **assessment regime** acts to privilege some and exclude others; it is the **gatekeeper** from the school to the wider world (Lingard et al., 2006).

This chapter is concerned with issues to do with monitoring, assessment, recording, reporting and accountability (referred to as MARRA). All these practical aspects of a teacher's job have complex theoretical backgrounds expounded in a range of weighty texts. The emphasis here is on equipping you with the knowledge and skills to meet your obligations and improve the teaching and learning in your classroom early in your teaching career. Practical considerations must, however, be informed by an understanding of some of the theoretical background and the terminology associated with assessment, as well as you reflecting on your initial experiences of assessing students.

A starting point for a critical look at the changing role of assessment in schooling might be the work of Lloyd-Jones et al. (1992: 6), in which the authors seek to identify trends in assessment. Some of their predictions have come to pass in full, for example, the move away from 'comparing pupils with each other to indicate final achievement and for ranking and selection purposes' towards 'comparing pupils' performance with predetermined criteria to provide feedback for improving performance' (1992: 6). Others have been partially fulfilled, but perhaps in ways that the authors were not expecting, such as the move away from academic assessment towards 'recognition given to skills such as listening, speaking, practical skills, attitudes, personal and social development' (1992: 6). Some of their other predictions sound unbelievable when compared with current assessment arrangements, such as the move away from examinations towards 'continuous assessment, often as a normal part of the teaching/learning process' (1992: 6). The introduction of standard assessment tasks (SATs) for the end of key stage test and modular examinations post-16 has intensified the formal examination experience of students to an unprecedented extent. Other developments were not anticipated by Lloyd-Jones et al. For example, it could be argued that the main purpose of formal assessment has shifted from the 'ranking and selection of pupils' (Lloyd-Jones 1992: 6) to the use of collective statistics for the ranking and selection of *schools*. Moreover, assessment arrangements are in a constant state of change, as governments introduce new or altered testing (for example, the significant changes anticipated in SATs in 2008–09).

These predictions raise a fundamental question in relation to any assessment regime, which is, 'what exactly is being assessed?' If you think about the complexity of human characteristics, it is difficult to envisage any ways in which an assessment system can encapsulate all the aspects of the human condition without serious testing overload. For example, a prospective employer might want to know how good you were intellectually, practically, or at theoretical knowledge, but would also be interested in your character, your ability to work socially, your values and personal dispositions that might impact upon your ability to do a good job (see Pring, 1984). Watkins (1992) identified seven 'selfs' that might be subject to testing: the bodily self, including health and environmental impact; the sexual self; the social self which includes communication skills; the vocational self and career trajectories; the moral self as a political actor, the self as a learner; and the self in the organization. Perhaps most influential on present day schooling in the UK, the work of Howard Gardner (see Gardner, 1993, for example) on multiple intelligences (see Chapter 2) raises problematic questions for any assessment system. Gardner proposes that there is not a single 'intelligence' that therefore can be simply measured, but that there are a number of 'intelligences' existing in everyone, but developed to different levels depending on the individual. The difficulty Gardner faced was in devising measures that could assess and profile the intelligences of an individual in a way that was practical and not too time-consuming (see Gardner, 2003).

Before looking at each of the five MARRA elements, gather your own thoughts about what you think assessment is for and how it has affected you.

Activity 5.1 Why assess?

This activity can be completed individually or with other beginning teachers.

Before you look at the list below, try to answer the question 'Why assess?' With other beginning teachers you could 'brainstorm' lots of ideas.

Then read these 15 suggested reasons and indicate with '++', '+' or '–' those which to you are very important (++), fairly important (+) or least important (–) to you as a teacher and, in your view, to students.

	Teacher	Student
1. To monitor student progress of a whole class.		
2. To identify strengths and weaknesses of individual students.		
3. To find out how well individual students are assimilating what is being taught.		
4. To provide feedback to students in order to help decide what action should be taken next.		
5. To provide information to students about how well they are doing against national standards.		
6. To accumulate records of progress.		
7. To inform other teachers who have to make decisions about students.		
8. To assess the benefits of a course.		
9. To evaluate the effectiveness of teaching methods.		
10. To provide motivation to students.		
11. To provide incentives to learn.		
12. To assist in guidance about choice of subject, course, career, and so on.		
13. To inform parents about progress.		

(Continued)

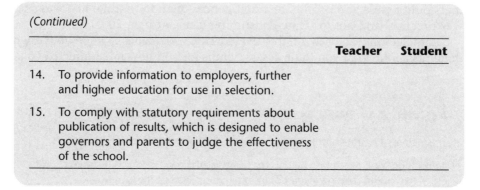

(Continued)

	Teacher	Student
14. To provide information to employers, further and higher education for use in selection.		
15. To comply with statutory requirements about publication of results, which is designed to enable governors and parents to judge the effectiveness of the school.		

MONITORING

An essential part of the everyday activity of all teachers is monitoring students' achievements and progress. This is often done in an informal and impressionistic way to allow the teacher to decide what has been learned and where there are still weaknesses in students' understanding. One of the most important skills you can develop in this regard is always to be aware of what is going on in your classroom. This is described as 'withitness' by Kounin (1970). Picking up quickly on the individual needs of students has a direct bearing on the quality of their learning experience, their behaviour and their motivation, and, by doing this, you will be able to teach more effectively.

Wragg (2001) suggested that observing students in the classroom is a key aspect of this monitoring process. It allows teachers to link informal assessment to learning. By looking at the interactions and individual circumstances of the students, the teacher can distinguish between those who might be making progress and those who might be having problems with the learning. However, Wragg warned against making simplistic judgements about student behaviour on the basis of observation alone. For example, what might seem to be a student concentrating on the task could be a student daydreaming. Therefore to monitor effectively, he argued that the teacher needs to interact verbally with students, both in groups and as individuals. However, what is vital in the monitoring process is *how* the teacher enquires about the student's engagement, what he called 'the language of discourse' (Wragg, 2001: 39) of the interaction. To monitor students' learning in a meaningful way, the teacher has to find the form of question that allows *the student* to identify what they have learned and achieved over the immediately preceding segment of the session.

Despite the apparent informality and spontaneity of classroom monitoring, planning will improve its effectiveness. Four aspects are worth looking at:

1. Very many lessons start with a teacher-led introduction, which includes a few questions and answers by way of a recapitulation of previous lessons. This is a rough and ready form of 'baseline assessment' (see page 167). To teachers, its main advantage is that it is a quick and efficient way to start a lesson, which helps to focus students' minds on the forthcoming topic. The drawback is that it is easy to rely on a few students to supply all the answers and the rest of the class get used to opting out. As a tool for monitoring what students already know or have recalled from previous work, it therefore has limited benefits unless the teacher consciously plans a sequence of questions and involves most if not all of the class. The use of directed questioning in this circumstance helps to spread the range of those who answer the questions. More formal methods of monitoring may be employed at this point, for example, requiring every student to come to the Interactive Whiteboard (IWB) and contribute to a **mind map**® or having a prepared written task on the desk as students come in to the class, which is designed to establish what the students have brought with them from a previous session.

2. The use of the 'three-part' lesson and its variations is one way in which monitoring student progress can have a built-in segment, usually called a plenary. While the use of the word 'plenary' would seem to indicate that it occurs at the end of a lesson, a plenary can occur at any stage, as it is the function that is important rather than its location. Plenaries are intended to provide an opportunity for students and teachers to review what has been learned in a previous learning episode and establish the foundations for future learning. They can be formal or informal, teacher- or student-led, and written or oral. Ofsted (2002) identifies the plenary as a way of ensuring that 'the whole class (is) moving forward together' (2002: 4) and teachers 'review with (students) the extent of their learning' (2002: 74).

3. Very many lessons also include a substantial amount of time when students are working on the task they have been set, with the teacher moving around the class responding to individuals. Beginning teachers are generally good at supporting students when they are working individually, but again practice could be improved by considering the nature of the questions asked in these interactions. Wragg (2001) distinguishes between lower-order and higher-order questions in which the former are concerned with asking students to give a factual response, that is recall a piece of knowledge, and the latter demanding some form of thinking beyond just remembering facts. The key skill of problem-solving is directly concerned with this higher-order questioning. Observations of the classroom have shown that many teachers give a very limited time for students to think about their answers, before the teacher moves on to someone else, or answers the question themselves! While factual recall can be a quick-fire activity, the thinking processes in higher-order questions need time to be thought through. The format of the question will also differ according to what you want to elicit

from the students. Higher-order questions are generally more open than factual recall questions (see also Chapter 4).

It is also worth considering why students may seem to be disengaged from activities in which you have planned for their active involvement. There is no one explanation for off-task behaviour. It may be that the student already knows a great deal about the topic or alternatively does not understand the task. It may that they have not had the chance to develop the skills to complete it or external factors may be affecting their performance. Some students for example are shy of engaging in public contributions in the classroom. As presentation is a central skill in many occupations, it is your responsibility to devise strategies that allow students to develop those skills in a structured and supported way, while monitoring their progress in this skill.

4. Teachers commonly attach considerable importance to written tasks such as homework or tests to judge how well students have understood a topic. The business of marking written work is looked at in the section on assessment (page 161), but it is worth considering its value as a way of monitoring students' progress. For the student who struggles with or dislikes writing, it has obvious limitations. A salutary experience is to observe and/or talk to an early years teacher who has to find ways of monitoring the progress of children too young to express themselves adequately on paper.

Over time, a good teacher also needs to monitor students' progress in terms of what kinds of task individuals find difficult and what skills they might be lacking. This should be closely linked to assessment, so that your mark book shows you significant ups and downs in a student's performance, and to planning, so that you can build in further opportunities for practice and improvement.

Activity 5.2   Definitions of assessment

This activity can be completed individually and responses shared with another beginning teacher.

Assessment and testing policies and practices are central structuring features of education systems, schools and classrooms, one important component of what Bernstein (1971) called the three message systems of schooling – curriculum, pedagogy and assessment. Assessment sits at the intersection of the educational field with its semi-autonomous character and the fields of the broader social arrangement. The varying forms of assessment and testing sit in different positions across these fields; compare for example, formative assessment and summative assessment, or the distinctions utilized by the contemporary Scottish project 'Assessment is for learning' of **assessment for, as and of learning** (see Hayward et al., 2000;

Hutchinson and Hayward, 2005). There are inherent tensions between assessment located within the educational field for educative purposes and that located at the intersection of that field and an unequally structured society for sorting and selecting purposes and within the bureaucratic state field for system accountability purposes. (Lingard et al., 2006: 83–4)

1. In three sentences, distinguish between **'curriculum**, **pedagogy** and **assessment'** in schooling.

2. Providing examples, identify the differences between assessment 'for, as and of learning'.

3. In discussion with another trainee teacher, establish what you understand by the authors' view that there are 'inherent tensions between assessment located within the educational field for educative purposes and that located at the intersection of that field and an unequally structured society for sorting and selecting purposes and within the bureaucratic state field for system accountability purposes'?

4. Individually, decide which of the three fields you think is the dominant one in contemporary schooling. Justify your answer to the other trainee.

ASSESSMENT

Assessment is any method of obtaining information about the progress and performance of your students. It is a big and complex area of a teacher's work, yet one that is undertaken every day. The research basis for awarding bodies' and teachers' practices in assessment is fraught with uncertainty. Some areas of schooling are more amenable to accurate testing than others. The more complex the understanding to be tested, the more difficult it is to devise assessment tasks that can validly measure that understanding. Take for example the issue of **key skills**. The 'harder' key skills such as numeracy can have assessment activities that can be fair and reliable to all the students who take them. However, with the 'softer' key skills, such as 'working with others', it is difficult to construct assessment circumstances in which we could be confident that everyone who participated was awarded the grade that their performance deserved. Because of this problem, data about schools' performance is expressed as attainment and achievement data. Attainment is the level of knowledge and skills that can be formally tested and presented as examination grades or test scores. Achievement is the broader range of knowledge, skills and attitudes that students acquire in schools and which are often part of the social and personal development of an individual student.

There is no generally agreed model for assessment. However, most commentators would agree that a useful starting point would be Thomas's (1990: 128) definition that 'assessing learning should involve not only terminal or summative assessment, but should also be a diagnostic process embracing learning as it proceeds'. Issues concerning assessment have come to the forefront of debates about how to improve student attainment, as evidence from Ofsted has accumulated that suggests that 'good assessment practice in the schools visited derives from scrupulous attention to pupils' progress and draws teachers together in working systematically on achievement. It has been key to improvement in these schools' (Ofsted, 2003: 4).

You will need to develop an understanding of how formal and informal approaches can work; of how you elicit information and form judgements about cognitive development (knowledge, understanding) as opposed to affective development (attitudes), and within the former, the difference between knowledge and skills; of differences between '**attainment**', '**ability**' and '**achievement**' and the importance of recognizing 'effort' and of using assessment in a way which motivates students. Assessment should never be seen as the last 'add-on' stage in the process of teaching and learning, but as an integral part of the planning cycle. In the 'virtuous circle of teaching' (see Figure 5.1) learning is at the very heart of what teachers do, and assessment is one of the four planks of teacher activity that promotes student learning. Alongside planning, delivery and evaluating, assessing is a vital component of teaching and has to be integrated into teachers' practices seamlessly.

Some of the terminology associated with assessment may be unfamiliar to you. Key concepts include the following.

Summative assessment

This takes place at the end of a course or period of schooling and is largely concerned with reporting results to an external audience such as parents, carers or a potential employer. End of year examinations or GCSE or **Level 3 examinations** (AS – Advanced Supplementary level taken at age 17, and A2 – Advanced level taken at 18, AVCEs – Vocational Advanced levels and the International Baccalaureate) are typical examples of summative assessment. While historically, summative assessment has taken a particular form, it is not a fixed format at all. Traditionally, discursive subjects such as history have relied on the essay-type question for their major form of assessment; the scientific and mathematical subjects relied on working through set problems; and the more artistic subjects have used practical tasks, but usually time-constrained and in a more formal setting. In the future, the involvement of ICT in summative assessment is likely to increase. Awarding bodies such as the Assessment and Qualification Alliance (AQA), Oxford, Cambridge and RSA (OCR) and Edexcel

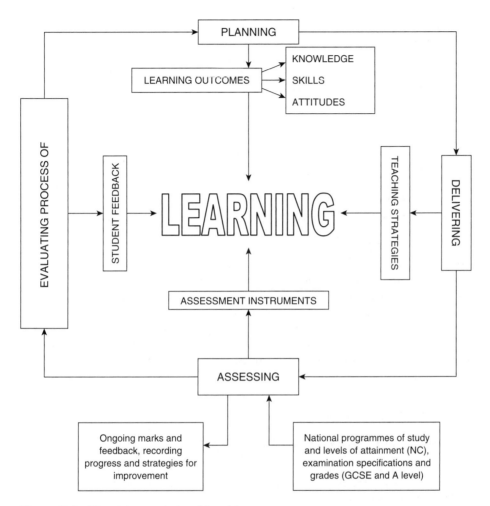

Figure 5.1 The virtuous circle of teaching

already use electronic marking in a wide range of subjects, including discursive ones, but there are also ways in which ICT can be utilized for direct assessment activities (see Richardson, 2003).

Since the 1980s, there has been a movement to less formal means of summative assessment, especially involving the project or coursework. The General Certificate of Secondary Education (GCSE) has had a compulsory element of coursework in all subjects since the 1980s (although this, at time of writing in 2007 is under review). The argument in favour of coursework was that it was a more 'authentic' way of assessing what students 'know, under-stand and can do'. It also allowed those students who did not perform well in the 'three-hour' examination format to have a different experience of assess-ment that might more closely fit their learning preferences. However, concerns about the reliability of coursework modes of assessment, in particular its potential for plagiarism with the rise of the Internet and the contributions that parents can make in a non-supervised mode of assessment has led to a rethink about the efficacy of coursework. At level 3, the proposals for change at AS and A2 include the idea that there should be one extended project for any student and that this should be separated from subjects.

One of the perceived problems with summative assessment, where nationally validated, is that it becomes a 'high-stakes' assessment. By this is meant that, because success in examinations is a passport to higher study, better jobs, more money, higher status, and so on, the investment of students in education can be aimed at achieving the certificate rather than learning about the subject. If you add in the fact that teachers are judged on the results that their students achieve, there can be a bias towards performance in examination rather than understanding the complexities of an area of study. This is often referred to as a focus on 'shallow' rather than 'deep' learning (see Harlen and James, 1997). Teachers may be aware of 'teaching to the test', but may still find their classroom strategies and interactions with students leaning towards more passive modes of learning in order to secure the best examination results (see Harlen, 2006).

Activity 5.3   Assessing your subject

Parts (a)–(c) of this activity can be completed individually and discussed with other beginning teachers. Parts (d)–(f) should be discussed with your mentor or another experienced teacher.

The approach to assessment in each National Curriculum subject represents one view of the matter: that of the people who devised the Order. You may agree with it, or parts of it; you may not. The fact that there are marked differences in this respect between the 1990, 1995 and 2000 (and 2008) Orders suggests the diffi-culties and contentiousness of assessment issues.

a) Before examining the National Curriculum, consider the following questions:

What should be assessed in your subject?

Are there aspects of your subject that should not or cannot be assessed?

b) Now examine the National Curriculum document in your subject (or one closely related if yours is not part of the National Curriculum) with these questions in mind:

To what extent do the assessment arrangements in your subject reflect your own views?

Are there aspects of those arrangements you would modify or remove?

c) Compare your views with beginning teachers from other subjects in order to decide whether some subjects are more problematic than others in the matter of assessment.

d) Examine closely the wording of the Level Descriptions for your subject or a closely related one. What are their strengths and weaknesses? Do they cover everything that you value in the learning activities to which they relate?

e) Carry out a marking exercise according to the marking criteria for your chosen subject to see how closely your judgements match those of a more experienced teacher. This will take you a long time, but is the best way of interpreting and applying National Curriculum assessment criteria.

f) Carry out a similar exercise for work at GCSE and A2 and AS levels. Do this as a 'blind' activity, marking work that a more experienced teacher has already marked but without knowing what mark it has been given.

Formative assessment

This is part of a continuous spiral of learning, the assessment of what has been learned in order to guide what should happen next, then more learning, more assessment, and so on. It is important to recognize that formative assessment can have negative as well as positive effects on achievement. Dweck (1986) distinguishes between 'mastery-oriented' responses to assessment, in which students seek challenge and deploy effort in pursuing goals, and 'maladaptive' responses, which are seen as a form of helplessness, where students avoid challenges and have low persistence when struggling with learning. Formative assessment is more diagnostic, should give more immediate feedback to student and teacher, and should be acted upon by them. Although allotting a mark to a piece of work does not seem to be as important in raising achievement as the provision of a commentary about how to improve it, Smith and Gorard (2005) showed that the students themselves valued a mark as a means of identifying where they were in terms of standards. Many would argue that self-assessment is an essential component of formative assessment. Theorists such as Earl (2003) argued that studies of assessment have concentrated on the assessment *of* learning, but that the investigation of assessment *for* learning and assessment *as* learning are equally important. Formative assessment is now most closely associated with the idea of assessment for learning (see page 169). Assessment as learning is used by teachers to gain access to students' understandings of an issue, to identify misunderstandings and plan for remedial action.

Normative assessment

This provides information about a student's ability or achievement compared with others in the same age cohort. Thus a mark or a grade tells us, for example, that a student is in the top 10 per cent for their age, or twenty-third in their class. Much assessment has traditionally been of this kind. The advantage of this type of assessment is that it establishes the relative position of students in relation to their peers. When entry to higher education or more prestigious occupations was limited to a relatively small percentage of the population, then this was probably an appropriate way of sorting individuals into a normal distribution curve, where the top percentile alone would be most likely to be recruited into higher education. However, the weakness of norm-referencing is that it does not describe what an individual student can actually do, only their position in relation to others' performance. As social policies have shifted towards increasing the proportion of each age cohort who is to be recruited to further study, norm-referencing has fallen out of favour as a principle of national examinations in the UK.

Criterion-referenced assessment

This is where a student's performance is judged against a clear and concrete statement (the criterion) of what is expected. It requires a careful analysis of the course concerned and its learning objectives, leading to unambiguously stated criteria. These require the formulation of a set of statements that enable the assessment to be expressed as a 'profile' of achievement rather than, or as well as, a single overall grade or mark. In national examinations, criterion-referencing usually appears as a number of level descriptions, with each paragraph defining what might be expected of a candidate at grade E, C and A (for AS and A2 examinations).

The link with formative assessment can be seen, as criterion referencing should give a clear statement of what a student can do or has achieved, which can be built upon in the next stage of their experience. Whilst the benefits of criterion-referenced assessment are now widely accepted, there can be practical difficulties. In particular the production of unambiguous and acceptable criteria can be highly problematic and time-consuming. General Certificate of Secondary Education and Advanced level are criterion-referenced examinations, but there are difficulties in putting them into practice. For example, the complexity of the original National Curriculum assessment regime included several criteria at each level of each attainment target. The testing regime was supposed to be short tests, but they could not cover all the criteria at all the levels (see Cullingford, 1997, for an account of this issue). The level description criteria used in GCSE and Advanced level examinations often contain within them norm-referenced statements, so that for example, a C-level candidate might be described as having a 'satisfactory' grasp of a piece of knowledge, which is implicitly contrasted with those who have a less or more satisfactory grasp (see Wragg, 1997).

Baseline assessment

In general terms, this means finding out what your students know and can do before you teach them more. Since September 1998 it has taken on a particular meaning as a statutory requirement for all children starting school – teachers must use an accredited baseline scheme capable of producing numerical outcomes related to a specific range of achievements. Schools that have adopted a dense form of assessment activity, use baseline type assessments to inform their future policies. For example, in the Sacred Heart High School, 'a range of assessment information is considered, including Key Stage 2 test and teacher assessment data, and the outcomes of standardised tests in mathematics, reading and non-verbal reasoning. These are used to provide a baseline for individual pupils and benchmarks for the school' (Ofsted, 2003: 7). These baseline assessment measures are also used by schools to identify those who have particular learning needs, or who are gifted and talented, or 'most able and more able' (MAMA).

Validity

This and reliability (next section) relate to technical issues of assessment and researchers in the area of assessment emphasize their importance. Validity concerns the extent to which an assessment actually assesses what it is supposed to be assessing. Most commonly this is judged by the opinions of those knowledgeable in the subject area concerned, but it is also sometimes possible to judge validity by some external criterion: for example, do results from this assessment predict performance in a subsequent course? This occurs for example when schools generate 'value added' measures of attainment.

Students are given predictions of what they should achieve at the next level of assessment on the basis of a previous assessment. When students achieve higher grades than previous performance would predict, the school is said to have 'added value' to that student's education. Another way that external criteria might be use to judge the validity of an assessment task is where the results from a test agree with ratings of achievement given by a teacher. You may be asked to engage in this predicted grade activity on post-16 examinations such as AS and A2 examinations.

However, there are certain areas of controversy around validity suggested by researchers that have to be considered. Different experts emphasize different types of validity in approaching assessment. Awarding bodies are particularly concerned with content validity, that is, how closely an examination paper matches the assessment objectives of the specification. For example, it would be unfair if an area of the specification studied by a group of students never had a question set on it. Lloyd-Jones et al. (1992) describe construct-validity as an important element for those programmes that cover a variety of skills, as well as knowledge. Construct-validity refers to how well an assessment task can provide judgements about higher-order cognitive skills, such as analysis and evaluation, rather than just the recall of relevant knowledge. The problem here is not just that it is more difficult to devise tasks that give all students who take them the possibility of demonstrating these skills if they have acquired them. There is also the problem that areas of affective skills such as feelings and attitudes that a subject might engender have proved to be very difficult to assess in a valid way (Messick, 1994). The search for reliability in assessment can therefore lead to only assessing those aspects of education that can more easily be assessed reliably (see Stobart, 2006: 135).

Finally, criterion-related validity refers to the ability of an assessment task to cover all the level descriptions connected to a particular examination. The difficulty of devising questions that all levels of ability can access fairly has led to the tiering of GCSE examinations, in which those who can access the higher criteria have additional or different assessment tasks to attempt.

Reliability

This relates to whether assessment results are consistent. Would the results be the same if the assessment was carried out on a different day, or in slightly different circumstances, or by a different teacher? Gipps (1994) distinguishes between consistency in student performance and consistency in assessing that performance. In the case of the former, reliability refers to how far the student would be able to replicate his or her performance on a different day with the same examination paper. The latter refers to whether different markers would arrive at the same mark for one candidate's paper. The awarding bodies try to achieve this through the technical device of defining reliability as all markers giving the same mark to a candidate's work that the chief examiner, who set the paper, would have given it. Reliability is clearly an important issue where results are for use outside the classroom, for example where they might influence selection for a job or for a place in higher education (see Black and Wiliam, 2006: 130–1). This is why all the awarding bodies are required by the **Qualifications and Curriculum Authority (QCA)** to have appeals procedures in place, so that candidates can challenge whether their individual papers have been reliably marked.

The question of the reliability of end of key stage tests in the National Curriculum has also been raised. The problem is that the tests can either assess a relatively small area of a subject in some depth or take a broader view and assess a greater range of skills more superficially. Wiliam (2000) has calculated that over 50 per cent of students who take end of key stage tests at Key Stage 3 are classified at the wrong level. Similarly Massey et al. (2003) argued that much of the apparent gain in test results at Key Stage 2 were attributable to variations in the standards of the tests, rather than a measure of real progress.

Activity 5.4   Identifying Good Practice in Assessment

All parts of this activity can be completed individually. Parts (c) and (d) can be shared with your tutor or mentor.

a) On the companion website is a link to an Ofsted document entitled *Good Assessment in Secondary Schools*, published in March 2003. You will need to read this or download all or part of it.

b) In Part 2, there are a number of vignettes of good assessment practice in various subjects. Choose a subject, OTHER THAN YOUR OWN, and select an account that you think has implications for good assessment practice in your own subject.

c) Write a 250-word report on the specific practice(s) that you have chosen, showing how it/they would be useful in your own subject and how you will introduce it/them into your own practice.

d) Choose another account from a different area of the curriculum where you think the assessment practice(s) is less useful for your subject and detail the reasons for your decision as another 250-word report.

ASSESSMENT FOR LEARNING

An extension of formative assessment, this is one of the key thrusts of the National Strategy for raising standards of student attainment. It is defined as 'the process of seeking and interpreting evidence for use by learners and their teachers to decide where the learners are in their learning, where they need to go and how best to get there' (ARG, 2002: 1). This can be seen as an element of an action planning process, in which students and teachers together review the evidence of what has been achieved, identify what still has to be done in terms of SMART (specific, measurable, achievable, realistic, time-defined) targets, draw up strategies to move the student towards those targets and provide a time frame when progress will be next checked.

The impetus for work in this area was created by the research by Black and Wiliam (1998), in which they reviewed the research evidence for the effectiveness of formative assessment. Their starting point was that international research suggested that the existence of formal external tests dominated the classroom and led to a focus on the outcomes of schooling rather than looking at the processes whereby learning could be analysed to promote improvements in learning. They concluded that implementing formative assessment could produce substantial gains in attainment but that major weaknesses in classroom assessment would need to be tackled if the potential of formative assessment is to be realized.

Three main categories of weakness are identified: the quality of assessment tasks on which the process of feedback is based; teachers' grading of students' work as part of the feedback process; and a failure to actively involve students in their own assessment in order to help them become increasingly responsible for their own learning.

Assessment for learning has the greatest potential for advancing students' progress, because it has the potential to close the gap between the current level of achievement and the desired level. Two crucial ingredients can turn this into reality: high-quality assessment tasks, which do actually find out what you think they will; effective feedback, which acknowledges achievement to date and indicates ways to improve. It is essential that students understand the processes so that self-assessment and target-setting can start to operate; in other words, assessment is not something that teachers do to students' work, but something in which all parties are involved.

Researchers have shown that classroom practice often demonstrates weaknesses in each of these areas (see Black and Wiliam, 1998), and offer the following recommendations.

Assessment tasks should:

- be planned as part of a deliberate sequence to achieve progression in students' learning over a minimum of a key stage
- be enjoyable but reasonably challenging and differentiated
- develop thinking skills, for example the ability to synthesize or evaluate
- require students to transform rather than transfer information

- make students aware of how they will be assessed
- sometimes be devised for students working in groups
- sometimes enable teachers to observe the process of decision-making
- sometimes make possible more than one acceptable solution or answer
- sometimes permit the student to select the form of response.

Feedback should:

- be directly related to the assessment task
- be related to the standards the teacher has set for the successful completion of the task
- concentrate on what the student particularly needs to do to improve which will make the most difference
- be communicated in a language the student can understand
- be positive but constructively critical
- be as immediate as is practical
- require action on the part of the student
- use consistent marking conventions across a department to acknowledge success and identify targets for improvement
- take advantage of a range of contexts, for example, pair or group work or homework.

This last point can be extended to include the importance of self- and peer-assessment as important elements of assessment for learning. Black et al. (2003) argue that self-assessment by students is a difficult skill to develop, as students do not automatically have the necessary analytical know-how to identify what has gone wrong or the ability to set realistic strategies for improvement. However, they claim that peer-assessment can help the students to develop these skills, because it motivates them to work more carefully, gives greater power to the student voice, thus commanding more attention and uses more accessible language to offer criticism that may more readily be taken on board.

Activity 5.5   Self-assessment

You can complete activity a) individually and b) in a small group.

a) Consider the experiences you have had of self-assessment. In what ways do you think they influenced your learning?

b) In a small group:

(Continued)

(Continued)

    i) list the possible benefits of students assessing their own work;

    ii) consider whether there are any drawbacks or potential difficulties;

    iii) drawing on experience from your own subject area collate ideas for supporting students' self-assessment;

    iv) discuss how schools can teach/encourage pupils to become autonomous learners;

    v) identify the skills you need as a teacher to help give young people the confidence to take responsibility for their own learning.

MARKING

During the early part of your teaching career, the priority is to mark in a way which is in line with departmental or school policy and therefore familiar to the students. One of the first difficulties that you might face is how to mark non-written work in a way that accords with the standards in your department. For example, the English National Curriculum has attainment targets related to speaking and listening, as well as reading and writing. Other subjects, such as drama, design and technology and PE, are involved in the marking of practical and performance work. In addition, you will have to familiarize yourself with national standards of attainment for your particular subject or subjects, especially if you are involved in marking coursework for national examinations or are preparing students for National Curriculum assessments. The difficulty that you face here is conforming to a standard that is fixed by remote awarding bodies and the Qualifications and Curriculum Authority. These organizations are charged with the responsibility of ensuring comparability in national examinations. By comparability, they mean three related aspects of examining:

- Examinations in the same subject should be comparable in standard year on year, so that a student achieving a B grade at GCSE in one year is at roughly the same standard as a student in the subsequent year.
- Examinations in different subjects at the same level in the same year should be of a comparable standard, so that a GCSE grade B in Maths represents a comparable difficulty to achieving a grade B GCSE in English.
- Examinations in the same subject but offered by different awarding bodies should be roughly comparable in standard, so that a C in History with OCR is the same level as a C with AQA.

Of course, it is not an easy or simple process to ensure that these elements of comparability are achieved. For example, schools may switch the awarding body they use for a particular subject because of a perception that one examination is easier than the other. However, there are procedures in place to try and ensure that comparability is as real as the human dimension of marking allows. So, subjects at a specific level are regularly scrutinized by QCA to ensure that they are at a comparable level of difficulty and the QCA runs constant checking projects to track standards over time and between subjects. However, the margin for error in marking remains a function of its human agency. As Sutton (1992: 2) puts it: 'Assessment is a human process conducted by and with human beings and subject to the frailties of human nature. However crisp and objective we might try to make it and however neatly quantifiable may be our results, assessment is closer to an art than a science.'

The difficulty that you will face in absorbing the national standards of marking is important because, when you mark your students' work, you need to give them a realistic assessment of where they stand in relation to the national standard. Giving a piece of work an accurate mark or grade is important for the students to understand where they are and the gap between that and where they want to be (for example, in terms of the grade they need to get to the course of their choice if they are going to go to university). It is also part of your job to support students with appropriate strategies to make that improvement – part of the assessment for learning agenda. There are a number of ways in which you can access the national standards. The awarding bodies offer training sessions for teachers to familiarize them with the processes of marking external examinations and internally assessed coursework. There are often clusters of schools that co-operate in moderating their own marking. In terms of your training year, the school or college department you are in will be the easiest place to access these standards.

Prompt, careful marking of students' work is one of the most important ways in which you can convey respect for their efforts and demand similarly high standards from them. It also has a special role in relating to parents/carers, who tend to make all sorts of judgements and assumptions about your teaching on the basis of the few comments they see on their child's work.

Marking is a form of assessment that gives teachers the chance to respond to an individual's work. It helps both teachers and students develop a shorthand language which facilitates efficient and clear communication. The problem is that marking is time-consuming and can easily feel burdensome. You will have to learn to fit marking into your working schedule, and plan the tasks which you set so that all your classes' work does not come in to be marked at the same time. Most departments select certain pieces of work – perhaps at the end of a topic – for careful assessment and prepare the students accordingly. You may need to target particular pieces of work for detailed marking and comments and treat others more superficially. Remember, too, the possibility of training students to use self- and paired-assessment.

Activity 5.6   Ways of assessing

Consider the following list of assessment strategies.

Oral evidence	Written evidence	Graphic evidence	Products
Questioning	Questionnaires		Models
Listening	Diaries	Diagrams	Artefacts
Discussing	Reports	Sketches	Games
Presentation	Essays	Drawings	Photographs
Interviewing	Notes	Graphs	Databases
Debates	Stories	Printouts	Dance
Audio recording	Newspaper	Overlays	Performance
Video recording	articles	Video clips	Theatrical show
Role play	Scripts	Spread sheets	PE or games
	Short answers to	PowerPoint	exhibition
	questions	presentations	
	Lists	Storyboard	
	Poems		
	Descriptions		
	Portfolios		
	Booklets		

1. Consider from your observation of others and your own experience of the classroom:

   - Which of these are produced frequently in the classroom?
   - Which of these are used infrequently?
   - Why?
   - Are any of the above underused in your own classroom?

2. Choose at least one example from each column of the table and consider the positive and negative aspects for each, for example:

Wallchart or display

Positive	Negative
Encourages discussion	Encourages copying
Co-operation	Assessing individual contribution
Skills other than writing	difficult
A guide to future lesson planning	Some pupils left out
Sharing ideas	Time-consuming
Demonstrates understanding	Has everyone a record of what they
Gives information about the topic	did?
for others to see	How do I record the work?
Interesting	Did everyone understand?

3. During your teaching experience, you must use a variety of teaching and assessment strategies. As part of your lesson evaluations, comment on the effectiveness of what you have tried and how this has informed your future planning to meet the needs of individuals.

RECORDING

Keeping tidy, accurate and informative records about students is a responsibility for every teacher and has become increasingly important as systems of public accountability for schooling have been refined. Records fulfil a number of functions for the individual teacher:

1. To support your memory and keep information for your own use, for example, formative assessment purposes.
2. To enable information to be passed on within school to other teachers, for example, as a student progresses up the school.
3. To inform contacts between school and parents/carers.

Records also provide functions for schools and colleges and the education system as a whole:

1. To provide information to other schools when children transfer.
2. To identify any patterns in a child's performance and thereby identify the need for intervention, in particular with regard to special educational needs, including gifted and talented students.
3. When aggregated, to provide information for outside agencies, for example inspection agencies, the national government, parents and the media.
4. To contribute to a school's improvement plans.

These different functions require varying amounts of detail and types of information. Good advice early in your career is to keep relatively full records, including notes and reminders to yourself from lesson to lesson. The mark book maintained by each teacher is an important record of student's work and progress. One of the problems with recording is that performance can be recorded in a number of forms (percentages, raw marks, grades, linear scales for effort – see Wragg, 2001: 76). You need therefore to organize your recording practice to fit in with the school's system of recording, but as long as it enables departmental records to be completed, it can be unique to each teacher. In addition, teachers are required to keep information about students' progress that contributes to the self-evaluation documents that departments and schools have to submit as part of their school improvement procedures.

Many schools have sophisticated systems for building up a profile of each student and groups of students throughout the school career, and as a class teacher you will contribute to that. Increasingly, these profiles are based on ICT software that allows a sophisticated analysis of an individual's performance, attendance, punctuality and the like. Ironically, one of the items of record-keeping that is often ignored is to build up a record of an individual student's exposure to various forms of ICT applications beyond the ICT classroom (see Comber et al., 2002). This record-keeping will therefore involve your role as a classroom teacher but also your pastoral role (see Chapter 7). As learning support teachers and teaching assistants take on duties within the classroom, you will also take responsibility for their record-keeping. Your duties in this regard will include both the collection of appropriate data, and also its accuracy.

RECORDS OF ACHIEVEMENT

The term 'records of achievement' first came into use in the 1970s. It developed from a concern to recognize the achievements of young people leaving school with no or few formal qualifications and primarily as an aid for employers to identify the skills of potential employees. However, the processes and principles of assessment that the term came to embrace steadily grew in their influence, and came to be seen as relevant to all students.

A large number of individual schools and local authorities developed their own versions of records of achievement, and in the mid-1980s the Department of Education and Science (DES) supported a number of pilot projects and a national evaluation (Broadfoot and Pollard, 1997) that resulted in a National Record of Achievement (ROA) in 1993. This was intended to have four purposes: documenting achievement; recognizing wider achievement; organizing the individual's curriculum; and motivating students towards personal development (see Latham, 1997).

Records of Achievement record the result of the processes of education and activities such as profiling (see later in this chapter). They therefore had the following features:

1. They use largely criterion-referenced methods to emphasise positive achievements.
2. They assess a wide range of achievements; including subject specific achievements, but also cross-curricular skills and extra-curricular and out of school achievements (and sometimes personal characteristics and attitudes).
3. They result in a summative document for use by the student on leaving school.
4. They incorporate elements of self-assessment by the student.

PROFILING

In developing ROAs, much emphasis was placed on the processes that resulted in the final document, as a way of students engaging in planning their own educational development (see Latham, 1997). That is to say, the formative processes of 'profiling' were seen, not only as a way of planning to achieve formal qualifications, but also as a means of promoting individual self-development in a number of areas. The central aspect of profiling includes discussions between individual teachers and students about each student's progress in relationship to desired outcomes (that could be a certificate or the development of skills and attitudes). These discussions would lead to targets being set for the student to focus on within a timescale, with strategies suggested for how the student could make progress in achieving these targets and evidence identified that would indicate when these targets had been achieved.

Therefore a process of individual action planning (IAP) lay at the heart of the profiling movement. The central theoretical idea behind action planning was the desire to engage students in their own learning and for them to take more responsibility for their progress. By encouraging a greater sense of ownership of learning, the intention was to 'empower' students, so that education was no longer something that happened to students, but became a process in which students were actively engaged in constructing their own profiles of achievements. The notion of empowerment is not without its controversies (see Lawson and Harrison, 1999). It has been argued that individual action planning, rather than passing control to students, gives only the illusion of freedom and instead, gets students to manage their own educational development within strict limits, as the end results (recognized qualifications or skills and attitudes desired by employers) are predetermined and outside of their control (see Lawson et al., 2004).

PORTFOLIOS

In many areas of education, the development of portfolios has been a significant development. The portfolio is 'a purposeful collection of student work that tells the story of the students' efforts, progress or achievement in (a) given area(s).' (Arter and Spandel, 1992: 36). However, portfolios can be used for a variety of purposes connected with assessment. They have been particularly deployed in vocational qualifications as a summative document for accreditation purposes. Criteria for making judgements about the level of performance indicated in a portfolio are usually built into the specification for the subject and identify, for example, the number and type of pieces of work to be included, the skills to be included and often a requirement of an element of self-evaluation as part of the content. Portfolios are increasingly used in professional courses such as the PGCE (see Groom and Maunonen-Eskelinen, 2006) or for threshold assessment for teachers as a means of logging evidence for the range of Standards that they have to reach in order to pass the course or proceed to higher pay levels. Grant and Huebner (1998) argued that the most effective portfolios in teacher education are those designed to promote reflective practice. To do this, the structure and processes associated with these portfolios should encourage a habit of mind that sees teaching as a continuous process of self-reflection and changes in practice as a result of collaborative working among professionals (see Chapter 1).

One of the main problems associated with portfolios as a means of assessment is their contrast to more traditional approaches in which reliability was assumed to be superior. The development of portfolios resulted from the search for more 'authentic' forms of assessment than traditional examinations. That is, many teachers and educationalists argued that reliance on end-of-course examinations alone meant many of the skills and attributes that students might have acquired during a course were not being assessed. By moving to portfolios, the range of criteria could be extended and therefore students would be allowed to show what they actually could do. However, because there were fears that portfolios did not provide a reliable measurement of the desired characteristics, the criteria for assessment were often drawn very tightly, with such a prescriptive and extensive number of assessment objectives that the portfolio was reduced to a bureaucratic exercise rather than an educational experience (see Klenowski, 2002). In addition, unless portfolio assessment is linked to some sort of reflective practice, there is a danger that it is seen by students as a hurdle to be overcome rather than a helpful device for demonstrating what they have learned (see Fernsten and Fernsten, 2005).

PROGRESS FILE

The Progress File is the planned successor to the National Record of Achievement. It supports the processes of planning, achieving and reviewing, which are at the heart of individual learning and development.

The Progress File aims to serve as a tool for:

- recording achievements
- helping students plan their learning and career development
- recognizing the knowledge, understanding and skills they are acquiring.

It consists of guidance materials for students from age 13 to adults and materials are downloadable from the Internet (www.dfes.gov.uk/progressfile/).

Schools can make use of Progress Files for tutoring, mentoring, target-setting and reviewing, key skills development, personal development via PSHE, careers education guidance, preparation for transition, and work-related approaches to learning. However, the DfES does not support any specific approach, but is more interested that the processes embedded in Progress Files are current in educational practice.

Activity 5.7   Recording achievement

Part a) of this activity can be completed individually. Part b) should be completed in consultation with other teachers.

a) In your school find out whether students have Records of Achievement or a Progress File. If so, what format are these in? How are they used? Who has overall responsibility for this in the school?

   What achievement do you think should be recorded:

   i)   in your subject area or one closely related to your subject?

   ii) generally for students?

b) If possible discuss this with experienced teachers and/or other beginning teachers:

   i)   What does your faculty/department regard as achievement? How is this recorded?
   ii) Discuss: Do you consider there is a relationship between use of Records of Achievement/Progress Files and styles of teaching and learning within a department?
   iii) Arrange to look at examples of Records of Achievement/Progress Files and, if possible, talk to students about them.

REPORTING

There will be, during your career, various ways in which you may be asked to report on your work – to your head of department, to senior management, to visiting inspectors, awarding bodies and to parents or carers. Reporting to external agencies has become part of the accountability system in education (see a later section in this chapter), while reports to internal lines of authority such as department heads, heads of division, and so on are often part of the process of self-evaluation and improvement that all schools and colleges are expected to engage in.

The style and timing of reports to parents and carers vary from school to school, but there are certain compulsory requirements. Schools must send a written report to parents on their children's achievements at least once during the school year and convey the results of National Curriculum assessments no later than 30 September of any year. Reports must include brief comments on the student's progress in each subject and activity studied as part of the school curriculum, highlighting strengths and development needs; the student's general progress; arrangements for parents to discuss the report with a teacher at the school; the total number of sessions (half days) since the student's last report or since the student entered the school, and the percentage missed through unauthorized absence. Many schools report more frequently than required as they view it as part of building a partnership between home and school.

At the end of each key stage, the QCA suggests including: the student's National Curriculum assessment levels; a statement that the levels have been arrived at by statutory assessment; a statement where any attainment target has been **dis-applied** for a student; the percentage of students at the school at each level of attainment at the end of the key stage; the most recent national percentage of students at each level of attainment at the end of the key stage. All reports written about a student must now be part of the student's educational record.

The purpose of reporting to parents in these formal ways is to provide parents with the necessary information so that a dialogue can take place about the best way forward for an individual child. As the personalized learning agenda (see Chapters 3 and 4) is implemented in schools and colleges, this dialogue will become increasingly important when individual students are entered for formal assessments at different ages rather than an age cohort. However, as assessment information has become more technical, there may be an increasing gap between parents/carers and the school in terms of a common understanding of this information. For example, the complexities of the statements of attainment and the levels that students can achieve may obscure rather than illuminate the overall progress of an individual student.

WRITING REPORTS

Report writing is, quite rightly, a time-consuming business – there are no short cuts! The terminology of the National Curriculum and, in particular, its level descriptors give teachers a neutral context in which to couch their comments, but a good report should also convey your personal response to a student's efforts (or lack of them) and be distinctive to that individual. Many styles and presentational formats of report writing are currently used by schools; these include detailed prose, tick boxes, combination of tick boxes and prose, prose generated from statement banks and so on. Most would agree that there is no single format for what constitutes a 'good report'.

The following is a suggested list of contents of a good report from a subject teacher:

- Brief outline of learning experiences
- What the child has achieved within the subject, especially in core/key skills
- Overall National Curriculum working level or GCSE level
- Where the student is in relation to the cohort/age-group
- Overall progress – target level/grade if appropriate
- Effort, behaviour, concentration, attitude
- Homework
- Examination/test results
- Coursework
- Future development and targets.

It is unlikely that during your training you will be given sole responsibility for report writing, but it is an excellent time to gain some practice and see how more experienced teachers go about the task.

Consider the following checklist:

- Read some previous reports to familiarize yourself with the general style.
- Start to collect some useful phrases.
- Invite the students to assess themselves or write their own version of their report.
- Think of the overall message you want to convey.
- Avoid jargon (even the use of levels to label attainment is baffling to many parents).
- Find something positive to say about every child and start with that.
- Convey criticism clearly but in positive terms, with advice about how to improve.
- Double check for any spelling or grammatical errors.

Activity 5.8   **Writing reports**

In consultation with your mentor or a teacher whose class you teach, try writing some reports taking account of the advice given here.

The sites below provide additional guidance and examples of good report writing.

www.qca.org/ca/2003 sample_reports.asp

www.completeteacher.co.uk/report_writing.htm

MEETING PARENTS/CARERS

Parents' evenings can be quite stressful events for all concerned. They are a very important point of contact between teachers and parents and so opportunities for fruitful exchanges of views should be maximized. They are situations in which you as a teacher can find out about your students rather than just a one-way flow of information (see Wragg, 1997: 77–8). Schools have tried out various formats to make the most of the occasion, and there may be variations in how they are handled for different age groups of students. It is always worth remembering that you are on familiar territory and that parents can be surprisingly anxious or reticent about visiting school, especially on formal occasions. Brooks (2002) argues that the teacher needs to pay particular attention to the language that is used at these events to avoid either oversimplifying information that will patronize parents or making it so complex that important messages about students' progress are lost to the parents/carers. She also suggests that parents/carers are as concerned about their child's social and personal development as they are about academic performance.

There are other occasions at which you will meet parents/carers, most notably at open or recruitment events. Here, your concerns are more likely to be subject based, in that you will be trying to engage students in the possibilities of your subject. Striking the balance between attracting the students themselves and keeping the parents/carers involved will be your most important consideration here. As you progress in your career, there may also be occasions when you carry out home visits to parents/carers, often in difficult circumstances, but you should be supported in your first forays into these activities.

Activity 5.9   Meeting parents/carers

Part a) of this activity can be completed individually and part b) discussed with your mentor or another teacher.

Reports very often lead towards a parents'/carers' evening. If the school's cycle of consultation evenings fits in with your time in school, be sure to take the opportunity to attend. Schools organize such events in different ways and you will no doubt form impressions about the value of the occasion. Try and see it from the parents' perspectives too.

The following comments were collected from parents after such an evening:

1. 'The information given me was insufficient. The teacher did not seem to know my son very well and could not advise me on the best way of assisting him with his Mathematics, which he said was weak.'

2. 'Some of the information given to me was inaccurate. I checked the marks which the teacher said that Debbie had gained in English this term with her exercise book and they did not match. Could more care be taken?'

3. 'It would have been useful to have been able to ask questions. The teacher talked all the time and gave me so much information that I could not absorb it all.'

4. 'I don't understand all this business about levels. What is a level 5c? Couldn't they simply tell us whether the children are doing better or worse than they should be?'

5. 'I'm sorry we did not attend the meeting as the notice was too short. Delvinder only gave us the information about it the previous day.'

6. 'Could the meeting be organised to give more privacy rather than in the school hall? My son was heavily criticised and I felt that other parents were listening. It was most embarrassing.'

7. 'Many thanks to all the teachers for attending and giving me such a good report on Nivraj.'

8. 'Mr Potter complained that John was lazy in class and also inattentive. John tells me that Mr Potter finds it difficult to control the class and that he cannot work with all the noise. Could something be done about this?'

9. 'The time given on the timetabled meetings was too short. We need at least half an hour with each teacher.'

10. 'It would have been a successful meeting if teachers and parents had kept to the timetable. I missed three appointments in this way.'

   a) Consider your response to some of the comments made above.

   b) Discuss advantages/disadvantages/possible improvements for such an event with your mentor or another teacher.

ACCOUNTABILITY

Accountability – 'the public face' of assessment – was a relatively new feature of education in the late twentieth century, though a familiar one in the late nineteenth century! The requirements for test and assessment data (key stage, GCSE and Advanced level results) to be made public have therefore made teachers much more accountable to a wider audience than their predecessors were. The publication of 'league tables' every year has resulted in a situation of competition between schools, as they seek to attract students to maximize their income. This means that every teacher has the burden of their students' results being part of the story of the success or failure of their school. The management of whole-school data and statistics is likely to be in the hands of a senior member of staff and to be more or less computerized. However, any teacher may be asked within school to account for a particular set of results (good or bad), and in due course, the measurable results of your work may have a bearing on your career prospects and salary.

One of the problems with the publication of assessment data is that they can be represented in several different ways and different types of data can be used to 'spin' the story of the school. For example, statistics may be represented as a raw 'pass rate' for the whole school or for selected subjects (usually mathematics and English to the fore). These may also be compared with the national averages in these areas, or against benchmark statistics for similar institutions, with the aim of showing better than average scores. Success might also be shown by the 'points scores' of individual students in the grades achieved across their examination subjects. Which of these is used can result in very different pictures of the work of the school (see Hewett, 1999). There are also value-added measures that compare actual results with the results that might be expected on the basis of students' previous performance (see Wragg, 2001: 82–5). As statistical analysis of assessment data becomes more sophisticated, then the potential for public misunderstanding of their significance is increased. However, careful use of this assessment data can also provide a picture of the complexity of school provision, for example, identifying 'coasting' schools – those that do not add much educational value to students who are already high attainers. **Performance data** can also be a 'tool in the service of school improvement' (Brooks, 2002: 144).

Activity 5.10   Accountability

Parts a), b) and d) of this activity can be completed individually. Part c) requires you to interview a specific member of your school or college staff.

a) Inform yourself of the meanings of some of the key terminology in relation to assessment-related data collection, such as: raw scores, value added, average, mean, median, mode, ratio, centile, quartile, standardized, histogram, scattergram, whiskergram, variables, normal curve of distribution, YELLIS. You may find Google useful in this activity.

b) Have a look at a sample Numeracy Test for beginning teachers (www.tta.gov.uk/skillstests). Many of the questions concentrate on the presentation and interpretation of data relating to student performance.

c) Arrange to interview the person in school who has most to do with whole-school assessment issues. Explore with them how they use data to analyse performance and develop plans for future action on a whole school basis. You may want to ask to look at the latest Self-Evaluation Report (SEF) to see how data is used.

d) Reflect on the view that the drive for accountability presupposes wrong-doing, inadequacy or guilt.

The other main engine of accountability is the 'light-touch' inspection of schools (and including PGCE provision) carried out by the Office for Standards in Education (Ofsted). In making judgements about the effectiveness of schools, Ofsted makes use of a great deal of statistical data, which emerge from your activities as a teacher. These data are connected to student performance in tests and examinations and to the ability of schools and colleges to make accurate judgements about the learning that takes place in the classroom to generate strategies for future improvements. The school or college has to complete a **SEF** (Self-Evaluation Form), in which the strengths and weaknesses of provision have to be identified. To do this, they make use of data about student performance contained in PANDA (Performance and Attainment) reports or their replacement RAISEonline (Reporting and Analysis for Improvement through School Self-Evaluation). While your classroom performance may seem a small cog in the chain of inspection – and the 'light touch' involves fewer classroom observations of actual teaching – the effect may be to increase the pressure to shape your activities in the classroom to the achievement of national targets, rather than wider educational objectives you may have (see, for example, Lawson, 2005).

Features of good practice

The Office for Standards in Education (2003) has identified these features as being examples of good practice in the use of data by secondary schools:

- Key Stage 2 data are gathered as early as possible and analysed carefully (including analysis by gender, ethnicity and mobility), supplemented by other test data (such as in English, mathematics or verbal reasoning), when available, for cross-referencing.
- Students with special educational needs (SEN) or those learning English as an additional language (EAL) are identified through individual consultation to enable smooth transfer from their primary school.

- Data are used as a baseline to monitor and review each student's progress, especially to identify signs of underachievement or unusual potential, and to help set targets for the students and subject departments.
- An effective management information system allows individual departments and teachers to access information independently and in a way tailored to their needs, and also allows new data to be easily entered and processed when required.
- Subject teachers and tutors use data and other assessment information to review the performance and expectations of students, maintaining a productive dialogue with the students about their progress.
- Test results and teacher assessments are analysed to illuminate aspects of students' performance and the extent to which progress is consistent with earlier data.
- Analysis of the performance of class groups is used to identify weaker aspects of teaching, which are then addressed through performance management and professional development.

Activity 5.11   Using data: aspects of best practice

Part a) of this activity needs to be discussed with teaching colleagues in your department. Parts b) and c) can be completed individually.

a) For each of the aspects of best practice identified by Ofsted, explore with your department how they seek to implement these. Be careful to maintain a professional attitude in discussing these matters – you need to learn about the departmental processes involved, not about the performance of the department in these regards.

b) Place the list of features above in order of importance from your point of view, from 1 to 6. For the items you have decided are the *most* important and the *least* important, provide a rationale for your decisions.

c) In relevant lesson evaluations, show where you have used data about performance with individual students to set targets and improve attainment.

Target-setting in schools and colleges

Target-setting to raise standards of student attainment became a statutory requirement for schools from September 1998. In Circular 11/98, *Target-Setting in Schools,* the government set out the following requirements for school governing bodies:

At *Key Stage 2* they set and publish targets for the percentages of pupils attaining

- Level 4 or above in English and Mathematics.

At *Key Stage 4* they set and publish targets for the percentages of pupils attaining

- Five or more GCSEs or equivalent at grades A* to C;
- One or more GCSEs or equivalent at grades A* to C;
- The average points score per pupil in GCSE or equivalent.

The setting of targets by central government was seen by them to be a key mechanism for school improvement. By identifying realistic steps that individual schools could take to achieve the required standards, it was believed that national targets for the percentage of students achieving at particular levels could be met. The idea was that the targets would provide motivation, direction and a measure of 'success' for schools and teachers alike. However, critics of target-setting raise issues about who sets the targets, how realistic they are and, most importantly, what targets are appropriate for an education system. By concentrating on rather narrow ranges of targets, especially literacy and numeracy, critics argue that this has the effect of 'shutting down' other areas of the curriculum as teachers 'teach to the test' to meet the targets by which they will be judged (see Wragg, 2003: 85–6).

The government has also provided schools and colleges with software called Pupil Achievement Tracker (PAT) that allows an institution or individual teachers to compare groups of students or even individuals with national and/or benchmark data as a basis for setting targets for the school, or an individual student. This software can also provide the school or teacher with value-added measures so that they can see how their students are doing compared to similar students elsewhere. The software and support material is available from the DfES at www.standards.dfes.gov.uk/performance/. The screen for the target-setting tool of PAT looks like that shown in Figure 5.2.

The National Public Service Agreements (PSA) Targets for Education in England in 2006 were as follows:

Key Stage 3

By 2007:

- 85 per cent of 14-year-olds to achieve at least Level 5 in English, mathematics and ICT, with 80 per cent achieving Level 5 in science, with this level of performance sustained to 2008.

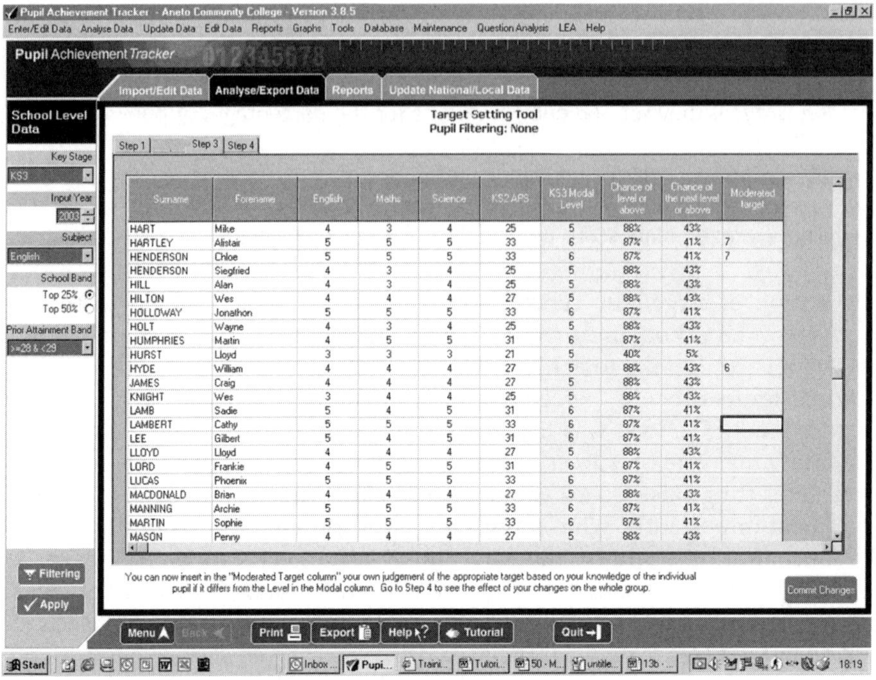

Figure 5.2   Example of pupil achievement tracker

By 2008:

- In all schools at least 50% of pupils achieve Level 5 or above in English, mathematics and science.

Key Stage 4

The national PSA targets are for:

- 60 per cent of pupils to achieve five or more A*–C GCSEs or equivalent by 2008.

In all schools at least 20 per cent of pupils will achieve five or more A*–C GCSEs or equivalent by 2004, 25 per cent by 2006 and 30 per cent by 2008.

However, we should be careful in interpreting what it means when national targets are apparently met. There are international attainment measures that offer an independent comparison with the validity and reliability of results from national measures of attainment. Brooks and Tough (2006) argue that while the proportion of students who gain benchmark levels at Key Stages 3 and 4 (that is, in end of Key Stage 3 tests and in GCSE scores) is increasing, international measures suggest that scores for students at these stages are stagnant rather than rising.

Activity 5.12   Analysing assessment data

All parts of this activity can be completed individually and then shared with your mentor in school or college.

The following tables are taken from anonymous PANDA (Performance and Assessment) data for secondary schools, published by Ofsted on the Internet.

GCE Results for 2004 by subject
School results Against All Maintained Secondary Schools
First line is the school result, second line is the national result.

Subject Area	**Percentage Achieving Grades**									% A*–C grades	% A*–G grades
	A*	A	B	C	D	E	F	G	U		
Art and	0.0	11.5	17.3	42.3	9.6	3.8	7.7	5.8	0.0	71.2	98.1
Design	4.7	13.3	19.7	27.6	14.4	10.0	5.9	2.6	0.5	65.2	98.1
Combined	0.0	0.0	0.0	4.8	11.1	25.4	31.7	19.0	7.9	4.8	92.1
Science	0.2	0.7	2.0	12.1	18.0	23.7	21.8	12.2	8.5	15.0	90.7
Computer	0.0	5.6	26.8	19.7	11.3	11.3	8.5	8.5	8.5	52.1	91.5
Studies	3.6	10.5	16.9	24.1	15.5	10.7	8.2	5.4	4.6	55.1	94.7
Design and	0.0	3.7	9.2	21.1	31.2	14.7	11.9	5.5	2.8	33.9	97.2
Technology	2.9	12.0	15.0	24.8	19.8	11.4	6.6	3.6	3.0	54.7	96.2
English	0.9	6.1	14.0	36.0	19.3	8.8	2.6	6.1	6.1	57.0	93.9
Language	3.1	10.2	18.5	26.0	20.0	11.5	6.0	2.6	1.7	57.7	97.9
English	0.0	1.3	16.3	51.3	17.5	5.0	6.3	0.0	2.5	68.8	97.5
Literature	3.3	11.6	20.9	26.2	17.0	10.4	5.5	2.5	2.2	62.0	97.4
French	0.0	13.5	18.9	32.4	24.3	10.8	0.0	0.0	0.0	64.9	100
	4.1	8.2	13.1	21.5	19.8	14.9	10.4	5.7	1.6	47.0	97.8

(Continued)

(Continued)

Subject Area	Percentage Achieving Grades									% A*–C grades	% A*–G grades
	A*	A	B	C	D	E	F	G	U		
Geography	0.0	20.0	25.0	15.0	10.0	20.0	5.0	0.0	5.0	60.0	95.0
	5.8	12.2	16.1	24.7	16.2	11.0	6.7	3.8	3.1	58.7	96.5
Maths	2.6	8.8	13.2	16.7	12.3	14.0	15.8	8.8	6.1	41.2	92.1
	3.3	7.2	17.3	22.3	17.5	15.5	9.3	4.0	3.2	50.0	96.3
PE	4.5	0.0	13.6	22.7	45.5	9.1	0.0	4.5	0.0	40.9	100
	3.8	11.9	19.8	21.5	24.3	12.4	4.5	1.2	0.3	57.0	99.4
RE	0.0	6.1	16.2	30.3	20.2	15.2	5.1	5.1	2.0	52.5	98.0
	6.8	16.0	20.4	19.0	13.9	9.8	6.7	3.9	2.5	62.3	96.6

AS and A2 Results 2004 by Subject
School Sixth Form Attainment Summary against national figures
First line is the school result, second line is the national result.

Subject	AS or A2	% A–B	% A–E	Average Points Score
Biology	AS	15.4	80.8	26.9
		10.4	63.5	19.8
	A2	39.1	100	80.6
		40.0	96.6	79.3
Business Studies	AS	11.1	61.1	22.2
		15.4	75.3	25.7
	A2	21.7	100	71.3
		39.4	98.9	81.8
Chemistry	AS	8.7	52.2	18.3
		13.2	70.3	23.0
	A2	36.5	100	80.6
		50.0	97.7	85.7
Communication Studies	AS	60.0	100	42.0
		24.9	87.2	32.8
	A2	47.5	100	87.5
		40.4	99.2	83.5
Drama	AS	0.0	100	30.0
		19.8	86.6	30.9
	A2	23.5	100	78.8
		42.8	99.6	85.1

Subject	AS or A2	% A–B	% A–E	Average Points Score
Economics	AS	28.6	71.4	31.4
		28.6	71.6	25.8
	A2	25.0	100	78.3
		54.3	98.8	89.8
History	AS	14.3	85.7	32.9
		20.8	82.2	29.2
	A2	68.8	100	99.4
		45.6	99.0	85.1
Information Technology	AS	6.7	73.3	22.7
		8.8	66.6	20.6
	A2	45.0	100	89.0
		25.7	96.3	71.1
Physics	AS	19.0	61.9	22.4
		14.8	66.4	22.4
	A2	56.3	100	88.8
		45.3	96.7	82.6
Psychology	AS	29.5	72.7	29.3
		15.1	67.8	23.2
	A2	42.4	100	85.5
		42.5	97.4	81.6
Sociology	AS	22.2	77.8	28.9
		19.6	72.1	25.9
	A2	31.3	100	82.5
		45.3	98.5	84.6

a) Imagine that you are TIC (teacher in charge) of your subject (or a closely related one) at this school. You have been asked by the senior management to analyse the performance of students in your subject against the national statistics. Produce a report on this data for the senior management that highlights the strengths and weaknesses in your curriculum area.

b) In the light of this analysis, you have to develop an action plan for your curriculum area for the next year. In your action plan, you have to suggest ways in which you will build on the strengths and address the weaknesses in your students' performance.

c) Senior management is so impressed with your handling of this data that they have asked you to support another curriculum area that has the opposite characteristics to your own. Choosing such an area from the data, carry out a similar analysis and action plan for that department.

CONCLUSION

While the issue of assessment is fraught with difficulty, it remains true that a great deal of your professional life will be caught up with this type of activity. Indeed, the argument for increased teacher assessment, rather than national testing, has never gone away and seems to be having a resurgence in the early twenty-first century. However, national testing systems are not going to go away, as they represent a huge industry and encapsulate a long tradition of measures of success in curriculum subjects at all secondary levels, that are independent from schools. The challenge will be to combine testing and teacher assessments in ways that will command the confidence of the government, employers, teachers, parents and students that they produce reliable and valid data.

REFERENCES

Arter, J. A. and Spandel, V. (1992) 'Using portfolios of student work in instruction and assessment', *Educational Measurement: Issues and Practice*, Spring: 36–44.

Assessment Reform Group (ARG) (2002) *Assessment for Learning: 10 Principles*. London: ARG.

Bernstein, B. (1971) 'On the classification and framing of educational knowledge', in M.F.D. Young (ed.), *Knowledge and Control: New Directions in the Sociology of Education*. London: Collier-Macmillan. pp. 47–69.

Black. P. and Wiliam, D. (1998) 'Assessment and classroom learning', *Assessment in Education: Principles, Policy and Practice*, 5(1): 7–74.

Black, P. and Wiliam, D. (2006) 'The reliability of assessments' in J. Gardner (ed.), *Assessment and Learning*. London: Sage. pp. 119–31.

Black, P., Harrison, C., Lee, C., Marshall B. and Wiliam, D. (2003) *Assessment for Learning: Putting It into Practice*. Maidenhead: Open University Press.

Broadfoot, P. and Pollard, A. (1997) *National Record of Achievement Review: Report of the Steering Group*. London: Department for Education and Employment.

Brooks. V. (2002) *Assessment in Secondary Schools: The New Teacher's Guide to Monitoring, Assessment, Recording, Reporting and Accountability*. Buckingham: Open University Press.

Comber, C., Watling, R., Lawson, T., Cavendish, S., McEune, R. and Paterson, F. (2002) *Impact2: Learning at Home and School: Case Studies*. Coventry: Becta.

Cullingford, C. (1997) *Assessment versus Evaluation*. London: Cassell.

Dweck, C. (1986) 'Motivational processes affecting learning', *American Psychologist*, 41(10): 1040–8.

Earl, L.M. (2003) *Assessment as Learning*. Thousand Oaks, CA: Corwin Press.

Fernsten, L. and Fernsten, J. (2005) 'Portfolio assessment and reflection: enhancing learning through effective practice', *Reflective Practice*, 6(2): 303–9.

Gardner, H. (1993) *Frames of Mind: The Theory of Multiple Intelligences*. New York: Basic Books.

Gardner, H. (2003) 'Multiple intelligences after twenty years', paper presented to the American Educational Research Association, Chicago, IL, 21 April.

Gipps, C. (1994) *Beyond Testing: Towards a Theory of Educational Assessment*. London: Falmer Press.

Grant, G.E. and Huebner, T.A. (1998) 'The portfolio question: the power of self-directed inquiry', in N. Lyons (ed.), *With Portfolio in Hand: Validating the New Teacher Professionalism*. New York: Teachers College Press. pp. 156–71.

Groom, B. and Maunonen-Eskelinen, I. (2006) 'The use of portfolios to develop reflective practice in teacher training: a comparative and collaborative approach between two teacher training providers in the UK and Finland', *Teaching in Higher Education*, 11(3): 291–300.

Harlen, W. (2006) 'The role of assessment in developing motivation for learning', in J. Gardner (ed.), *Assessment and Learning*. London: Sage.

Harlen, W. and James, M. (1997) 'Assessment and learning: differences and relationships between formative and summative assessment', *Assessment in Education*, 4(3): 365–80.

Hayward, L., Kane, J. and Cogan, N. (2000) *Improving Assessment in Scotland: Report of the National Consultation on Assessment in Scotland*, Glasgow: University of Glasgow.

Hewett, P. (1999) 'The role of target setting in the school improvement', in C. Conner (ed.), *Assessment in Action in the Primary School*. London: Falmer Press. pp. 71–83.

Hutchinson, C. and Hayward, L. (2006) 'The journey so far: assessment for learning in Scotland', *The Curriculum Journal*, 16(2): 225–48.

Klenowski, V. (2002) *Developing Portfolios for Assessment and Learning*. London: RoutledgeFalmer.

Kounin, J.S. (1970) *Discipline and Group Management in Classrooms*. New York: Holt, Reinhart & Winston.

Latham, A.M. (1997) 'Profiling and self-assessment', in C. Cullingford (ed.), *Assessment versus Education*. London: Cassell. pp. 203–21.

Lawson, T. (2005) 'The new framework for the inspection of schools: implications for sociology teachers', *Social Science Teacher*, 35(1): 15–16.

Lawson, T. and Harrison, J. K. (1999) 'Individual action planning in initial teacher training: empowerment or discipline?', *British Journal of Sociology of Education*, 20(1): 89–105.

Lawson, T., Harrison, J. and Cavendish, S. (2004) 'Individual action planning: a case of self-surveillance?', *British Journal of Sociology of Education*, 25(1): 81–94.

Lingard, B., Mills, M. and Hayes, D. (2006) 'Enabling and aligning assessment for learning: some research and policy lessons from Queensland', *International Studies in Sociology of Education*, 16 (2): 83–103.

Lloyd-Jones, L.J., Bray, E., Johnson, G. and Currie, R. (1992) *Assessment: From Principles to Practice*. London: Routledge.

Massey, A., Green, S., Dexter, T. and Hamnett, L. (2003) *Comparability of the National Tests over Time: Key Stage Test Standards between 1996 and 2001: Final Report to the QCA*. Cambridge: University of Cambridge, Local Examinations Syndicate.

Messick, S. (1994) 'The interplay of evidence and consequences in the validation of performance assessments', *Educational Researcher*, 23(2): 13–23.

Office for Standards in Education (Ofsted) (2002) *Good teaching, effective departments*. London: Ofsted.

Office for Standards in Education (Ofsted) (2003) *Good Assessment in Secondary Schools.* London: Ofsted.

Pring, R. (1984) *Personal and Social Education.* London: Hodder.

Richardson, C. (2003) *Whither Assessment?* London: Qualifications and Curriculum Authority.

Smith, E. and Gorard, S. (2005) '"They don't give us our marks": the role of formative feedback in student progress', *Assessment in Education*, 12(1): 21–38.

Stobart, G. (2006) 'The validity of formative assessment', in J. Gardner (ed.), *Assessment and Learning.* London: Sage. pp. 133–46.

Sutton, R. (1992) *Assessment: A Framework for Teachers.* London: Routledge.

Thomas, E. (1990) *Assessing Learning Unit 11 MA and Diploma Course in Distance Learning.* London: Institute of Education.

Watkins, C. (1992) *Whole School Personal and Social Education: Policy and Practice.* Coventry: NAPCE Publications.

Wiliam, D. (2000) 'Reliability, validity and all that jazz', *Education 3–13*, 29(3): 9–13.

Wragg, E.C. (1997) *Assessment and Learning: Primary and Secondary.* London: Routledge.

Wragg, E.C. (2001) *Assessment and Learning in the Secondary School.* London: RoutledgeFalmer.

EDUCATION AS A SOCIAL AND POLITICAL PROCESS
Hilary Cremin

By the end of this chapter you will:

- know about key legislation and policy that has impacted on the education system in England from the start of the twentieth century to the present day
- be able to reflect on your own values and perspectives as a beginning teacher
- know how to engage colleagues and students in debate about issues of citizenship, diversity, inclusion and sustainability
- have formulated ideas about whole issues that you may wish to take forward as an early career leader.

INTRODUCTION

Everyone has an opinion on how schools and schooling should be organized. Many adults also believe that their own experiences of schooling (and those of their children) provide them with important insights into how teachers and schools could be more effective. Politicians appear to have turned this to advantage, using education as a means of promising voters that schools and teachers will continue to improve. It cannot have escaped anyone's notice that various governments, beginning in the UK with Margaret Thatcher's Conservative government and continuing with New Labour's government, have missions to reform education. Schools in England and Wales have been subjected to over 20 years of unprecedented government interference in the processes of schooling, involving teachers in constant innovation, regular inspection, public scrutiny, and increasingly high levels of paperwork and bureaucracy. This can be frustrating for many teachers who can see beyond the sound bites and national statistics to situations that are complex and contradictory. Teachers and head teachers see education in the round. They educate children from all social and ethnic groups. They see the impact of poverty on teaching and learning, and the impact of parental pressure on children who must perform well in tests. They themselves exert pressure on underachieving children and their parents. When they articulate such insights, these are not always well received. As a critically reflective education professional, you will need to decide where you stand on issues of teaching, learning and accountability, and you will need to draw on your own values, beliefs and motivations for teaching. Whether you like it or not, teaching is a political process, and you will find yourself defending the decisions that you have made on more than one occasion in your professional life. Teachers in the twenty-first century may even need to add image management skills to their portfolio. Importantly, they need to be absolutely clear about why they came into teaching. We believe teaching in schools and colleges remains one of the most important jobs that anyone can do.

This chapter introduces you to some of the key policy directives in education in England – the major legislation in the 1980s, 1990s and early twenty-first century. It draws on and uses the thread of reflective practice that runs through this book, and reviews debates about standards, new forms of funding, the National Curriculum, the comprehensive ideal, the inspection role of **Ofsted** and the numerous whole-school initiatives which aim to prepare young people for the diverse, complex and globalized contexts of the twenty-first century and beyond.

THE TWENTIETH-CENTURY LEGACY: A SUMMARY

The twentieth century can be seen as a time when issues of equality, rights, access and inclusion were played out in education. As the century progressed, however, it became clear that the modernist, emancipatory dream of equality for all through education was not as simple as it seemed. Education was not, after all, the great leveller. Elements of parental choice and competition between schools would re-emerge to ensure that, although all students are equal, some students are more equal than others. Children's rights emerged as a central concern in the late twentieth century, but British children have recently been identified as suffering from greater deprivation and worse relationships with their parents than children in any other wealthy country in the world (UNICEF, 2006). They are also at greater risk from alcohol, drugs and unsafe sex.

We currently have certain tensions within the education system: on the one hand there is an ongoing drive for improvements in educational attainment and achievement, with no let up in the imposition of externally driven targets; and on the other, there is a drive for education to be personalized. The *Every*

Child Matters (**ECM**) agenda is emphasizing health and enjoyment of young people. The Office for Standards in Education is emphasizing lighter-touch institutional inspections and methods of school self-evaluation. In order to make sense of these often conflicting drivers, it is useful to review where the impetus for these initiatives has come from. An overview of some of the major political events and legislation of the twentieth century serves to provide a context for some of the current challenges that teachers now face.

As in most areas of life in Britain, the law relating to education has arisen from a combination of statutes and precedent, so that the present situation is very complicated, and there are many instances in which it is impossible to give a final ruling until a court makes a decision. Nevertheless, the day-to-day business of teaching and caring for young people continues, with, on the whole, few legal problems. The Secretary of State has the power to make Orders in Parliament relating to specific matters, which have the force of law. The way in which such statutory instruments are to be carried out is described in Circulars, issued by the Department for Education and Employment. Their publication is often preceded by draft consultation documents which enable teachers and others to express their views. In recent history, these Circulars have been relatively weighty documents containing detailed instructions to schools, governors, local education authorities (**LEAs**) or, since 2004, local authorities (**LAs**), and teacher trainers. There is an increasing move to using the Internet for on-line consultation and uploading documentation. The legality of action taken in interpreting the Acts and the Circulars is however open to being tested in courts of law. It must be stressed that many aspects of the Acts, especially the most recent measures, have never been tested by court cases. Each governing body must work within the school's Articles of Government which prescribe the nature of the provision and lay down procedures for the organization of the school. Nothing can occur in the school which is contrary to the Articles of Government, which have legal status in that institution. The task of keeping up to date with all of this paperwork has become an onerous one for schools and teachers!

Education for all?

The state became fully involved in education for the first time in 1870. The Education Act of that year required local school boards to provide elementary schools. It coincided with a Revised Code that ushered in the first period of payment by results. The architect of the Code, Robert Lowe, declared at the time that the, 'education of the poorer classes should be just sufficient to give them that sense of awe for higher education the leaders of the nation demand' (cited in Brighouse, 2007: 2). This perhaps gives a flavour of the motivations, values and attitudes that existed at the time. Government control over elementary education was extended by the Education Act 1902 (Balfour's Act) which put schooling under local authority control, but it is important to remember that until the Education Act 1944 (Butler's Act), most children in England received elementary school education only.

The Education Act 1944 required that there should be compulsory, free education for all children from the age of 5 to 15, and that all-age schools were to be replaced by separate primary and secondary institutions. This act came into force just after the war, and was part of an optimistic post-war vision of a strong welfare state. (The National Health Service Act followed in 1946.) Although there was a strong drive for equal rights to education for all, there was little challenge to the idea that different types of schools would serve different types of children, and that schooling for the majority would involve preparation for life as unqualified manual or semi-skilled workers. Harber (1995) has argued that school was seen as a place to prepare the mass of ordinary children for workplaces that require punctuality, quiet orderly work in groups, respect for authority, and for tolerance of monotony, boredom, punishment and lack of reward. It is a matter of debate as to whether these early education reformers were concerned to reduce social inequalities, or to perpetuate them through ensuring a steady supply of compliant workers to work in the factories and businesses of the educated classes.

Whatever the intention, the selective education system that ensued from the 1944 Act resulted in the majority of children (80 per cent) receiving largely vocational education in secondary modern and technical schools from the age of 11. This was the age at which their abilities were tested via the national eleven-plus (11+) examination. A minority of children (20 per cent) passed their 11+ examination and they were educated at the more prestigious grammar schools rather than secondary modern schools. They took Ordinary (O) (GCSE) and Advanced (A) level examinations, and, unlike their secondary modern counterparts, they had the greater opportunity of progressing to higher education. There was very little movement of pupils between the two systems following the decisions taken at the time of the 11+.

Activity 6.1   Selective and independent schools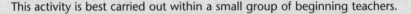

This activity is best carried out within a small group of beginning teachers.

a) Find out about selective schools that still exist in your area. They may be Grammar schools, or Independent schools. Try to establish more about the views of local parents/carers on the impact of these schools on the community. What are the schools' admissions policies? Do they have a particular faith or philosophical perspectives?

b) Go to the website of the National Grammar School Association (or similar website) www.ngsa.org.uk/comment/com_004.htm. Do you agree with what is said there about the on-going value of the selective education system? Here are a few examples of the *myths* that this website seeks to explode:

- *Pupils who do not get into grammar schools are labelled as failures.*

Not by anyone in the grammar school system! It is only the opponents of selection that use this disparaging term. Children develop at different rates and therefore need different educational opportunities.

- *You can't get into a grammar school if you don't make it at 11.*

All grammars admit pupils into their sixth form, although most youngsters prefer to stay in familiar surroundings for their sixth form experience.

- *Abolishing grammar schools would bring about more equality of opportunity in education.*

Just the opposite in fact would be likely to happen. Existing independent schools would be in even greater demand and new ones would be established to provide a fee-paying grammar school education no longer available free of charge. The gap in educational opportunity would widen, not close.

- *Grammar schools are middle class.*

This is most certainly not the case. All grammars have children from the complete range of backgrounds and help families on income support or family credit with costs of trips and uniforms.

c) With other members of your small group, present your responses to these points. Try to agree to locate exactly where the myths might lie.

By the 1950s there was growing concern that the processes for selection via the 11+ examination were stunting the work of primary teachers, were proving traumatic for children and parents, were dominated by the middle classes, and that the selection process was a poor indicator of a child's potential. Experimental comprehensive schools, originally known as *multilaterals* in London, Coventry and Anglesey were providing evidence that children who had been denied a grammar school place could still be successful at O (GCSE) and A level. In the 1960s more LEAs softened their processes for 11+ selection, while others abandoned schemes altogether and established comprehensive schools which were open to all students. By the 1970s comprehensive schools were the norm, as selection was overwhelmingly rejected. Although a selective education system persists to this day in some areas, by and large most schools are comprehensive in their intake.

Activity 6.2 Examining the effects of the 11+

This activity can be conducted individually and followed up with a presentation of your findings to a group of beginning teachers.

a) Find references to the effects of grammar school selection, or the effects of poverty and social class on educational achievement in art or literature. Write a reflective piece of 500 words responding to the ideas and feelings generated by this stimulus material. The poem *The Choosing* by Liz Lochhead (n.d.) may be a place to start or the book *Once in a House on Fire* by Andrea Ashworth (2004).

b) Carry out a personal survey by interviewing an older friend or relative who was educated before the days of comprehensive schools and consider what they say. Did they pass the 11+? What have been the implications for them of their success or failure at that age? Do they still have contact with children from their community who had a different test result? How have these other lives been differently affected by their test results at age 11?

Many of these new 1970s comprehensive schools developed humanistic, progressive and child-centred education, based on notions of empowerment, student autonomy and equality of opportunity. Largely influenced by writers such as Dewey (1964), Holt (1984) and Illich (1973) a good number of head teachers and teachers introduced active and experiential learning into their schools and classrooms, encouraging students to take responsibility for their own learning, rather than feeling marginalized by an impersonal education system (Cremin, 2007). Moves towards more active, child-centred, teaching and learning styles were stimulated and legitimized by the Plowden Report (1968) which emphasized the importance of children learning through discovery, group work and discussion.

The 1970s were also characterized by a growing human rights-driven agenda to promote equal opportunities in society generally, and equality of educational opportunity for young people in schools in particular. The Sex Discrimination Act 1975 and the Race Relations Act 1976 date from this time, as do their related public bodies, the Commission for Racial Equality (CRE) and the equal opportunities commission (**EOC**). Each Act makes it unlawful to discriminate on the grounds of gender, or on the grounds of nationality or race respectively. The Race Relations Act 1976 makes reference to education in Sections 17, 18 and 19, and makes it clear that responsible organizations that provide education (for example, LEAs and individual schools) should take care not to discriminate in any way on the grounds of nationality or ethnic origin when carrying out their duty of provision, and when making decisions about admission, grants or any other benefits. Many local authorities set up multicultural advisory services during the 1970s to combat racism and intolerance in young people and their communities. These services, along with charities and non-government organizations (**NGOs**), such as Development Education

Centres, set about providing resources and in-service training for teachers. Many of these programmes were based on *multiculturalism*, which promotes understanding and celebration of different cultures. Recent criticisms of multiculturalism have highlighted the superficiality of initiatives which gloss over difference and inequality in order to promote false notions of harmonious communities (Phillips, 2006). Thirty years on, there is still much to be done to promote racial and gender equality in the UK and, indeed, in the rest of Europe and the world. The following paragraphs provide a further focus on aspects of diversity and inclusion.

It is widely recognized that when young people experience a clash of home and school cultures, there is a great danger of discrimination. Anti-discrimination statements always appear in the legal provisions for the protection of human rights. Race, colour, sex, language, religion, political or other opinion, national, ethnic or social origin, property, disability, birth or other status are all related to cultural differences. These can all impact on the young person's self perception as a learner as well as on his or her values and ways of interacting and approaching different types of knowledge and learning. Teachers need to consider how their students are different. Tomlinson (2003) refers to the diversity of student cultures, learning environments and traits that influence students' engagement with learning; these being interest, learning profile, affect and readiness to learn. In Chapters 2 and 3 of this book you may have read about different learning styles and how to plan your teaching to allow more students to learn effectively and efficiently. In conjunction with this, how the students feel about themselves, their work and the classrooms as a whole is closely bound up with the quality of learning that goes on. In addition, their readiness to learn (rather than their *ability*) will determine the type of work that you, as teacher, can require of them. Knowing more about their readiness and how it has been influenced by prior experiences and attitudes to school should help you understand your learners better and adapt to their particular needs.

It is important to take time to reflect on the difference between the attempt to make a student fit into a given school environment – *integration* – and changing the educational environment to meet the particular needs of the student – *inclusion*. The two terms are sometimes used interchangeably, but it should be recognized that inclusion goes far beyond integration. Inclusive schools will have 'pedagogy … that will lead them to respond positively to pupil diversity – seeing individual problems not as problems to be fixed, but as opportunities for enriching learning' (UNESCO, 2005: 9).

Activity 6.3 should help to develop your thinking and reflection in the area of inclusion and discrimination. Adams et al. (1997) identified four levels of discrimination which interact and overlap. They are:

1. *Structural.* These are the ways in which different statuses and access to benefits in society are structured in society physically, politically and legally.
2. *Institutional.* These are the usual procedures and practices which work against the interests of certain groups (even with no conscious decision to discriminate).

3. *Cultural*. These are the shared assumptions about normality and ideas that are not questioned.

4. *Personal*. These are individual acts of stereotyping, discrimination, abuse, harassment and physical assault.

Activity 6.3   Challenging your awareness of discriminatory attitudes, policies and practices (adapted from support materials in Bartolo et al., 2007)

The importance of this activity is to provide opportunity through dialogue for some critical reflection on your perceptions and attitudes towards one underprivileged group at risk of discrimination. You should work both in pairs and with a larger group of beginning teachers.

a) In pairs.

Recall a first meeting with another person/student who differed from you in culture, gender or any other exceptionality. How did you react? Share a description of your remembered meeting, and your reactions to it, with another beginning teacher. In turn, help the other to draw out the implications for their attitudes and the personal reflection to be done on these attitudes.

Summarize as:

My initial reaction to difference ....

b) Work in small groups of 3 to 4 beginning teachers.

Using the four levels of discrimation (Adams et al., 1997) described on pages 201–2 of this chapter, provide some examples from your own experiences to complete Table 6.1.

c) Work in a group of five to eight beginning teachers with a more experienced teacher or a mentor.

Discuss how diversity issues that arise in school can be turned into opportunities for celebrating diversity. Members of the group should contribute different examples or scenarios for discussion.

Examples might include:

- a student in a wheelchair cannot gain easy access to the ecology work carried out in the field

- comments to students about being terrorists based on the colour of their skin

- stereotypes of black students being good at sport.

Table 6.1 can be used in association with Activity 6.3. The table provides some examples of how Activity 6.3 might be completed.

Table 6.1 Dimensions of diversity and discrimination at structural, institutional, cultural and personal levels

Dimension of diversity	Structural	Institutional	Cultural	Personal
Social class	Access to Independent schools based on family economic status			
Ethnicity		More black students suspended proportionately than white students		
Language			Status of non-European languages in school	
Disability				Use of language such as 'spastic'
Religion	Banning of wearing the hijab in school			
Sexual orientation		Assumptions of heterosexuality in school's resources		
Special education needs			SEN as a 'problem' to be addressed separately and after mainstream needs.	

Source: adapted from training resources in Bartolo, 2007: 23

Thus for teachers to provide equality of access to educational success, they need to be aware not only of what knowledge is needed for learning, but also more about the knowledge and skills that students bring from their linguistic and cultural backgrounds. Schools are still seen as socializing young people into the dominant culture of the nation. There is a huge challenge for teachers in many countries to enable young people from many cultures to interrelate and contribute to each other's lives.

To help you think more deeply about aspects of gender in relation to schooling in the UK the following data is presented for consideration in Activity 6.4. It is drawn from Equal Opportunities Commission (2006). Note, the EOC became the CEHR (Commission for Equality and Human Rights) from October 2007.

In 1975

- Girls' and boys' achievements were almost identical. 25 per cent of school leavers in England and Wales passed at least five O (GCSE) levels
- 50 per cent of mothers with dependent children worked
- Men in full-time work earned on average 29 per cent more than women in full-time work
- 4.3 per cent of Members of Parliament (MPs) were women.

In 2005

- 49 per cent of boys and 59 per cent of girls in England and Wales passed at least five GCSEs (grade A–C)
- 66 per cent of mothers with dependent children worked
- Men in full-time work earned on average 17 per cent more than women in full-time work
- 20 per cent of MPs were women
- 71 per cent of students taking A level English literature were girls. 24 per cent of students taking A level physics were girls
- 17 per cent of directors and chief executives of major organizations were women
- 33 per cent of secondary head teachers and college principals were women
- 9 per cent of the senior judiciary were women
- 76 per cent of cleaners and domestics were female.

Activity 6.4   Gender equality?

All parts can be carried out individually. Once you have accessed the reading, analyses and thinking you can join with others, perhaps for a seminar, led by a mentor for more critical reflection.

a) Gender biases?

A link to the EOC (or CEHR) the publication *Facts about Women and Men in Great Britain 2006* www.equalityhumanrights.com/en/publicationsandresources/Gender/Pages/Research.aspx is available on the companion website.

Note, the EOC became the CEHR (Commission for Equality and Human Rights) from October 2007. This document reviews gender-related social trends between 1975 and 2005.

Examine the data. Do any of the changes/lack of changes surprise you? What are your own reflections on the current status of gender equality in the UK?

Some of the data are extracted and presented on pages 206–7.

- What do these statistics tell you?

- How might you respond to this as a teacher?

b) Boys' underachievement?

There are a range of views in the media and academic journals and books about the possible reasons behind the current differences in boys' and girls' achievement worldwide. The following documents may help you to form your own views on the extent of the problem (if any) and what can be done about it.

Younger and Warrington (2005) *Raising Boys' Achievement*. Research Report 636. London: DfES. This can be accessed at

www.dfes.gov.uk/research/data/uploadfiles/RR 636.pdf

Gorard, Rees and Salisbury (2001) 'Investigating the patterns of differential attainment of boys and girls at school', *British Educational Research Journal*, 27(2): 125–39.

Having read the documents, you should in discussion with others reflect on:

- the impact of race and class on gender debates within the context of schooling

- the role of creativity, flexibility and choice in raising the achievement of both boys and girls.

Before we return to think about the broader social and global dimensions of education and the political influences on them, here is another opportunity for you to explore critically your own values and beliefs in relation to aspects of race.

Activity 6.5   Race equality: where do you stand?

This is a paired activity.

Take a look at the quotes below, all from Trevor Phillips the chair of the Commission for Racial Equality.

For each statement provide a grade, on a continuum from 1 to 5, (with 1 = no/ strongly disagree; 5 = yes/strongly agree. Ask a partner to do the same. Compare your grades to see how much agreement there is between you. Can you use persuasive argument and critical analysis to get your partner to adopt your point of view for each statement?

> On July 6 2005 (the day before the London bombings) the day we won the Olympics of 2012, Britain emerged as a beacon of diversity across the globe. There is no doubt that the IOC saw London as a place where anyone, whatever their background, could come and feel at home, could visit and know they would find a kindred spirit … July 6 and the days after showed that one thing that makes us special is our comfort with diversity.

a) Do you see Britain as a place that is comfortable with diversity?
     (1/2/3/4/5)

b) Are schools more diverse (and more comfortable with diversity) than the rest of society?
     (1/2/3/4/5)

> (*Talking about a policy of multiculturalism*) In recent years we've focused far too much on the 'multi' and not enough on the common culture. We've emphasized what divides us over what unites us. We have allowed tolerance of diversity to harden into the effective isolation of communities, in which some people think special separate values ought to apply.

c) Do you agree that people in the UK should spend more time thinking about what unites us culturally, and less time emphasizing our separate identities?
     (1/2/3/4/5)

d) Should schools celebrate multiculturalism?
     (1/2/3/4/5)

> Faith leaders can make … discord worse by insisting on fundamentalist and purist interpretations of faith that cut off their followers from the rest of society. They can isolate their congregations if they fail to accept that in the modern world, faith is part of our identity but it is not a complete description of any of us.

e) Should it be possible for people to live their lives according to fundamentalist religious principles in the UK?
     (1/2/3/4/5)

f)   Should we encourage faith schools?
(1/2/3/4/5)

g)   Is it hypocritical to be against Islamic faith schools while supporting Catholic schools?
(1/2/3/4/5)

For over a year now, the French state has banned the display of any significant religious display in public – famously banning the hijab, but also the yarmulke and the turban – but not, significantly, the Christmas tree, today perhaps more a celebration of the material and commercial than the spiritual.

h)   Should the hijab, the turban and the crucifix be banned in UK schools?
(1/2/3/4/5)

i)   What about the Christmas tree?
(1/2/3/4/5)

The full text of these speeches, including detailed references, can be found at www.cre.gov.uk/diversity/integration/index.html.

For information about the duty to promote community cohesion in schools from 2007 see www.teachernet.gov.uk/wholeschool/Communitycohesion/.

For more general information about community cohesion in the public sector see www.coventry.ac.uk/researchnet/icoco

Standardization, testing and accountability

Although James Callaghan, the Labour Prime Minister, first placed education on the political agenda in 1976 through his famous Ruskin College speech (www.education.guardian.co.uk/thegreatdebate/story/0,9860,574645,00.html), it was the Conservative Party who 'took the bull by horns' when it came to power in 1979. Progressive child-centred education and individualized learning did not find favour. Margaret Thatcher, followed by John Major, took it upon herself to bring teachers to heel on behalf of parents and employers. Many at that time felt that education was becoming too much of a lottery, with schools and teachers free to educate children as they saw fit. Major stated at the 1992 Conservative Party Conference, for example: 'Let us return to basic subject teaching and get rid of courses in the theory of education … Our primary school teachers should learn how to teach children to read, not waste their time on the politics of gender, race and class' (cited in Chitty, 2004: 186). The Conservatives rode high on two powerful social trends – the first associated with conservatism (with a small *c*) and the second associated with market liberalism. The first heralded a return to an age of innocence, with children sitting in rows, chanting their timestables, and respecting their teacher – the second demanded school improvement, with the marketization of schooling leading to greater accountability and improved educational attainment.

Within education, of course, real markets were not available, but ingenious proxy markets, designed to force (or enable?) teachers and head teachers to enter into the enterprise culture, were created with alacrity. Increased financial autonomy, national testing of students at ages 7, 11 and 14, the publication of *league tables* of schools' performances (there is more on these later in this chapter), and the introduction of school inspection by Ofsted, all contributed to a developing culture of entrepreneurship, audit, measurement and control.

Many of these measures were introduced in the Education Reform Act (ERA) 1988, the most fundamental legislative change since 1944. These included:

- the introduction of a National Curriculum, composed of specific subjects, to which all children are entitled during the compulsory years of education, overseen by the newly formed National Curriculum Council (NCC)
- arrangements for assessment of children's progress through the National Curriculum
- arrangements for religious worship and education
- requirements to provide information to parents and hold an annual parents' meeting
- reduction of LEA powers over admissions to schools (open enrolment)
- delegation of budgets to governing bodies (local management of schools – LMS)
- new powers of appointment and dismissal given to governors
- the establishment of grant maintained status (GMS), to promote state independent schools funded (generously) by the central authority and independent of the LEAs
- the establishment of city technology colleges (CTCs), envisaged as specially equipped inner city institutions funded in part by industry and commerce.

These measures stressed the importance of entitlement, standardized provision for all children and *parent power*. They were designed to take power out of the hands of local educational authorities, and to ensure that policy and practice in schools would be grounded in *common sense* notions of what schooling should involve. This extended to children with special educational needs (SEN), with government responding to increasing pressure from a variety of sources for all children to be educated in the mainstream wherever possible. Following the influential Warnock Report (DES, 1978), the Education Act 1981 required LEAs to make provision within mainstream schools for children with special educational needs (estimated to be 20 per cent of schoolchildren at some time in their school career) and introduced the procedure of *statementing* for categorizing those who needed and were eligible for different types of extra support and resources. (See Chapter 3 for more on SEN.)

The Conservative government also tackled the teaching unions, effectively taking away their right to withdraw their labour following strikes over pay in 1986, and mandating for the first time what was required of a teacher in some detail. They introduced the Teachers' Pay and Conditions Act 1987 which enabled the Secretary of State to make orders relating to pay and conditions for teachers in maintained schools. The orders relating to conditions of service identified certain professional duties that a teacher may be required to perform. These include planning, preparing and giving lessons; setting and marking students' work and reporting on their progress; promoting the general progress and well-being of students; providing guidance and advice; making records and reports; consulting with parents; participating in arrangements within an agreed national framework of appraisal; participating in further training; maintaining good order and discipline; participating in staff meetings; and supervising students when their teacher is not available. The teacher's working year is 195 days, of which 190 are days when students are in school. The head teacher directs the teacher's time for a maximum of 1,265 hours in this year, but the teacher is required to work such additional hours as are necessary to enable him or her to discharge effectively the professional duties. This is usually taken to mean that there is no definition of time to be spent on preparation, marking and report-writing, and so on. The salaries of teachers in the public sector are now reviewed annually, and usually new arrangements date from 1 April in any one year.

The Education (Schools) Act 1992, enacted key aspects of the government's *Parents' Charter*, and made schools more publicly accountable than ever before. For example, schools must be inspected every four years by a team of Ofsted inspectors, and schools' National Curriculum test scores, external examination results and truancy levels would be published (in what became known as *league tables*). The Education Act 1996 was a major exercise in consolidation of existing legislation relating to primary and secondary education and is currently the principal source of statute law on education. The Education Act 1997 covered Ofsted's role in inspecting LEAs and teacher training and the establishment of the Qualifications and Curriculum Authority (**QCA**).

Thus the Conservatives changed the face of education in the UK. For better or for worse, a culture of audit, entrepreneurship accountability and control are set to stay. It is no longer the case that teachers are trusted to educate the nation's children according to what they feel is best. These decisions are now made by government, and ultimately the voting public. Teachers must learn to walk the tightrope between doing what they feel is right, and obeying a common consensus on what their role should be.

Activity 6.6   Judging what feels right

This can be an individual or a group activity.

Read the extract below that is based on an unpublished interview that the author of this chapter carried out in 1997 and respond to the questions below:

> I was a reception teacher in Manchester, and I really loved my job. I had been teaching for a couple of years, and I felt that I was beginning to do quite well. Then the dreaded Ofsted experience came around! On day three I had an inspector sitting in the back of my class observing me teaching. Half way through it started to snow. The whole class of four and five year-olds ran to the window. It was when it hadn't snowed for a few years, and I suddenly realized that this was the first time in their young lives that they had seen the snow. I tried to get them back in to their seats (because of the inspector) but they were enthralled! I eventually gave up and we went outside and 'experienced' the snow. We came up with lots of really good words to describe the snow, and I made a note to bring this in to our science work.
>
> The inspector failed the lesson because I had not stuck to my lesson plan, and none of my learning objectives had been met. I made a decision there and then to leave teaching, and that is what I did. I now work as an administrator in local government.

- Was the inspector right to insist that the teacher stuck to the original lesson plan?

- How do you feel about this person's decision to leave teaching?

- What would you have done in this situation?

NEW LABOUR: EDUCATION, EDUCATION, EDUCATION

A Labour government was elected in May 1997 on a platform of *education, education, education,* with David Blunkett becoming the Secretary of State for Education. Large numbers of teachers, academics, famous people and other experts were drafted into various working groups and task forces. A new *National Schools Standards Task Force* was set to work immediately and a government Green Paper on special educational needs, *Excellence for all Children,* 'caused considerable excitement and optimism in the education world, particularly amongst those favouring a move towards greater educational inclusion' (Thomas and Vaughan, 2004: 130). It appeared, to many of us at that time, that we had entered a new era of education.

Legislative changes

New Labour's major legislative changes were set out in the Education (Schools) Act 1997, the School Standards and Framework Act 1998, the Teaching and Higher Education Act 1998 and the Education Act 2002. Changes in financial arrangements included the abolition of the Assisted Places Scheme, guaranteed free early years places for all 4-year-olds, extra money for school budgets paid directly to schools, extra funding to reduce infant classes to a maximum of 30 and the trialling of education maintenance allowances for 16- to 18-year-olds. One of the first announcements by Gordon Brown when he became Prime Minister in July 2007 was his intention to extend the school leaving age to 18.

Curricular changes

Curricular changes provided a new emphasis on literacy and numeracy, initially in primary schools; including tough performance targets in these areas. For example, 80 per cent of 11-year-olds were to achieve level 4 in English and 75 per cent in mathematics by 2002. September 1998 saw the introduction of *baseline assessment* for all 4- and 5-year-olds, and the introduction of the *National Literacy Strategy* followed by the *Numeracy Strategy* in 1999. (See also Chapter 3.) There was also a rapid expansion of ICT provision, and from September 2001 the *National Strategies* were extended into Key Stage 3, and later into Key Stage 4. A major reform of the 14–19 Curriculum was described in the government Green Paper, *14–19: Opportunity and Excellence* (DfES, 2003). A new National Curriculum came into effect from September 2000, and included a *new* subject – Citizenship.

Citizenship

There appear to have been two key motivating forces behind the introduction of this new subject into the school curriculum; it is statutory at Key Stages 3 and 4, and non-statutory at Key Stages 1 and 2. First, there was a increase in the perception of political apathy amongst young people, illustrated by low voter turnout among 18- to 24-year-olds (Crick, 1998: para. 3.5); second, there were worries about antisocial behaviour, personified by the highly publicized, brutal murders of the black teenager Stephen Lawrence in 1993 and the London headmaster Philip Lawrence (no relation) in 1995. Citizenship education would, it was hoped, help to create a more politically engaged and civil population. David Blunkett outlined these expectations at the report's launch:

> Education for Citizenship is vital to revive and sustain an active democratic society in the new century. We cannot leave it to chance … We must provide

opportunities for all our young people to develop an understanding of what democracy means and how government works in practice — locally and nationally — and encourage them to take an active part in the lives of their communities. Linking rights and responsibilities and emphasizing socially acceptable behaviour to others, underpins the development of active citizenship. (1998: 1)

The report of the Advisory Group on Education for Citizenship and the Teaching of Democracy in Schools (Crick, 1998) identifies three interrelated components that should run through all education for citizenship:

- social and moral responsibility
- community involvement
- political literacy.

These found their way into the National Curriculum documents for citizenship, which had all-party support. The DfES has suggested in their guidance that,

Pupils develop skills of enquiry, communication, participation and responsible action through learning about and becoming informed and interested citizens. This will be achieved through creating links between pupils' learning in the classroom and activities that take place across the school, in the community and the wider world. (2004b: 2)

This guidance is significant, as the emphasis is on participation and skill development, rather than on a knowledge-based curriculum. Knowledge (becoming informed citizens) is seen as important only in as much as it enables young people to be active citizens. Cautious, restrictive schemes of work, where young people are given worksheets and passive activities in order to protect ill-informed and poorly trained teachers cannot achieve such broad aims. The programme of study for citizenship covers such areas as:

- crime, justice, law and human rights
- diversity and ethnic identity in the UK
- local, national and European government
- parliament and democracy
- pressure groups and the voluntary sector
- war and conflict resolution
- media and ICT in society
- the world as a global community
- sustainable development
- business, employment and trade.

It is clear that while some of these areas are covered in other parts of the curriculum, many are not, and a personal, social and health education (PSHE)-driven curriculum, provided by non-specialist tutors, is unlikely to be adequate to deliver National Curriculum citizenship (see Chapter 7 for further discussion about the development of the personal–social curriculum). Many secondary schools wrongly place drug education, for example, within citizenship lessons. Whilst the international and social implications of the drugs trade would indeed form part of a citizenship curriculum, other issues to do with personal decisions on drug-taking are better placed in a personal–social curriculum.

The most important aspect of citizenship education, however, is the acquisition of the skills necessary to be an active citizen. In order to develop the skills of Key Stages 3 and 4 citizenship, students should be taught the skills to:

- research and think about topical issues
- analyse information and its sources
- justify a personal opinion orally and in writing
- contribute to discussion and debate
- use imagination to consider other people's experiences and viewpoints
- organize and participate in school and community-based activities
- reflect on the process of participating.

These skills can be taught by providing young people with opportunities to contribute towards a better quality of life in school and beyond. Some can be involved socially and politically through schools councils, initiatives such as young people's parliament, and local government consultation processes. They can link with a school or an NGO in another part of the world in order to better understand the challenges that are faced by others globally, and the ways in which they can help to bring about change. They can work towards a more sustainable environment through initiatives such as recycling, sustainable schools or engagement with ventures such as *Fair Trade*, and they can take part in volunteering to improve their local community, or the lives of vulnerable people within it. Where young people feel strongly about particular issues (animal welfare, recycling, human rights, and so on) they can be supported to lobby their MP, and to begin to understand the mechanisms by which pressure groups and individuals can bring about change. Fundamental of course to any *education for citizenship* is the use of ICT, from videoconferencing to using the internet for research and communication purposes. Young people need to understand the uses and abuses of various forms of media, and how these can impact on social and political life. This knowledge and understanding are the responsibility of all teachers, and need to take place in all teaching rooms, not just the citizenship classroom.

Activity 6.7 Contributing to the whole school Citizenship curriculum

This activity can be completed either on your own or, preferably, as part of a small group of beginning teachers. Use the mapping as a basis of reflection and discussion, either with fellow subject specialists, or with colleagues from across subject disciplines.

a) Together write the word 'Citizenship' on a large piece of poster paper halfway down, towards the left. Write the name of your own teaching subject halfway down towards the right. Draw a large circle around each of these words in such as way that they overlap in the middle. This is a Venn diagram.

- In the left-hand circle write the skills, attitudes, knowledge, values and learning opportunities that are fundamental to your own subject.

- In the right-hand circle write the skills, attitudes, knowledge, values and learning opportunities that are fundamental to Citizenship.

- In the bit in the middle where the two circles overlap write in the skills, attitudes, knowledge, values and learning opportunities that are fundamental to both.

b) Find ways of representing how the two subjects are distinct, and how they are linked. You may prefer to do this activity using a different form of diagram, for example, a spider diagram, or a mind map®. You may also wish to extend this to create a mind map® of citizenship as it is taught across the curriculum if you are working with fellow beginning teachers from other disciplines.

c) Individually, make your own action-plan for integrating citizenship into your teaching area. Use the following questions to assist your thinking:

- How will you ensure that any schemes of work involve active participation of the students in the life of the school, or the local or global community?

- How can you integrate a critical or a political perspective into what you are doing?

- How does your work with students prepare them as active and committed citizens?

Unfortunately, aspects of citizenship continue to present challenges for teaching across the curriculum in some schools. Recent reports and research from three different sources, the Office for Standards in Education (Ofsted, 2005a), National Foundation for Educational Research (Kerr and Cleaver, 2004) and the Community Service Volunteers (CSV, 2004), show that it is often poorly taught. It can lose its distinct identity if it is taught as part of the personal–social curriculum and thus it may be seen as *everywhere* and yet *nowhere* in the whole-school curriculum. It can be badly organized and co-ordinated, poorly assessed, and taught by non-specialists with little training or enthusiasm for the subject. This is partly due to under-investment in training, partly to reluctance by government to mandate how schools should go about teaching this eclectic and politicized subject, and partly to the way in which citizenship education was conceived in the original Crick report. It seems that the high aims of the Labour government in introducing education for citizenship may still be some way off.

The DfES (since July 2007, **DCSF**) produced a self-evaluation toolkit for schools in 2004. This is a very useful document for auditing citizenship, and can be obtained from their website. While it would be beyond your remit as a beginning teacher to carry out such an audit in your placement school, it should be of interest for you to read what is involved in the four different categories of school provision for citizenship, and to reflect on where you feel your placement school is situated in relation to these four areas (DfES, 2004c).

Activity 6.8   Whole-school citizenship: conducting an audit

This is best carried out with other beginning teachers and the citizenship co-ordinator in your placement school.

The four categories of school provision for citizenship have been identified as (DfES, 2004b):

- *focusing* (only just beginning)

- *developing* (some progress made)

- *established* (effective management and provision)

- *advanced* (excellent practice, innovation and self-review).

Go to and download the self-evaluation toolkit as a word file or PDF file.

a) Read through the descriptors and estimate where you feel the school is in relation to these.

b) If necessary, arrange to meet and interview the citizenship co-ordinator for the school. Have they carried out this audit, or a similar one? What do they feel are the development points for the school for citizenship education? How do they think that you (in your curriculum areas) can contribute towards the citizenship goals of the school?

Social exclusion

New Labour in 1997 was keen to tackle social exclusion, and education was seen as a means of achieving this. Accordingly, Education Action Zones (EAZs) (initially there were 12 identified from September 1998) were established to tackle urban poverty. Each comprised 10 to 20 schools run by a forum, and funded by both government and private money. They were expected to demonstrate *innovative practice*, and were enabled to suspend the National Curriculum, and increase the nationally agreed pay and conditions for teachers and *head teachers*. Special programmes, such as free summer schools to enhance achievement and opportunities, were made available to gifted and talented inner city children. Rural poverty received less attention, and was to re-emerge as an issue later in Labour's period of office.

So-called *Failing Schools* were named and shamed in New Labour's first month in office, in line with the government's zero tolerance of failure. This resulted in their abandonment by some students whose parents had the mobility, to the detriment of the students who were left. Other schools quickly became over-subscribed, with many families, especially in London, having to accept places in schools that were their third or fourth choice. The private sector was involved in organizing *Fresh Start* schools, and in running poorly performing LEAs (as identified through new Ofsted procedures for inspecting LEAs). New measures of *value-added* school/student performance were introduced. These aimed to take account of achievement on entry, and thereby show progress during school career. Percentages of students taking free school meals were used as a way of banding comparable schools. Home–school contracts were introduced in all schools. They were intended to formalize parental commitment, boost homework and cut truancy, and contained guidelines on homework and bedtimes for young people of all ages.

New roles for governors

From September 1998 governors were required to set and publish targets for student performance. The school and the LEA had to work together in setting these *challenging* targets, and from April 1999 they were included in the LEA's Education Development Plan. This process of target-setting was a central plank in the national drive to meet the national performance targets. School governing bodies now had wide-ranging powers and duties including the appointment of head teachers; conducting the school with a view to promoting high standards of educational achievement; establishing and approving the whole curriculum on offer (ensuring that the National Curriculum and religious education are taught); and managing the school or college budget. They were given significant new responsibilities in areas as diverse as determining teachers' salaries (pay policy); setting appropriate targets for student achievement at GCSE level;

drawing up and monitoring an action plan after an inspection; providing appropriate working conditions (health and safety); holding teachers directly accountable for the quality of their work (performance management); adopting and reviewing the home–school agreement; ensuring that sex education is given in a way that encourages students to have due regard to moral considerations and the value of family life; prohibiting political indoctrination; approving the school prospectus and approving the annual report to parents. Many of these governors' duties developed from the government initiatives to raise national standards of attainment.

Activity 6.9   School governors: What do they do and how do they do it?

This can be an individual or collaborative activity. You may be able to arrange for the chair of the governing body, for example, to meet with a group of beginning teachers for a wide-ranging discussion. Alternatively you may be able to carry out some research by interviewing one of the governors from your school (preferably not one of the teacher governors).

Find out:

- Why did they wish to become a governor?

- How are governors appointed in this school?

- What training is provided for governors?

- What is the mix of the governing body in terms of gender, age, socio-economic background and ethnicity?

- How are roles and tasks allocated within the governing body?

- Have their expectations of the role and its rewards been fulfilled?

- How do governors ensure that they are able to represent the interests of:

    - the local community (including residents, businesses and other educational establishments)

    - parents

    - teaching and non-teaching staff

    - students?

- How do governors in this school ensure that all students achieve the highest possible standards?

- How do governors in this school ensure that students' social and emotional needs are met?

Inclusion and SEN

The government Green Paper 1998 *Excellence for All Children* on special educational needs, made the government's commitment to inclusion very clear. The foreword by David Blunkett, Secretary of State for Education, stated:

> Schools have to prepare all children ... That is a strong reason for educating all children with special educational needs, as far as possible, with their peers. Where all children are included as equal partners in the school community, the benefits are felt by all. That is why we are committed to comprehensive and enforceable civil rights for disabled people. (DfEE, 1998: 130)

The Green Paper endorsed the UNESCO Salamanca Statement (1994), and named the important *social and moral grounds* for inclusion, highlighting the need for education to prepare all young people to flourish in their various communities as adults. It also made it clear that special schools still had a role to play, stating that the government's approach to inclusion would be practical not dogmatic. Separate education would continue to be a reality for some, especially those whose parents favoured it. New legislation, in the form the Special Educational Needs and Disability Act (SENDA) 2001, further strengthened the rights of parents to choose whether or not their child should be educated in the mainstream (provided that the education of other children would not be adversely affected) and increased the obligation on schools to make reasonable provision to ensure that students with disabilities would not be excluded from the curriculum or physical environment, should they opt for inclusion.

Although many schools embraced full inclusion, for others it remained problematic. For teachers, the move from integration (which involved the student *fitting in* with the environment) to inclusion (which involves the teacher changing the learning environment to cater for the needs of all students) was significant. Additional resources, training and teaching assistants were not always readily available. The paraphernalia and requirements of the medical model of SEN have been a hindrance here. As Thomas et al. powerfully state, 'A central aspect of an inclusion project must therefore lie in the deconstruction of the idea that only special people are equipped and qualified to teach special children' (1998: 14). In comparing more traditional approaches to SEN (which may include integration) with more inclusionary approaches, Porter (1995) shows that there are clear differences in emphasis in these two extremes. One places its focus on the student, with assessment by specialists and diagnostic outcomes. The other places its focus on the classroom, collaborative problem-solving and the quality of teaching and learning. The first involves a special programme or placement for the student, the second involves teacher innovation, and new strategies for adapting and strengthening normal classroom practice. All of this has workload and financial implications for teachers, and is not to be undertaken lightly. Rustemier and Vaughan noticed that very little progress towards inclusion had been made nationally in the period from 2002 to 2004. Indeed, one-third of local authorities had increased segregation of disabled students over the three years. They found there were 'disturbing, local variations in placement across England' (2005: 1), with students with statements of special educational needs in South Tyneside 24 times more likely to receive a segregated education than those in Newham, London in 2004. These issues continue to challenge schools as they try to balance the need to raise the attainment of all children with the need to make adequate provision for children who experience difficulties with schooling.

Issues of inclusion raise heated debate among teachers, parents and others. A variety of pressure groups, whose aim is to promote inclusion wherever possible, have produced a range of websites and other resources. See also Lupton and Power (2002) and the index developed by Booth and Ainscow (2002) for further reading on social inclusion. A recommended key text is Nind et al.'s *Inclusive Education: Diverse Perspective* (2003).

Activity 6.10   Knowing more about inclusion

This is an individual activity.

This task will support you to conduct some personal research into the issues of inclusion, and perhaps then, to interview experienced teachers and others in your placement school about what they believe about the benefits, challenges and limitations of inclusion. You should then be in a position to engage in informed debate on the subject.

a) Go to the websites listed below and draw up a list of the main arguments for and against inclusion.

b) Read some or all of the listed books, chapters and articles on inclusion and add more references to this list.

c) Interview three or four people in school about their views on inclusion (teachers, learning support assistants, mentors).

d) If possible, try to arrange to visit a special school with a group of beginning teachers and talk to students, parents and teachers there.

e) Complete the list of arguments for and against inclusion, adding evidence from such interviews.

f) Write a 500-word summary to share with your mentor on your own position on inclusion.

(Continued)

(Continued)

www.//inclusion.uwe.ac.uk/csie
www.diseed.org.uk

Florian, L. (1996) 'An examination of the practical problems associated with the implementation of inclusive education policies', *Support for Learning*, 13(3): 105–8.

Nind et al. (2003) *Inclusive Education: Diverse Perspectives.*

Thomas and Loxley (2007) *Deconstructing Special Education and Constructing Inclusion*. 2nd edn. (See the final two chapters for some arguments for inclusion.)

Undermining the comprehensive ideal?

There are those who have argued that New Labour's policy decisions to reduce social exclusion have, paradoxically, undermined the comprehensive ideal (Cremin and Faulks, 2005). After all, is it not comprehensive education, the local school where all young people are educated, that is the best guarantor of social inclusion? This is at odds with a belief that schools are improved through increased parental choice and competition for places. Local schools have been replaced by schools offering greater specialization, selection and diversity in the name of *choice* and standards. In a review of Labour's policies in this area, Taylor et al. conclude that 'pursuing a programme of school diversity leads to greater social inequality' (2005: 66). As schools are encouraged to compete for students, the better-funded, popular schools can use their extra resources and admissions policy to attract and select the most able and advantaged children. Current government policies will only exacerbate existing inequalities and exclusion by shifting 'major aspects of educational decision making out of the public into the private realm with potentially significant consequences for social justice' (Whitty, 2002: 87). Of particular concern in this respect is the encouragement by government of private sponsorship of schools. The *hidden agendas* of such marketization cannot help but influence the context, ethos and values of a school.

Teacher training and employment

Other changes introduced by New Labour included the establishment of a **General Teaching Council in England** (GTCE), in 2000. This oversees entry to the profession, defines standards of professional behaviour and is empowered to dismiss bad teachers. A further change was the introduction of advanced skills teachers (see **professional standards**) by giving them enhanced rewards and responsibilities to disseminate good practice to colleagues, other schools and trainee teachers. There has been substantial government investment in management training for head teachers and in the creation of a National College for School Leadership – located in Nottingham. The introduction of performance-related pay in 2000, and workforce remodelling in 2005 are two initiatives that have contributed to the stronger links made between teacher pay and student attainment. See Chapter 7 for more on the impacts of workforce remodelling. There have been changes in teacher training, including the introduction of a National Curriculum in English, Mathematics, Science and Information and Communications Technology (ICT) at primary level, and a compulsory induction period for new teachers. Ofsted's gradings of teacher training courses are published, and there are numeracy, literacy and ICT tests for trainee teachers (see Chapter 3). From September 2000 there have been training bursaries for beginning teachers, and national standards for Qualified Teacher Status have been introduced. These standards are extended to include professional standards for induction, professional, excellent and advanced skills teachers from 2007, and will mean that teachers are subject to ongoing scrutiny throughout much of their professional lives.

THE TWENTY-FIRST CENTURY: A NEW ERA FOR EDUCATIONAL CHANGE

In some ways there has been a sea change in education within the past five years, with moves towards better relationships between government and teachers, and a more holistic view of educational outcomes for young people. In other ways the same pressure on teachers to comply with a standards-driven agenda continues apace. There is private acknowledgement from government figures that performance-based league tables and high stakes testing have negative consequences as well as the desired ones, but the political will to get rid of them appears lacking. Attainment continues to improve slowly, but the gap between the attainment of students from the richest and the poorest homes is also widening (UNICEF, 2006). The testing of 7-year-olds in England has been school based and is less formal than previously, but children in England seem to be among the most frequently tested children in the world. More recent government policy documentation aims to improve children's health and general life experiences as members of a fairer and more sustainable global community, but there is no let-up in requirements to ensure that all students perform ever better in tests and examinations.

The documentation for yet another *new* National Curriculum from September 2008 (DfES, 2007a) includes a focus on testing core competences in literacy, numeracy and ICT, following complaints from British industry that productivity is lost due to low levels of skills in these areas. As a beginning teacher, you may not be aware that it was these same complaints from industry that heralded the first National Curriculum in 1988, the *back-to-basics* campaign of the Conservative goverment, and New Labour's *National Strategies* for literacy and numeracy. Young people now going into the workplace will have had their entire life in schools centred on providing for these key skills and as participants in initiative after initiative to drive up student attainment in these key areas. It is certainly worth asking the question as to whether there are other things going on here. Are there other factors beyond the classroom which impact on low levels of literacy and numeracy? Does *more* really mean better? Might there be other ways of raising levels of attainment in core skills? The final section of this chapter aims to review some of these questions, and to reflect on where schools and schooling might be heading over the coming years.

Every Child Matters

Anyone entering schools at the current time cannot help but know about the *Every Child Matters* (ECM) agenda. The trigger for ECM was the murder of 8-year-old Victoria Climbié in February 2000. Her death, and the subsequent media coverage, exposed fragmentation in the care services – she had been seen by a range of services including health, social services and the police – and the lack of communication systems for sharing information about at-risk children. Lord Laming's damning report recommended the urgent establishment of a co-ordinated approach to dealing with such children. Government acted quickly and the government Green Paper *Every Child Matters* (DfES 2004a) started a fierce debate about how to achieve an integrated children's service to ensure that no children slip through the net. The Children Act 2004 put the recommendations of ECM into law. In effect, this Act abolished local education authorities and replaced them with Children's Services Authorities headed by a Director of Children's Services. Inevitably this has involved all schools in responding to the act by ensuring that they play their part in an integrated and coherent provision for children and young people.

To recap, ECM sets out five outcomes for children and young people. They are that they should:

- be healthy
- stay safe
- enjoy and achieve
- make a positive contribution
- achieve economic well-being.

One possible response to these outcomes is to ask whether any teacher would want their students to be unhealthy, unsafe, unhappy, underachieving, unproductive or poor! On a less fractious note, the new emphasis on a more holistic idea of educational outcomes is to be welcomed, especially if it means that teachers can return to some of the activities that they were forced to shelve due to the standards agenda. Other initiatives which support this more holistic approach to education include (among others) personalized learning, healthy schools, learning in a global context, education for sustainable development, **extended schools** and initiatives connected with student consultation, and engagement with the voice of the child. Taken together, these initiatives provide a mandate for teachers to engage in a wider interpretation of their role than has been the case in the recent past. These areas are now explored further.

Personalized learning

As discussed in Chapters 3 and 4, personalized learning represents an attempt to ensure that as many schools as possible tailor the curriculum and teaching methods to meet the diverse needs of young people. David Miliband, in his speech to the North of England Education Conference, described it as:

> High expectations of every child, given practical form by high quality teaching based on a sound knowledge and understanding of each child's needs. It is not individualised learning where pupils sit alone. Nor is it pupils left to their own devices – which too often reinforces low aspirations. It means shaping teaching around the way different youngsters learn; it means taking the care to nurture the unique talents of every pupil. (2004: 8)

It is interesting to note the reference to individualized learning here. Individualized learning was popular in the 1970s and 1980s in contexts where students were encouraged to take more responsibility for their own learning, in some cases negotiating their own curriculum and pace and style of learning (see Brandes, 1986; Rogers and Freiberg, 1994). Advocates of such approaches claimed high levels of academic achievement as well as improved social and study skills and an ongoing love of learning. These progressive methods have been much criticized and ridiculed by policy- makers and the media, and have all but died out except in some post-16 contexts or with vulnerable, excluded or home-educated children. However a growing number of families who choose to educate their offspring at home are a testimony to their ongoing appeal.

 If we pause for a moment to conceptualize the shift from individualized learning to personalized learning we might begin to understand the fundamental shift that has occurred in education over the past few decades. We could imagine it as a shift from an *inside-to-outside* model of learning to an *outside-to-inside* model of learning. In the former model, learning is seen as natural and motivating, and young people are supported to follow their curiosity and enthusiasm. Outcomes depend on the particular skills and talents of the individuals involved. In the latter model learning is seen as something that teachers structure for learners, and students are taken through a series of activities to achieve a predetermined set of learning objectives. Outcomes are set by teachers, and ultimately by government/international indicators of excellence. The former model learning can be seen as similar to the lighting of the fuse of a firework, the latter model more as a *leg-up* model of learning, ensuring that as many children as possible are able to achieve against a standardized set of descriptors. Each model is based on different sets of learning theories, and their relative worth and success is an ongoing matter of debate. Advocates of the former will draw on Finland as a country which uses individualized learning to stunning effect. The Finns consistently outperform every other nation in terms of what their 15-year-olds know and are able to do (OECD, 2004). Advocates of the latter in the UK will draw on examples of schools which have been able to drive up levels of attainment through structured learning. As a beginning career teacher, you may find international comparative perspectives useful in grappling with these issues. Published research in this area can fall short, owing to the fact that it often confirms the ideas of those who commission it, but looking at research outcomes from other countries often provides us with a wider lens, and opportunities for thinking *outside the box*. A good place to start is the British Education Research Association (BERA) special interest group – Comparative and International Education. This group can be accessed at www.bera.ac.uk/sigs/sigdetails.php?id=32.

Healthier schools?

The National Healthy Schools programme covers a wide range of activities and to achieve National Healthy School Standard (NHSS) is a challenging one for schools. It is a long-term, whole-school approach that provides for maximizing students' academic and social potential. At its heart is the intention to produce the right environment for effective learning to take place while at the same time providing a template for healthy living into adult life.

To achieve NHSS a school enrols onto a nationally accredited local scheme and has to show it is committed to four core themes: personal, social and health education, healthy eating, physical activity and emotional health and well-being. All LAs now have a local healthy schools programme and coordinator who assists schools who join the scheme to meet planned objectives. Generally it takes three to five years to establish the **school ethos** needed to bring about change. Some schools already have a head-start because, for example, they have negotiated, and put in place, an anti-bullying policy, or have negotiated with catering services for better-quality school meals. The programme works by accrediting those schools which are able to show through a process of self-audit, improvement and self-review that they have met the national criteria across the four specified areas. Once accredited, they achieve NHSS. Schools are able to select from a range of programmes, offering a *kitemark* against various criteria to show their particular strengths and specialisms. To find out more go to www.healthyschools.gov.uk/.

The programme for Healthy Schools is jointly funded by the Department of Health (DoH) and the DfES. It was launched in 1999 and has, at least in theory, been able to link neatly with initiatives such as the *National Service Framework* by the DoH/DfES (2004) – a 10-year plan to stimulate improvement in children's health – and to dovetail with government programme targets for schools sports, where there are plans for a minimum two hours a week of physical education (PE) by 2010. In theory the *Healthy Schools* initiative fits well in the ECM programme, because the common aims of ensuring the safety and emotional and economic well-being of every child can be addressed. In practice it is difficult to see a successful connection between the stresses and strains of a target-led, performance-driven school and the wider healthy outcomes expected when the focus is also on emotional health and well-being, for example. Interestingly there is some limited evidence (see the related website above) that the emphasis of the *Healthy Schools* initiative on improving attainment and league tables has pushed the healthy schools agenda forward and where it has been successful it has been shown that it can underpin everything that a school does. The current review of the Healthy Schools Programme should reveal more evidence of its impact in time. (For more on Healthy Schools, see Chapter 7.)

Meanwhile it is well worth you finding out more about the health-related concerns in the immediate community of the school in which you teach. National and regional health-related statistics can only tell you so much about incidences and targets for reducing obesity, sexually transmitted infections, incidences of drug and alcohol use and abuse, and so on. Young people are some of the least healthy members of our society. School medical officers and nurses, together with annual published local data, can tell you much about the particular health needs in pockets of the wider local community and you can begin to target your teaching to meet specific individual needs and health concerns. This is where *joined-up* thinking and action can really begin to have an impact on young people's lives.

Some key health-related questions for you in your own teaching and pastoral work are:

- How do I encourage students to eat healthily, use the school canteen, keep the social areas clean and tidy, use the waste bins and remove unwanted litter?
- How do I provide consistent messages and provided opportunities for debate about good health?
- How do I work with parents/carers over aspects of good nutrition, physical activity, raising self-esteem or empowering students to take charge of their own learning?
- How do I ensure I have a good work–life balance?
- How do I work with specialist services, including school nurses, health visitors, educational psychologists and others to support the emotional and psychological as well as the physical well-being of students?
- How do I consult with students so they can express their views and feel they have a say in the health-related aspects of the school?

'Putting the world into world-class education'

Three more initiatives that aim to broaden educational provision and introduce modern globalized perspectives include Charles Clarke's *Putting the World into World-Class Education* (DfES, 2004d), the *Sustainable Schools* initiative (DfES, 2007b) and the Keith Ajegbo's *Diversity and Citizenship Curriculum Review* (2007). The first of these has the following aims:

- equipping our children, young people and adults for life in a global society and work in a global economy
- engaging with our international partners to achieve their goals and ours
- maximizing the contribution of our education and training sector and university research to overseas' trade and inward investment.

Schools can work towards these aims through international teacher exchanges and through linking with schools in different parts of the world. Some schools link with schools in the towns with whom their town is twinned, others link with schools in the global South and East in order to extend their students' awareness of the challenges that are faced by children living in poorer parts of the world. Videoconferencing can be used to very good effect, as can a simple exchange of letters or emails. It is important with any twinning programme that it is integrated across the curriculum, and that it is based on genuine exchange and mutuality, and not on paternalistic ideas of what *we* can do for *them*. The citizenship curriculum can contribute by supporting young people's understanding of how unfair trade in the West contributes to poverty, and the ways in which their personal choices have an impact globally, and these perspectives can enhance the learning that can take place through global linking across the curriculum.

The *Sustainable Schools* initiative (DfES, 2007b) aims to challenge schools and to empower young people to become models of good practice for their communities. Schools account for 15 per cent of UK public sector carbon emissions, half of which arises through electricity and heating, the rest from areas like travel, purchasing and waste. Through careful planning and a more managed approach these emissions can be reduced, and young people can be supported to contribute to a reduction in the carbon emissions of their school and homes. A total of 347 children and young people aged 19 and under responded to the sustainable schools consultation that helped to launch this initiative. These young people felt frustration with the state of the environment and their communities, typically road danger, noise, pollution, vandalism, litter, graffiti and the destruction of nature for building/industry. They were concerned about antisocial behaviour, racism, vandalism and litter, and a lack of respect demonstrated by young and old people alike. They were concerned about the continuing presence of poverty and injustice in the world, and the backdrop of war. They were angry at the careless use of natural resourses at the expense of future (their) generations (DfES, 2007b). The young people in our schools, including the very youngest, have sophisticated and strongly-held views on these issues, and teachers who treat them as empty vessels do them a disservice. Young people may indeed be more apathetic about voting than older people, but their interest in politics (sometimes referred to as *single issue politics* or politics with a small *p*) is as keen as ever. Knowing how to tap into young people's concerns and special interests is a skill that increasingly needs to be developed by beginning teachers.

Keith Ajegbo's *Diversity and Citizenship Curriculum Review* (2007) notes that a number of factors continue to inhibit effective education for diversity in schools. These include weak leadership in these areas, teachers' lack of confidence and training in dealing with issues of diversity in the curriculum and elsewhere, and not enough consideration of student voice and the contributions that can be made through links with the community. Stereotypes, ignorance and prejudice still abound in schools, as elsewhere, and some indigenous white students have negative ideas about diverse UK/English identities. Recommendations include developing mechanisms for ensuring that the *student voice* is heard and acted upon, curriculum audits and more formal links between predominantly monocultural and multicultural schools. His report calls for a fourth strand within citizenship which develops critical thinking on ethnicity, religion and race, and the history and values that unite us as UK citizens. This has been hailed in the media as a new focus on *Britishness* and community cohesion.

Activity 6.11   The voice of the child

This can be an individual practitioner research project or it can form the basis of collaborative professional enquiry with two or more peers and your mentor.

a) Put together a specific question, or questions, that you would like to address by researching the particular perspectives of young people. Keep it relatively simple and ensure you can address it within the constraints of the available time and resource.

Examples to start your thinking:

- How much bullying has taken place in my tutor group since the beginning of this school year, and what can I do to reduce it?

- How much homework do year 10 students get each night. What are the factors that influence whether or not it gets done?

b) Decide how you are going to draw out the student perspectives. Will you:

- devise a simple questionnaire?

- interview a representative sample of young people?

- approach the task in some other way?

- involve young people themselves as researchers?

c) Decide how will you record and the analyse data.

d) Now negotiate what you would like to investigate with your mentor. Some further questions and points may now arise:

- Is there anything that the school would like to know more about what you intend to investigate?

- Are there any existing findings that you could build on?

- Are there any procedural or ethical issues that you should take into account? You may need to complete an ethical checklist. (This will depend on what the students are doing – student consultation is a normal part of school life, and does not need parental consent. More in-depth research of course needs parental consent.)

e) Talk with the students concerned about what you would like to investigate and why you are carrying out this study. You need to reassure them about the steps you will take to maintain confidentiality, why you feel the research is important and what you hope to do with the findings. Ensure that at every new stage of the project you gain formally their informed consent.

f) Talk to your school mentor about the ways in which this research could be useful to the school or the wider community. Find a suitable audience to share your conclusions.

The voice of the child

The notion of engaging with the voice of the child is all-pervasive in current education policy documentation. Indeed, there is a legal duty in the Education Act 2002 for local authorities and governing bodies of maintained schools to consult with students when making decisions on matters that affect them. The DfES (2004b) has published guidance on this in *Working Together – Giving Children and Young People a Say*. David Bell, Chief Inspector of schools, made it clear in 2005 that citizenship education could be used as a vehicle for meeting the outcomes of ECM through student consultation:

> I would like to make the link between 'participation' in citizenship and the 'making a contribution' element of *Every Child Matters*. Making a contribution involves asking children and young people what works, what doesn't and what could work better, and involving them on an on-going basis in the design, delivery and evaluation of services. (2005: 4).

Ruddock and Flutter note that, 'out of school many young people find themselves involved in complex relationships and situations, and carry tough responsibilities', but that 'in contrast, the structures of secondary schooling offer, on the whole, less responsibility and autonomy than many young people are accustomed to' (2004: 1). Ruddock and Flutter outline five *advocacies* for engaging with the voice of the child in schools. These are: the importance of helping students to develop their identities and individual voices; the need for young people to be able to *speak out* about matters that concern them; a recognition that in the task of change, students are the *expert witnesses*; the need for policy-makers and schools to understand and respect the world of young people; and the importance of preparing young people to be citizens in a democratic society' Ruddock and Flutter, (2004: 101).

Huddleston and Rowe stress the importance of teacher skill and patience in working to create an atmosphere 'in which all students feel they have something to contribute and are able to express themselves freely' (2003: 122). Huddleston and Kerr argue that students should be consulted about school issues because, 'they have a right to be involved in decisions that affect them; it is an important opportunity for citizenship learning; and it improves relationships and promotes dialogue in school' (2006: 84). They point out that taking on positions of responsibility helps students to see themselves as active members of a community, grow in confidence and maturity, acquire new skills, knowledge and understanding, and prepare for a world beyond school. For this to happen, students need to be fully briefed about their responsibilities, given support and training, and to have opportunities to discuss their experiences and reflect on them in their personal portfolio and/or progress file. They give the *Students-as-Researchers* movement as an example of one of the most significant student participation developments in recent years, 'because of its potential to re-draw organisational lines of responsibility and accountability in school' (2006: 94). Hastingsbury Upper School in Bedford was one of the first schools in England to set up a *Students-as-Researchers* group. The group developed as a sub-committee of the student council. The students involved collected and analysed information and evidence on specific school issues and reported their findings to students and staff.

In 2004, Hannam, in association with Community Service Volunteers (CSV), carried out a study investigating young people's views on consultation, and the methods they found to be preferable. The main focus of the data collection was on four schools known to have active and effective school student councils. Students in these listening schools were willing to *give it a try*, participate and communicate their ideas to a wide range of audiences, including national government. They were motivated to share their perceptions in order to benefit themselves and other students. They had some confidence that such an exercise would be worthwhile, although there was also scepticism about the extent to which their ideas would be acted upon. Individual students in these schools believed that they could enhance the quality of information provided by young people through their participation in the consultation process. They felt that they were better placed than adults to reach out to peers who were reluctant to be drawn into consultative processes, and had ideas about how these peers could be involved. In fact, they doubted that any consultation project that failed to listen to the full spectrum of student voices could ever be successful.

Key texts for you to read in relation to this part of the chapter are Keith Ajegbo's *Diversity and Citizenship Curriculum Review* (2007). Ruddock and Flutter's *How to Improve your School: Giving Pupils a Voice* (2004); and Huddleston and Kerr's *Making Sense of Citizenship: A Continuing Professional Development Handbook* (2006).

For Activity 6.12 you have the opportunity to engage in some practitioner research into students' voices. Although beginning and early career teachers may find it difficult to find quality time to engage with research, as we have seen in Chapter 1, forms of professional or practitioner enquiry are core features of critical reflective practice. Engaging with this activity should provide you with the confidence and necessary impetus for any future investigation and review. A useful book for any enquiry or school-based review is Bell (1999) *Doing your Research Project: A Guide for First-Time Researchers in Education and Social Science.*

Activity 6.12   Responding to the challenges of ECM

This activity can be carried out individually or within a small group such as a collaborative enquiry group.

a) Carry out some research into your school's action plan for implementing ECM. Interview a deputy head teacher or other senior manager with responsibility for ECM.

- Who are the key players in local partnership?

- How are partners working towards a shared vision for children and young people? What are the barriers?

- How does the Children and Young Persons Plan (CAYP) and the Common Assessment Framework work in practice?

- What have been the key benefits/challenges of ECM so far?

- What further changes are planned in this school and its locality?

b) Find about how your school is responding to the various initiatives discussed above to do with health, globalization, diversity and sustainability. Has your school got any *kitemarks* or special status in any of these areas?

c) Write a list of your special interests, hobbies or areas of study in the past that would equip you to take at least one of these initiatives forward, either in your own teaching or across the school? Write an action plan for what you might do to further these aims in your first teaching post, and reflect on what you would like to achieve.

Teacher voice!

For student voice to have a significant impact on schools, teacher voice (and teaching assistants' voices!) should also be taken into account. How can teachers empower students when they themselves do not feel that anyone is interested in their perspectives? This is an important piece in the jigsaw of a newly emerging picture of greater holism, diversity and responsiveness within in the education system. In 2003 the government announced workforce remodelling, and in 2005 Ofsted announced its new relationship with schools. Both were highly significant in enabling teachers' voices to be heard.

The signing of a new agreement on tackling workload amongst teachers introduced important changes to teachers' conditions of service. This agreement acknowledged the pressure on schools to raise standards and tackle unacceptable levels of workload for teachers, and introduced a series of significant changes to teachers' conditions of service to be introduced in three annual phases from September 2003. Significantly the agreement does not focus solely on teachers. It acknowledges the vital role played by school support staff and has led directly to the establishment of higher-level teaching assistant (**HLTA**) standards and the certificate in school business management (CSBM). The agreement has also helped create other new roles in schools for adults who support teachers' work and students' learning. It called for a structured change process which would help schools implement the contractual changes and embrace wider workforce reform. The three phases of contractual changes arising from the agreement for teachers were:

1 September 2003

- Routine delegation of administrative and clerical tasks
- Introduction of work–life balance clauses
- Introduction of leadership and management time for those with corresponding responsibilities

1 September 2004

- Introduction of new limits on covering for absent colleagues (38 hours per year)

1 September 2005

- Introduction of guaranteed professional time for planning, preparation and assessment (PPA)
- Introduction of dedicated headship time
- Introduction of new invigilation arrangements.

This move, in combination with the ECM agenda, and extended schools (where schools are open longer and provide a base for a range of services for children and their families) has shifted the teacher's role more heavily towards planning, teaching and assessment and away from administration and the more traditional pastoral role. Teachers are increasingly seen as managers of learning, supported by a plethora of classroom and non-classroom-based professionals. With some routine and administrative activities taken away from teachers, the hope is that they will be released to do what only they can do best – teach! As these initiatives bed in over the coming years, it is likely that the nature of schools and schooling will continue to evolve quite significantly.

In 2005 Ofsted announced a *New Relationship with Schools* (NRwS) with clearer priorities, less bureaucracy for schools, and more information for parents (Ofsted, 2005b). It will support schools as they implement the *Every Child*

Matters agenda and joined-up local services for children and families. The NRwS aims to:

- introduce a school improvement partner (SIP) into every school
- reduce unnecessary bureaucracy
- build the capacity of schools to drive their own improvement
- establish a more intelligent, coherent, evidence-based accountability framework
- make better use of data
- secure better alignment between schools' priorities and the priorities of local and central government.

Ofsted inspections are now shorter and more frequent. Schools are given only a few days' notice of an impending inspection, reducing time for retrospective paperwork and sustained levels of stress! There is a greater emphasis on self-evaluation, and on co-ordination with local agencies. All of this contributes to a feeling that schools are being placed at the heart of plans for reform in the lives of children and young people, and that government and policy-makers are finally beginning to recognize the professionalism and expertise of teachers, and the harmful effects of undue criticism, regulation and control of the teaching profession.

For beginning teachers, these initiatives provide much scope for developing a special interest in a whole-school initiative at an early stage in your career. Notions of *distributed leadership* (see Harris 2005; Woods et al. 2004) have resulted in many head teachers delegating responsibility for various aspects of whole-school change to key teachers who show commitment and enthusiasm. It is no longer the case that you have to wait to *do your time* before your perspectives on education are seen as valid and worthy of support. This means that, even as a newly qualifed teacher (NQT), there may be an area that you are interested in leading, and your knowledge as someone who is recently trained may place you in a strong position to drive forward an initiative which you feel passionately about.

It may feel at times like a trying time to be entering the profession. In reality, however, teaching has never been easy, especially in the previous two decades. The scene is now set for some innovative and impactful work to take place in schools. The profession needs critically reflective beginning teachers with professional insights who are able to think *outside the box*, who are committed to the social, emotional and economic well-being of young people, and who are determined to make a difference. Is this the journey you wish to make?

In the final activity in this chapter, you are asked to think about where you think education and schooling are heading over the coming decade.

Activity 6.13 Visions for schools of the future

This is an individual activity.

a) Read through the characteristics shown in Table 6.2 of a vision for future schools set out by *Vision 2020* – a network of practising head teachers affiliated to the Specialist Colleges and Academies Trust (Walsh, 2004).

- Which of the characteristics listed do you agree with, and which do you feel are off the mark? Use this as a basis for further reflection and discussion with your peers.

- What do you think will be the significant drivers of ongoing change?

- What aspects of education do you think are here to stay?

The references below will assist you in researching a variety of perspectives on these matters. The full report can be found at www.ncsl.org.uk/media/B2D/ 53/leading-and-managing-the-future-school.pdf

b) Read the chapter by McIntyre (2003) 'Has classroom teaching served its day?', in Nind, Rix, Sheehy and Simmons (eds), *Inclusive Education: Diverse Perspectives*, pp. 95–115.

c) Visit the *Building Schools for the Future* website: www.bsf.gov.uk/index.html.

d) Read all or part of the book Beare (2002) *Creating the Future School: Ready, Coming or Not (Student Outcomes and the Reform of Education).*

e) Based on all of the above and your own imagination put together a fictional diary extract from 2020.

- What are your reflections at the end of a typical working day?

- What are your hopes and fears for education and young people?

- How has your working life changed over the previous decade?

Table 6.2 Characteristics of schools in the future

Characteristics for future schools	Agree (A)/ Disagree (D)?	Your further comments
• Schools are learning centres and part of learning networks or communities of 5 to 20 schools		
• The best networks are part of a global group of world-class schools		
• The home is an extension of the learning network and families choose to belong to several public and private learning networks online		
• All students have individual education plans and, from the age of 14, considerable control of their own learning		
• The previous structures of the school day and school terms no longer exist		
• The boundaries between types and age ranges of schools no longer exist		
• Schools are part private, part state funded		
• Adults who work in the learning centre are teachers, para-professionals, business people and other volunteers		
• Teachers' professional training involves the study of neuroscience, cognitive psychology, emotional intelligence and creativity as well as detailed study of teaching and learning styles and thinking skills		
• The uses of ICT as both a management tool for the teacher and an essential way in which students learn allow learning to take place anytime, anywhere		
• A local learning centre is the main provider of training to the business community and promotes services to local, national and international communities		

REFERENCES

Adams, M., Bell, L. and Griffin, P. (1997) *Teaching for Diversity and Social Justice: A Sourcebook.* London: RoutledgeFalmer.

Ajegbo, K. (2007) *Diversity and Citizenship Curriculum Review.* London: DfES.

Ashworth, A. (2004) *Once in a House on Fire.* London: Picador.

Bartolo, P. (ed.) (2007) *Responding to Student Diversity: Tutor's Handbook.* Malta: Faculty of Education, University of Malta. www.dtmp.org (from January 2008).

Beare, H. (2002) *Creating the Future School: Ready Coming or Not (Student Outcomes and the Reform of Education).* Abingdon: RoutledgeFalmer.

Bell, J. (1999) *Doing your Research Project: A Guide for First-Time Researchers in Education and Social Science.* Buckingham: Open University Press.

Bell, D. (2005) *Citizenship,* Hansard Society lecture, 17 January. www.ofsted.gov.uk/assets/3821.doc (accessed 6 July 2007).

Blunkett, D. (1998) *Speech at the Launch of the Crick Report.* London: DfES.

Booth, T. and Ainscow, M. (2002) *Index for Inclusion: Developing Learning and Participation in Schools.* Revd edn. Bristol: CSIE inclusion.uwe.ac.uk/csie/indexlaunch.htm (accessed 12 July 2007).

Brandes, D. (1986) *A Guide to Student-Centred Learning.* Oxford: Blackwell.

Brighouse, T. (2007) *Futures, Meeting the Challenge: Accidents can Happen.* London: QCA.

Chitty, C. (2004) *Education Policy in Britain.* Basingstoke: Palgrave.

Community Service Volunteers (CSV) (2004) *CSV Reports on Citizenship in the Curriculum Two Years on.* London: CSV.

Cremin, H. (2007) *Peer Mediation: Citizenship and social inclusion revisited.* Buckingham: Open University Press.

Cremin, H. and Faulks, K. (2005) 'Citizenship education past, present and future: reflections from research and practice', paper presented at the British Educational Research Association conference, Glamorgan, September.

Crick, B. (1998) *Education for Citizenship and the Teaching of Democracy in Schools: Final Report of the Advisory Group on Citizenship.* London: QCA.

Dewey, J. (1964) *Democracy and Education: An Introduction to the Philosophy of education.* London: Macmillan.

Department for Education and Employment (DfEE) (1998) *Excellence for all children.* London: HMSO.

Department for Education and Skills (DfES) (2003) *14–19: Opportunity and Excellence.* London: DfES.

Department for Education and Skills (DfES) (2004a) *Every Child Matters: Change for Children in Schools.* London: DfES.

Department for Education and Skills (DfES) (2004b) *Working Together – Giving Children and Young People a Say.* London: DfES.

Department for Education and Skills (DfES) (2004c) *The School Self-evaluation Tool for Citizenship Education.* London: DfES.

Department for Education and Skills (DfES) (2004d) *Putting the World into World-Class Education: An International Strategy for Education, Skills and Children's Services.* London: DfES.

Department for Education and Skills (DfES) (2007a) *The National Curriculum*. London: HMSO.

Department for Education and Skills (DfES) (2007b) *Sustainable Schools for Pupils, Communities and the Environment*. London: DfES.

Department of Education and Science (DES) (1978) *The Warnock Report: Special Educational Needs*. London: HMSO.

Department of Health and Department for Education and Skills (DoH/DfES) (2004) *National Service Framework for Children, Young People and Maternity Services. Executive Summary*. London: DoH/DfES.

Equal Opportunities Commission (2006) *Facts about Women and Men in Great Britain*. www.eoc.org.uk/pdf/facts_about_GB_2006.pdf (accessed 2 May 2007).

Florian, L. (1996) 'An examination of the practical problems associated with the implementation of inclusive education policies', *Support for Learning*, 13(3): 105–8.

Gorard, S., Rees, G. and Salisbury, J. (2001) 'Investigating the patterns of differential attainment of boys and girls at school', *British Educational Research Journal*, 27(2): 125–39.

Hannam, D. (2004) *Involving Young People in Identifying Ways of Gathering their Views on the Curriculum*. London: QCA.

Harber, C. (1995) *Developing Democratic Education*. Ticknall: Education Now Books.

Harris, A. (2005) 'Leading or misleading? Distributed leadership and school improvement', *Journal of Curriculum Studies*, 37: 255–65.

Holt, J. (1984) *How Children Fail*. London: Penguin.

Huddleston, T. and Kerr, D. (2006) *Making Sense of Citizenship: A Continuing Professional Development Handbook*. London: HodderMurray.

Huddleston, T. and Rowe, D. (2003) 'Citizenship and the role of language', in L. Gearon (ed.), *Learning to Teach Citizenship in the Secondary School*. London: RoutledgeFalmer. pp. 115–27.

Illich, I. (1973) *Deschooling Society*. London: Penguin.

Kerr, D., and Cleaver, E. (2004) *Citizenship Education Longitudinal Study: Literature review – Citizenship Education One Year On – What Does It Mean? Emerging Definitions and Approaches in the First Year of National Curriculum Citizenship in England*. London: DfES.

Lochhead, L. (n.d.) 'The Choosing', in J. Leggett and R. Moger (eds), *Yesterday Today Tomorrow*. London: English Centre. pp. 12–13.

Lupton, R. and Power, R. (2002) 'Social exclusion and neighbourhoods', in J. Hills, J. Le Grand and D. Piachaud (eds), *Understanding Social Exclusion*. Oxford: Oxford University Press. pp. 118–40.

McIntyre, D. (2003) 'Has classroom teaching served its day?', in M. Nind, J. Rix, K. Sheehy and K. Simmons (eds.), *Inclusive Education: Diverse Perspectives*. London: David Fulton. pp. 95–115.

Miliband, D. (2004) *Personalised Learning: Building a New Relationship with school*. Speech given at the North of England Education Conference, 8 January. London: DfES.

Nind, M., Rix, J., Sheehy, K. and Simmons, K. (2003) *Inclusive Education: Diverse Perspective*. London: David Fulton.

Office for Standards in Education (Ofsted) (2005a) *Citizenship in Secondary Schools: Evidence from Ofsted Inspections (2003–2004)*. London: HMSO.

Office for Standards in Education (Ofsted) (2005b) *New Relationship with Schools*. London: HMSO.

Organisation for Economic co-operation and Development (OECD) (2004) *Top-performer Finland Improves Further in PISA Survey as Gap Between* Countries Widens. www.oecd.org/document/28/0,2340,en_2649_201185_34010524_1_1_1_1,00.html (accessed 24 July 2007).

Phillips, T. (2006) *Speech by Trevor Phillips to the Royal Geographical Society Annual Conference, 30 August 2006.* www.cre.gov.uk/Default.aspx.LocID-0hgnew0jl.RefLocID-0hg00900c002.Lang-EN.htm (accessed 4 July 2007).

Plowden, D. (1968) *Children and their Primary Schools: A Report of the central Advisory Council for Education.* (Plowden Report.) London: HMSO.

Porter, G. (1995) 'Organisation of schooling: achieving access and quality through inclusion', *Prospects,* 25(2): 299–309.

Rogers, C. and Freiberg, H.J. (1994) *Freedom to Learn.* New York: Macmillan.

Ruddock, J. and Flutter, J. (2004) *How to Improve your School: Giving Pupils a Voice.* London: Continuum Books.

Rustemier, S. and Vaughan, M. (2005) *Are LEAs in England Abandoning Inclusive Education?* Bristol: CSIE.

Taylor, C., Fitz, J. and Gorard, S. (2005) 'Diversity, specialisation and equity in education', *Oxford Review of Education,* 31(1): 47–70.

Thomas, G. and Loxley, A. (2007) *Deconstructing Special Education and constructing inclusion.* 2nd edn. Maidenhead: Open University Press.

Thomas, G. and Vaughan, M. (2004) *Inclusive Education: Readings and Reflections.* Buckingham: Open University Press.

Thomas, G. Walker, D. and Webb, J. (1998) *The Making of the Inclusive School.* London: Routledge.

Tomlinson, C. (2003) *Fulfilling the Promise of the Differentiated Classroom.* Alexandria: ASCD.

United Nations Children's Fund (UNICEF) (2006) *The State of the World's Children 2007.* Geneva: UNICEF. www.unicef.org/publications/index_36587.html (accessed 14 July 2007).

United Nations Educational, Scientific, and Cultural Organization (UNESCO) (1994) *The UNESCO Salamanca Statement 1994.* Paris: UNESCO.

United Nations Educational, Scientific, and Cultural Organization (UNESCO) (2005) *Guidelines for Inclusion: Ensuring Access to Education for All.* Paris: UNESCO.

Walsh, K. (2004) *Leading and Managing the Future School – Developing Organisational and Management Structure in Secondary Schools.* Nottingham: NCSL.

Whitty, G. (2002) *Making Sense of Education Policy.* London: Paul Chapman Publishing.

Woods, P.A., Bennett, N., Harvey, J.A. and Wise, C. (2004) 'Variabilities and dualities in distributed leadership: findings from a systematic literature review', *Education Management Administration and Leadership,* 32: 439–57.

Younger, M. and Warrington, M. (2005) *Raising Boys' Achievement.* Research Report 636. London: DfES.

7 PASTORAL CARE AND TUTORIAL ROLES

Angela Wortley and Jennifer Harrison

By the end of this chapter you will:

- have developed your understanding of the nature of pastoral care and how it has developed
- have gained awareness of the many aspects of pastoral roles and responsibilities you will take on
- be aware of the links between pastoral care and other areas of the personal–social curriculum, including personal, social and health education (PSHE)
- be able to think critically about your contribution to tutorial roles in school in the future and about the range of personal and professional attributes, professional skills and professional behaviours required for this part of your teaching role.

INTRODUCTION

The pastoral roles and responsibilities of a secondary teacher are varied and complex; some, such as acting **in loco parentis**, are statutory. Other roles and responsibilities such as contributing to the 'all-round well-being and development of the child as a person (and not just as a pupil)' (Best, 1999: 57) are more open to interpretation by both schools and teachers. Pastoral care is a distinctly British concept and one that deserves much more critical examination than has been the case since the term became generally used in schools from the late 1960s. As you have read in Chapter 6, schools and **LEAs** gained increasing autonomy for their whole-school curriculum until the introduction of a

National Curriculum in 1989. This earlier relative freedom for curriculum development resulted in a range of imaginative initiatives in terms of pastoral curricula, for example, *Active Tutorial Work* by Baldwin and Wells (1983), as well as providing for neglect or oversight in other contexts (see DES, 1988). By 1992 the National Curriculum Council had produced guidance documents for cross-curricular elements to be included in the (then) new National Curriculum in order to assist schools in preparing their students for adult life. However, as Whitty et al. concluded, 'themes which did not have a significant presence in school prior to the introduction of the National Curriculum have generally lacked status and resources' (1994: 159). This illustrates the particular tensions that exist for curriculum planners in schools. They are caught between the demands of ensuring statutory provision and implementing ministerial guidance, and the recognition that school ethos, devolution of appropriate resources and individual teachers' commitment to the pastoral care and curriculum are also crucial factors in developing successful pastoral curricula.

Best also draws our attention to an important point in evaluating pastoral curricula, the

> separation of content and outcomes from process is dubious in regard to any aspect of the curriculum. In the realm of personal and social education, it seems particularly so. Here the **'hidden curriculum'** of teachers' attitudes towards, and relationships with, their students is arguably more likely to have a lasting impact than the formal content of the lesson. (2002: 21)

In addition, as you have read in Chapter 6, we have seen the impact of increasing political interference on aspects of education in areas such as careers and vocational education, education for citizenship, religious education and spirituality, sex education, many aspects of health education, and, more recently, in the relationship between pastoral care and academic support for students.

In the sections which follow in this final chapter of the book, you will be helped to explore some of the whole field of pastoral care and personal–social education. We shall start with the development of pastoral care in schools, look at the organization of pastoral care, then consider the pastoral aspects of your work as class subject teacher and your role as tutor, and finally consider its relationship with other areas of the work of the school. Since schools vary enormously in terms of the time and resources they allocate to pastoral care, and the importance they attach to it, this chapter should provide you with the chance to interpret what pastoral care means to you as a new professional and what it should entail in your various roles as you enter this *caring* profession.

THE DEVELOPMENT OF PASTORAL CARE IN SCHOOLS

What is pastoral care?

Pastoral care is often rather poorly defined in the literature. Here is an older but still useful, authoritative definition taken from a report on aspects of pastoral care undertaken by Her Majesty's Inspectorate:

> Pastoral care is concerned with promoting pupils' personal and social development and fostering positive attitudes: through the quality of teaching and learning; through the nature of relationships amongst pupils, teachers and adults other than teachers; through the arrangements for monitoring pupils' overall progress; through academic systems; and through extra-curricular activities and the school ethos. Pastoral care, accordingly, should help a school achieve success. (DES, 1989: 3)

This definition probably bears some resemblance to your own pastoral experiences in your schooling. Underpinning all pastoral care in schools and colleges is the vision of education as a moral endeavour, one that is aimed at human development in its widest sense. Nevertheless, issues of school management, at a time when target-setting and performance indicators are given high priority for raising student attainment, mean that there must also be a planned and purposeful approach to pastoral care in the school. Thus, however altruistic a teacher's *caring* might be, institutionalized care has its own costs. Hence schools have to consider the efficiency of their pastoral provision, however *uncaring* that might seem.

Since the late 1980s there has been a particular emphasis placed on tutorial aspects of the pastoral role to facilitate and support students' academic learning. Indeed one can justify this by arguing that there is nothing *less* caring than allowing students to work to standards below those of which they are capable. Consequently teachers have to find ways to blend academic *challenge* with help and compassion, and to remove obstacles and to enhance self-esteem.

The origins of the concept of pastoral care

Early influences

The term *pastoral care* has its origin in the teachings and organization of the Christian Church in which the term *pastor* remains in common usage. Most formal institutionalized schooling in the UK in the nineteenth century was provided through Church schools which probably accounts for the application of this term to education. In the eighteenth century these schools tended to be brutal, inhuman places with the masters competing with the boys to establish authority. The boarding of students required round-the-clock supervision and it was often during non-teaching time that the worst excesses of bullying occurred.

Subsequently, eminent head teachers of some public schools, such as Arnold at Rugby School (1828–42) and Thring at Uppingham School (1853–87) were influential in challenging the situations they had inherited. They reformed their schools to become ones in which the ethos was more rooted in religious and moral principles, and in gentlemanly conduct. Schools, in recognizing that their sheer size contributed to some extent to indiscipline, established structures to support the development of these educational ideals. A common response was to organize students and teaching staff into smaller units such as *houses*, with students from all year groups within one house. The allocated masters would therefore have responsibility for a small number of students throughout their time at the school. This responsibility covered all that could not be expected of the regular class teacher and so began the principle of what is now known as the *duty of care*. Such house structures were also able to provide for learning outside the classroom and inter-house competitions for school games, for example, provided a strong component of such learning. A prefect system supported the masters in maintaining order and organizing activities.

These early pastoral systems revealed the tension that exists even today between concern and support for the well-being of the students and the task of controlling behaviour and difficult students. Such pastoral structures can therefore provide hierarchies for referral and correction of misdemeanours rather than a means for accessing expert guidance and counselling. A good deal of the pastoral curriculum (which may be informal rather than formal) was, and is, concerned with promoting personal and social skills, and developing values and attitudes which are focused on self-discipline and socially acceptable behaviour.

Later influences

As we have seen in Chapter 6, the Education Act 1944 established free, compulsory secondary education in England with a tripartite system of grammar, secondary modern and technical or central schools. Grammar schools in particular became established academic places often with house systems based on those of the public schools. With the advent of comprehensive education in England and Wales from the 1960s, schools increased greatly in size, were often formed from the amalgamation of several schools and were sometimes located on several school sites. In recognizing the pastoral difficulties that might ensue in these large establishments, house systems, or similar, were introduced to develop a sense of belonging and bring about loyalty of students to the new school. House leaders, together with designated teaching staff to forms or tutor groups within each house, allowed new traditions and a house culture and identity to develop. Where schools have adopted methods of streaming or setting (see Chapter 3), having one teacher who can take overall responsibility for supporting and knowing each member of the form group well becomes still more important for both pastoral and academic care.

Pastoral structures generally refer to the organizational structures and systems to:

- manage and control student behaviours
- ensure provision of an individual member of teaching staff who could know, monitor, record and report on the progress of each student
- provide a way of dealing with student problems.

The raising of the school leaving age to 16 in 1972 coincided with the time that many comprehensive and other schools were setting up pastoral systems. How could schools make provision for an additional year of compulsory schooling for these often reluctant and unmotivated students? New pastoral structures often emerged to cater for the needs of this particular group. Meanwhile most teachers remained unclear about their caring role and received little or no professional help to support their pastoral and tutorial work.

Activity 7.1   Your pastoral memories

Part a) is an individual activity; part b) can be carried out in small groups or individually.

a) Take a few minutes to think about your own pastoral experiences as a secondary school student.

   - Make a **mind-map**®, or **spider diagram**, or put together some notes arranged in a sequence, in order to illustrate your experiences of pastoral care.

   - Identify the school tutors or significant events that played a part in the experience.

   Would you have described your schools as *caring*?
   Would you have described any provision in the school as *uncaring*?

b) Do you think it is helpful if students stay with the same tutor throughout the school, or is regular change more useful to them? Talk to some students in your placement school about their experiences and preferences of such pastoral systems.

   With other beginning teachers, make a list of the arguments *for* and *against* each system.

In the remaining sections of this chapter we shall refer to the informal and formal curricula that are associated with the variety of pastoral structures and tutorial roles as the *personal–social curriculum*. The separate development of pastoral and academic structures and curricula in schools has militated against the development of whole-school responsibility and understanding of non-subject teaching and learning. Pastoral and academic teams of teachers were separated. These teams rarely met to develop coherent and complementary pastoral and academic curricula or to develop a shared understanding of how students could be helped to achieve their potential in a caring community.

From the early 1970s a number of key books were written to assist practitioners in schools. These influenced practices and still have a place in supporting teacher development today (see Blackburn, 1975; Hamblin, 1978; Marland, 1974; 1989). Best, et al. (1980) were critical of prevailing practices that went under the guise of pastoral care, noting the over-emphasis on structures rather than the process and practice of pastoral work. The books by Best et al. (1980) and Lang and Marland (1985) were both edited collections, influential in supporting schools to develop whole-school practice in their pastoral work. Rather than providing detailed pre-scriptive models they offered frameworks and guiding principles so schools could put in place pastoral practices that were consistent with pastoral aims. A further significant development in 1982 was the establishment of a professional associa-tion for those involved in pastoral work in schools: the *National Association for Pastoral Care in Education* (NAPCE). Its professional journal, *Pastoral Care in Education*, has become well known for its coverage of both research and prac-tice on issues such as bullying, aspects of the personal–social curriculum and more recently introduced areas of the school curriculum such as education for citizenship.

It is not possible to make any general statements about the level and effec-tiveness of provision and quality of pastoral care as the evidence base from research and other bodies such as Ofsted is limited. A great many books and articles in this area make use of, but do not report, research. Best et al. noted the overall

> growth of personal–social education in and across the curriculum, the elaboration and increasing complexity of the role of the form tutor, a greater awareness of the relationship between pastoral work and the curriculum, and more integrated approaches to meeting children's personal, social, emotional and learning needs over this period. (1995: 288)

Ofsted (2005; 2007a) show that many schools have recognized the value of good pastoral care in meeting the needs of individuals and have largely good practice in this area. This situation was by no means universal.

THE ORGANIZATION OF PASTORAL CARE

This section focuses on the relationship between the school ethos and the overall arrangements for its pastoral care provision including all members of the wider school community. **School ethos** is revealed in many ways: in the quality of inter-personal relationships between all the so-called stake-holders (students, teaching, support and non-teaching staff, parents/carers, local authority (**LA**), local health/medical personnel, local police and so on). It is revealed in the quality of the pastoral structures, the arrangements for inclusion (see Chapter 6 for more on this topic), the quality of the teaching, the provision of out-of-classroom learning and the range of extra-curricular activities. Here we shall focus on the pastoral structures. Activity 7.2 allows you to build a picture of how one school begins to identify its pastoral structures. First you should review the following terms.

1. *Pastoral structures.* These are the ways a school organizes the pastoral teams of teaching and non-teaching staff, allocating particular roles and responsibilities. Schools may refer to a *year* or *house* structure and designate key titles to particular managerial or support roles.
2. *Pastoral and tutor activities.* These can include a range of general administrative tasks, disciplinary procedures, tasks for form/tutor time, a taught tutorial programme, meetings for parents/carers, induction of new students, support for/acting as advocate for groups of students, **academic tutoring**, counselling, keeping individual records and monitoring progress.
3. *Relationships in school.* These contribute to, and are indicators of, the significant quality of *caring* in the school. They include in particular relationships between: teacher–student, student–student, teacher–parent, teacher–support worker, teacher–youth worker.
4. *School ethos.* In addition to the information given at the start of this section, ask yourself:

   (a) What do members of the school community say when asked if they belong to a *caring* school?

   (b) How are members of the school community expected and supported to work in a way that fosters co-operation and overall inclusion of all its members?

5. *Attitudes of members of the school community to each other.* The values we hold are generally reflected in the attitudes we have towards all members of the school community and towards students and teaching colleagues. Day-to-day exchanges demonstrate the level of mutual respect, willingness to listen and understand, and overall fairness, justice and consistency of action in such settings.

Activity 7.2 Identifying personal, social and academic exclusion amongst students

This is a small mixed subject group activity (parts a and c), also to be carried out in conjunction with an experienced teacher or mentor (parts b and d).

a) Try to find out just how common some individual critical incidents are in your placement school. For example, what is the incidence of personal trauma amongst students as a result of separation or divorce of parents; of child abuse; of depression and suicide; of bereavement; of eating disorders; of unplanned pregnancy; of drug misuse/abuse; of criminal actions?

b) Share your findings with each other, as a group and with an experienced teacher or mentor. You may be surprised just how frequently these events occur and supporting pupils in distress requires much more than having appropriate policies in place. How has the school been able to deal with the minor and more major traumas /incidents?

c) Find some examples of how your placement school:

- listens to the problems/difficulties of its students, their families, their communities

- provides effective support to bring about increased: (i) student attendance; (ii) pupil motivation

- helps pupils feel physically and emotionally safe in school

- provides for each pupil to have at least two trusted members of staff, as well as fellow students, in which they can confide

- has a clear picture of any drugs misuse in the school/community and has an effective programme against drugs misuse

- has good links with health and social agencies, community policing, local employers, other agencies

- has effective programmes on sex and relationships education

- knows when individual pupils are *at risk* (for example, through drugs, health problems, crime, depression, family crises) and acts on their behalf

- has fair and impartial equity policies (for example, for gender, ethnic and social issues)

- incorporates all these issues in the whole curriculum.

d) As a result of examining some aspects of care such as those listed above, you can now reflect as a group on the quality of staff co-ordination and the level of co-ordination with other agencies in the community.

Summarize together some of the particular challenges and the further training/support that members of the whole school community might now need.

e) Look at the framework of *pastoral tasks* (Best, 1999) – see page 249 of this chapter. Take one of the aspects for which you gathered evidence in part c). Consider how the first pastoral task of *reactive pastoral casework* accounts for most of these critical incidents you (as a group) have described. Explore how the other four pastoral tasks might be used to provide further educational support to students experiencing this particular critical incident in the future.

Every Child Matters agenda

At this point we should try to establish the links between the pastoral curriculum and structures in a school and the five key outcomes of the *Every Child Matters* agenda (see Chapter 6) before we describe in more detail the structures in which teachers' general pastoral responsibilities are located. Pastoral structures are discussed later in this chapter. First, remind yourself of the definition of *pastoral care* (DES, 1989: 3) given at the start of Chapter 7. Then, consider the statement below taken from the *National Curriculum Handbook* over 10 years later. It is headed *The importance of personal, social and health education*:

Personal, social and health education (PSHE) at key stages 3 and 4 helps pupils to lead confident, healthy and responsible lives as individuals and members of society. Through work in lesson time and a wide range of activities across and beyond the curriculum, pupils gain practical knowledge and skills to help them live healthily and deal with the spiritual, moral, social and cultural issues they face as they approach adulthood. PSHE gives pupils opportunities to reflect on their experiences and how they are developing. It helps them to understand and manage responsibly a wider range of relationships as they mature, and to show respect for the diversity of, and differences between, people. It also develops pupils' well-being and self-esteem, encouraging belief in their ability to succeed and enabling them to take responsibility for their learning and future choice of courses or career. PSHE at key stages 3 and 4 builds on pupils' own experiences and on work at key stages 1 and 2 and complements citizenship in the curriculum, which covers public policy dilemmas related to health, law and family. (DfEE/QCA, 2000: 188)

The following extract is taken from *Inspecting schools: The Framework* (Ofsted):

Where welfare and guidance are good, each pupil's needs and progress are identified and monitored by a member of staff who has the confidence of the pupil, and to whom there is a ready and regular access. Pupils are able to maximise their opportunities; they feel secure and have high but realistic expectations based on a sound assessment of what they have achieved. Class teachers or tutors monitor pupils' progress and regularly discuss it with them and their parents. The school has clear, well-documented procedures for assuring pupils' well being and health and safety when in the school's care. Governors, staff, parents and pupils are aware of these and observe them. A carefully structured and co-ordinated guidance programme, which includes health education and careers education and guidance, ensures that pupils are well-informed and are counselled wisely, particularly at points of transition. Teachers have skills appropriate to their responsibilities for guidance and have access to, and make use of, professional support both from within the school and from specialist services. (1999: 73).

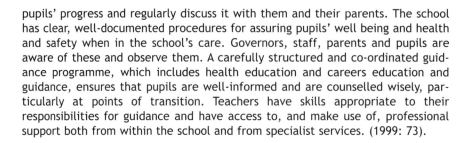

Activity 7.3   Pastoral care and the *Every Child Matters* agenda

This is a mixed-subject, small group activity.

a) Using Table 7.1, try to map the three statements/extracts already provided in the main text of this chapter:

- definition of pastoral care (DES/HMI, 1989: 3)

- 'The importance of personal social and health education' (DfEE/QCA, 2000: 188)

- 'Inspecting schools: the Framework' (Ofsted, 2000: 73)

against the five outcomes of *Every Child Matters*.

b) Discuss your responses to the following questions:

- Is it possible to identify changes in expectations for pastoral provision or has there been consistency in these expectations over time?

- Are there aspects of the ECM outcomes not identified in these three statements published prior to 2004? Clarify any new emphases, if they exist.

- Is academic achievement the most important aim as set out in these extracts? Should it be?

The nature and scope of pastoral care

One way of considering the interrelationship of pastoral work with other areas of work in schools is to look at activities undertaken by schools to fulfil their statutory pastoral responsibilities. As a beginning teacher you may be required to contribute to the pastoral work in your school in a number of ways: first, as a subject teacher, then as a form tutor and a member of a specialist pastoral team,

Table 7.1 A mapping exercise for ECM

Outcomes of *Every Child Matters*		Quotes/extracts from key documents		
	DES/HMI (1989: 3)	*National Curriculum Handbook (DfEE/QCA, 2000)*	*Framework for the Inspection of Schools (Ofsted, 2000)*
Be healthy			
Stay safe			
Enjoy and achieve			
Make a positive contribution			
Achieve economic well-being			

and, finally, in your wider whole-school responsibilities, for example, undertaking enrichment activities, or managing teaching groups when moving around the school site. What follows is a framework of five pastoral tasks which Best developed, drawing on his extensive work and the work of other experts in the field identified earlier in this chapter:

1. *Reactive pastoral casework,* undertaken on a one-to-one basis in response to the needs of children with problems of a social, emotional, physical, behavioural, moral or spiritual nature;
2. *Proactive, preventative pastoral care,* often in the form of presentations or activities undertaken in tutor or form periods and assemblies, which anticipate 'critical incidents' in children's lives and are aimed at pre-empting the need for reactive casework;
3. *Developmental pastoral curricula,* aimed at promoting the personal, social, moral, spiritual and cultural development and well-being of children through distinctive programmes of Personal and Social Education (PSE), tutorial work and cross-curricular activities;
4. *The promotion and maintenance of an orderly and supportive environment* by building a community within the school, through extra-curricular activities, the 'hidden curriculum' of supportive systems and positive relations between all members, and the promotion of a pervasive ethos of mutual care and concern;
5. *The management and administration of pastoral care* in the form of planning, motivating, resourcing, monitoring, supporting, evaluating, encouraging and otherwise facilitating all of the above. (1999: 58–9)

You should find this framework useful when considering you own pastoral experiences in Activity 7.1 and when thinking further about the particular skills teachers need when undertaking these tasks. These five pastoral tasks are comprehensive. However, they do not take account of one of the recent developments that is assuming an increasingly important aspect of the role of form teachers, namely, tutoring to support students' academic progress and achievement. This has been seen to be effective in motivating students particularly at key assessment points and is becoming a common feature of the tutor's brief.

Web activity 7(1) – Under the umbrella of pastoral care

Pastoral structures

These generally fall into two categories: those which have their origins in the early forms of organization for pastoral care in the independent schools which are described as *vertical* (for example, the house system with its house head and tutorial team), and those which involve *horizontal* groupings (such as year groups with year heads and tutors each attached to a year tutor group). There are key advantages to both ways of operating such structures (see Hamblin, 1978; Ireson, 1999; Lang, 1980, Marland, 1974, for further discussion of these points).

Whichever pastoral system is used, the allocation of students to particular tutor/form groups may be done randomly, alphabetically, by friendship groups, or by ability. For secondary schools with many feeder primary schools, students may be involved with some consultation prior to entry as to which friends they would like be aligned with in a new tutor group. Generally great care is taken. Siblings may be placed in the same house. Tutor groups may be balanced to bring about a mix of talent, ability and personality in an attempt to establish mutually supportive units from the outset. In such organizational systems the emphasis is clearly on *care*.

Recent political influences on arrangements for pastoral structures

This extract, taken from a newspaper advertisement for a Head of House post for Clevedon Community School in Somerset, sets out reasons for why it chose to change its pastoral structure.

> Clevedon Community School has moved from a horizontal year structure to a vertical tutor group House structure. This has facilitated our student centred vision and helped develop student responsibility, leadership and identity whilst at the same time promoting a positive ethos.

It asks if applicants have the skills to:

drive forward a whole school ethos ... motivate and enthuse students to raise expectations, aspirations and self esteem; lead students and staff in developing a school and House identity promoting the support of this 'family' group; play a high profile role within the school and with parents to encourage higher student achievement and success. (*Times Educational Supplement*, 2007: 288).

It illustrates the result of a whole school review that is taking place in many such schools as they begin to identify effective ways to support learning and personal development of both students and staff.

Responding to the national agreement on workloads and the increasing emphasis on student achievement

The notion of *workforce remodelling* has been introduced in Chapter 6. From 2003 there have been further statutory requirements for schools to implement the *National Secondary Strategy* (see Chapter 3) as well as meeting schools' own developmental plans to reach their academic targets. Thus there is frequently a redefinition within schools of tutorial roles and responsibilities, with consequent realignments of pastoral structures. The article by Phil Jones (2006), referred to in Activity 7.4, illustrates the move towards a vertical structure based on mixed-age groups, and which his school refers to as *learning communities*. In these new vertical structures different or alternative ways have to be found to provide for the personal–social curriculum.

Super-tutors

In some sixth-form colleges for 16–19-year-olds the need for a daily tutorial meeting is seen as neither practical nor important. Here there has been the introduction of super-tutors. These teachers, identified by the quality of their tutoring skills, are allocated multiple tutor groups. Within designated tutor periods they may:

- induct students into the new setting
- support students to develop skills to work independently
- monitor student progress and liaise with subject teachers and parents/carers
- set challenging academic targets and provide guidance to achieve these
- help students to achieve balance between academic and social opportunities
- support students in making important vocational and career choices and preparing applications for employment, training and higher education.

Such tutors play a significant part in preparing students for their independent adult lives.

Good enough care?

A further dimension of the organization of pastoral care is the amount of time allocated to it. This will vary from school to school and may depend on how the form tutor's role includes responsibility for the pastoral and personal–social curricula. It is becoming more common for schools to include time for academic tutoring and to provide time for progress review meetings periodically through the year. However, having sufficient time to undertake this aspect of tutoring is seen as a major factor in its effectiveness in supporting students, learning (Carnell and Lodge, 2002a).

Other personnel

Where teachers have been freed from the more mundane administrative tasks to concentrate on raising student achievement, new systems have been put in place. Examples include the appointment of non-teaching staff to support the pastoral managers. The *Remodelling the Workforce* website, www.tda.gov.uk/remodelling.aspx, contains illuminative case studies of these new ways of working. It is clear that in the future pastoral managers will co-ordinate teams of teaching and non-teaching staff working in flexible teams to provide for continuity of pastoral care. A key part of the work of the team will be to plan for learning and support where it is likely to be most effective. This will require regular monitoring and evaluation to ensure that responsibilities are shared according to expertise. There is more on these aspects in a later section of this chapter. Meanwhile it is important to note that the increasing appointment of non-teaching staff within pastoral teams has raised some serious professional concerns about the possible diminution of the pastoral, caring role of the teacher and the apparent de-professionalizing of most teachers in relation to pastoral care.

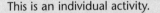

Activity 7.4   Changes to the pastoral team

This is an individual activity.

Schools are responding in different ways to implementing the National Workforce Agreement that has removed many administrative tasks from teachers. Many tasks were formerly undertaken by form tutors. Other initiatives have impacted on pastoral provision causing schools to review structures and priorities for tutors.

a) Read the following articles to find out more about how schools are responding to these intiatives.

- Jones, P. (2006) 'Status of pastoral care in schools in the 21st century', *Pastoral Care in Education*, 24(2): 64.

- Andrews, D. (2006) 'Non-teachers moving into roles traditionally undertaken by teachers: benefits and challenges – for whom?' *Pastoral Care in Education*, 24(3): 28–31.

Access the *Remodelling of the Workforce* website to locate case studies of schools that have used some non-teaching staff in pastoral support roles.

b) Summarize the benefits and challenges of using non-teaching staff in pastoral teams. Do you consider that there will be long-term advantages for (i) teachers and (ii) students?

c) Find a very recent copy of the *Situations Vacant* section of the *Times Educational Supplement* and go to the posts advertised for pastoral leaders. Jot down the titles and main responsibilities described and note phrases that are new to you.

  - Is there anything that surprises you about the language used in the advertisements?

  - What impression do these advertisements give you of the status of pastoral leaders?

  - Find out if there have been any recent changes to pastoral roles and responsibilities in your placement schools and ask a pastoral leader what they think have been the benefits to students and teachers?

  - From your experiences and your reading so far would you consider pastoral leadership as a future career choice? Explain why.

Pastoral aspects of your work as class teacher and your role as tutor

This section focuses on the skills and attributes you need to develop in order to carry out your duties as a tutor and to recognize and develop your caring role in your classroom subject or other teaching.

The following quotations have been taken from newly-qualified teachers towards the end of their first year in teaching (induction year).

I have found working with my form one of the most rewarding experiences of my teaching this year. I feel I've really got to know them well and I always look forward to our tutor periods.

I have a number of challenging students in my form. I have found my responsibilities overwhelming at times and I've often had to seek help. I did not realise how time-consuming personal tutoring would be.

I've really had to think about my own values and attitudes when planning PSHE (personal, social and health education) lessons. I've become more confident in approaching some of the topics, like aspects of the sex and relationships programme. I'm sure I've learned much more about myself and what I teach than any of my students have this year!

Activity 7.5 should be carried out in each of your school placements so you gain as wide a set of experiences of tutorial work as possible. Focus particularly on the range of skills, attributes and attitudes that are necessary to become an effective form tutor. You cannot copy the tutorial style of another teacher directly but aim to observe and analyse good practice and to unpack the qualities that such teachers demonstrate in this part of their work.

Activity 7.5   Studying the role of the form tutor

Part a) is an individual activity. Parts b), c) and d) require you to work with one or more others, as indicated. During your time in school you should take the opportunity to be assigned to a tutor group and work alongside an experienced, enthusiastic form tutor.

a) Below is a list of some of the responsibilities of the form tutor. Keep a log (for a minimum of two weeks in each school placement) of all the things that the form tutor does in their designated tutor role. Then classify them under the following headings:

- Administrative tasks

- Liaising with others

- Guidance/counselling

- Monitoring student progress (see Chapter 5)

- Pastoral/curriculum (for example, PSHE)

b) Consult the list of tutor tasks given on page 255. Which of these tasks require a tutor to develop *specific skills* to assist them to do the work effectively? List those skills. Compare your list with that of another beginning teacher. Each of you should identify one skill which you may need to improve; identify strategies to do this and how you will recognize any improvements.

c) It is important to make time for your students. Listen to what they say and watch for non-verbal cues, too. Give them some time and attention and get to know them and about their lives.

Put together some *case-study* notes on one student (or a small group of students) and be prepared to share these (confidentially) with another beginning teacher.

Pseudonyms for each student studied help to prevent recognition and misuse of information about each person. Take great care with any written material and keep it in a safe place, destroying it later. Try to identify any skills/attitudes that you, as beginning teachers, need to develop to become effective tutors.

d) If possible, arrange a 15-minute interview with a manager of pastoral work in your school (for example, head of year). Prepare some specific questions from a group of beginning teachers, for example:

- Please describe in detail one (of the many) concerns or critical incidents that you have had to deal with today.

- How is this situation followed up/explored further/shared with others (inside or outside the school)?

Responsibilities including required administrative tasks

The list below includes some routine responsibilities that you might expect to undertake as a form tutor during daily registration or a tutor period. Some of these tasks may now be undertaken by a member of the support staff whom you will need to liaise with to share information and maintain accurate records and procedures. You can use this list when undertaking Activity 7.5(a).

Responsibilities include:

- completing formal registration of the tutor group; marking if a student is late, or has brought in a letter to explain absences
- informing the pastoral manager (for example, head of year), following the school procedures, if a student is continually late
- ensuring that you have correct titles, names and spellings for parents/carers
- keeping up to date all home and work contact numbers for your students
- signing and dating all letters received, passing them on to appropriate colleagues/filing them
- ensuring that students receive any messages through the school bulletin, or from colleagues and the school office
- checking personal pigeonhole to receive concerns/incidents/student absences noted by other staff regarding students in your form group, and acting upon these
- checking students' homework diaries/planners; signing them
- ensuring that contact is made with their home via a letter/phone call, if a student is away for more than three days
- responding to concerns expressed to you by parents/carers or your students.

In the first chapter of *How to Be a Successful Form Tutor*, Marland and Rogers propose that the core task of a tutor is 'enabling a child to become a student and develop more fully as a person' (2004: 1). They explain how a tutor has a special responsibility for nurturing students, particularly in those aspects that help to develop their confidence, self-esteem and interpersonal skills that enable them to take increasing responsibility for themselves as they negotiate the difficulties of adolescence and the move to adulthood and economic independence. In *Personal and Social Education in the Curriculum* Richard Pring (1984), an influential philosopher and authority in the field of pastoral care, considers fundamental questions about education and its role in the development of the person. He explores what it means to *be a person* and how education can contribute to the developing personhood of students. His writing complements well that of Marland and Rogers and reading both key texts should help you to articulate your own developing philosophy of education. For example, consider some of the theoretical perspectives of personal development and what we mean by *personal* in the pastoral education debate and the implications for you of what it might mean to be *professional*. Try to question any previous assumptions you held about the relative importance of the pastoral role and the subject teacher role in secondary schools.

Activity 7.6   Understanding the *person* in *personal*

This is an individual activity. Part a) can also be carried out usefully in a pair or small group.

a) On your own, or with other beginning teachers, make notes on your responses to the following challenging questions.

- What does it mean to be a person?

- How would you describe yourself as a person?

- What is the role of education in developing persons?

b) Read chapter 2 in *Personal and Social Education in the Curriculum* (Pring, 1984).

Go back to your responses to a) and review them in the light of your reading.

- In what ways do his concluding questions have significance for you as a teacher?

- How will knowledge affect the way you think about your daily interactions with your students?

Share your responses with colleagues if possible.

Establishing relationships

As a form tutor you are usually the students' first point of contact as they join the school and then at the start (or middle) of each school day. It falls to you to establish and reinforce standards of behaviour and dress and to set the tone for academic work in the day ahead. Aim to set high expectations of all your students, and provide a positive model for personal conduct and interpersonal relationships. You are responsible for promoting the values of the school, maintaining a positive school ethos and clarifying information about the school, its rules, routines and rituals that everyone is expected to adhere to.

The relationship you have with your tutor group should be based on mutual trust and respect. It can be one of your most satisfying roles in school and you can play an important part in creating a happy atmosphere in the school. Such relationships do not happen by chance. They are facilitated through planned activities with your group and building on your personal knowledge of their collective backgrounds, prior achievements, abilities, interests, dispositions and attitudes. These early meetings with your tutor group should also serve to develop cohesive and mutually supportive relationships between all members of the group which are fundamental to creating classrooms where all students' contributions are listened to and are valued. It is reassuring for most students to know that their tutor appreciates, understands and cares about their academic and broader educational progress. The strategies described later in this chapter can help you refine these ways of working in tutor time.

The effort you put into establishing such relationships very much reflects your personal attitude to the tutoring role as well as the importance attached to the role more generally within the school you teach. Such effort might be reflected in the extent to which you can establish the tutor room as a welcoming, homely base for your students. Posters, student bulletins and cheery messages can help to mark it as special for them all. The student-researchers investigating the workings of the newly implemented pastoral structure based on *learning communities*, referred to earlier in this chapter, reported that the way in which the tutor interacted with their group in the short morning registration period 'determined their (students') attitude to learning for the rest of the day' (Jones, 2006: 65).

Supporting individual students

It is important for you to be aware of any changes in student behaviour that might be early warning signs of personal or other difficulties. By seeking opportunities for regular individual talks and discussion you can help to create a climate of trust in which students will be encouraged to discuss more with you if they wish to. Your early intervention, on behalf of a student, might mean that you can provide support for them to cope with school work while they try to resolve other challenges.

Confidential and sensitive information given to you by a student means you may be responsible for transmitting this to certain colleagues. Some students experience significant personal events (for example, serious illness in the family; changes to family circumstances caused by loss of employment) and schools can provide the much needed stability and support for coping in such crises. Effective tutors can protect individual confidences and take account of the individual's situation and its likely impact on their behaviour, attitude and ability to meet deadlines.

Recognizing signs of child abuse and knowing about child protection procedures

It is often a form tutor or class teacher who is first aware of physical or behavioural changes that might reflect more serious problems in a student's life. Therefore you should take steps to know well in advance who you can turn to for support and advice in such serious situations. Suspicion of child abuse obliges you to act responsibly and within required school procedures. As a new teacher, find out from the start as much as you can about your school's child protection policy and procedures, and particularly the **designated senior person** for child protection issues. Prompt collective action can be crucial.

Child abuse includes physical injury, emotional harm, sexual abuse and severe neglect. In situations that might include these, keep written records of what has been noticed, said and done and pass these on to the designated senior person to follow up. In any situation where a student asks to talk to you confidentially you should:

- treat the matter seriously and reassure the student if necessary
- not overreact, or frighten the student
- not pursue details – keep your questions to a minimum
- never *lead* or interrogate the student (this may jeopardize any future legal action)
- try to use the everyday vocabulary that the student uses
- not promise confidentiality
- explain what will happen next
- make a written record as soon as possible of what was said and how the student behaved
- get support for yourself from your own pastoral manager or head of department.

Tutor as student advocate or mediator

Not all students progress smoothly through their schooling and some come into conflict with individual teachers or other students, or seriously transgress school rules. Tutors can take on the role of a respected adult who knows the student well enough to speak on their behalf. They can provide insight into contributing reasons and may suggest ways forward that are seen as fair by all parties, during a case conference, for example. A tutor can also support a student in expressing his or her own view, in ways that might be better listened to and taken notice of.

Tutoring as a process for raising achievement

The term **academic tutor** describes a role in school that is becoming increasingly significant as a school strengthens its provision to support students to maximize their potential. Some schools apply the traditional divide between pastoral and classroom based tutoring but this is beginning to disappear. Tutoring and guidance is seen increasingly as a task for all teachers, aimed at helping students taking responsibility for themselves and their learning in taught subject time as well as in form time. However, the form tutor is the only person who has an overview of their tutees and their relative strengths and weaknesses in all aspects of their learning, and it falls to them to act as both academic and personal tutor. You may wish to refer back to Chapters 2 and 4 for more on the variety of approaches to *personalized learning*. Flexible timetabling may place even greater responsibility on the form tutor's role in monitoring academic and personal performance, maintaining good records and reporting to school managers as well as parents/carers.

Academic tutoring requires teachers to develop an understanding of their students as learners and what motivates or impedes their progress. Form tutors who know their students well take early action to support students appropriately. In undertaking this role tutors draw heavily on their own knowledge about the school – its planned and hidden curricula – to help students make informed choices, to interpret and make sense of different approaches used by subject teachers, and to intercede on their behalf.

Munby (1995) has described three challenging principles to learner-centred assessment (see also Chapter 5) which are critical to effective academic tutoring. One is based on understanding the essential difference between **achievement** and **attainment**. An achievement-based approach is crucial, with opportunities for students to self-assess. A whole-school tutorial system can help the student make sense of attainment information and provide a person-centred context. A second principle is to involve the students in the assessment process, not only because it is motivating as a learner, but also because, by involving them, the assessment judgements are more likely to be accurate. A third is that there should be effective strategies for raising individual achievement which involve the **SMART** framework for target-setting (see also Chapter 5).

By applying these principles, the form tutor's role becomes clearer, helping students: to make sense of advice, (or sometimes conflicting advice given by different subject teachers); to make links between learning in different contexts; and, to help students set priorities and develop strategies to succeed. Carnell and Lodge (2002a) present a strong argument for developing *learning to learn* programmes in school. They develop their evidence and arguments further in 'Support for students' learning: what the form tutor can do' (2002b). In this article you will find practical ideas on how to put in place these approaches with a tutor group. The role of dialogue between tutor and student(s) and between student and student is rooted in constructivist approaches to learning (see Chapter 2) and is central to the success of developing effective learners. In advocating that form tutors take a lead role in this process, Carnell and Lodge (2002b) highlight the fact that only they have an overall view of their students as learners (see also Table 7.2). Target-setting using the *plan, do, review* cycle (see Chapter 1) is also a central part of the process. Such ways of working with students are not new. Waterhouse (1991) claimed that academic, as well as personal and social benefits can be gained by using the tutoring strategies such as small-group tutorials with carefully structured agendas. These have a place in both pastoral and subject tutorial work. The **Excellence in Cities** initiative specified a new role of **Learning Mentor** to support students whose progress is below that expected for their key stage. The idea has been further developed through the *National Secondary Strategy* (see Chapter 3). Learning mentors can form close relationships with form tutors and other teachers, sharing information to support the students.

Web activity 7(2) – Tutoring students

To gain a wider international perspective on the role of the tutor in raising standards in schools, have a look at the article by Nadge (2005). Its focus on developing *resilient* students resonates with both the ECM outcomes (see Chapter 6), and the aims and purposes of the most recent guidance for a new type of personal–social curriculum as set out in the two new non-statutory programmes of study of the new secondary curriculum for England: Personal Social Health and Economic Education (*PSHEE*) (QCA, 2007a; 2007b).

Activity 7.7 provides you with an opportunity to develop your skills in conducting a *learning conversation* (see also Chapter 1). It builds on the reflective processes described in Chapter 1. You will find it useful to refer to the information in Table 7.2 first. The table sets out the four stages of a 'learning conversation', identifying the skills tutors need to use at each stage, and suggests prompts to focus on both how and what students are learning.

Table 7.2 Stages in a learning conversation for tutor–student dialogue

Stage of learning conversation	The tutor can:	Tutor prompts to support reflective learning of student	Tutor prompts to support development of student's subject knowledge/skills/ …
1. Explore the situation	• listen actively • ask open questions • be non-judgemental	What is going well? What are the challenges? What is not going so well …? How do you feel (about this)?	What has excited you in your learning (about teaching this subject)? What are you finding interesting …?
2. Identify new insights/ understandings	• empathize • reflect back • share new insights	How do you make sense of what is happening? What new insights have you have gained? Have you noticed any patterns in your learning? What helps your learning? What seems to stop your learning?	Does this lesson link to previous knowledge? Have you noticed any patterns in this topic? Describe something you found difficult to understand in the topic? … something you were unsure of in the topic?
3. Take the learning forward	• help establish clear, negotiated goals • help with action planning and target-setting (focus targets on the *learning* to be achieved, rather than on the *performance*)	What will your next steps be …? What, or who, do you need to help you progress? If you get stuck, who will you talk to? When will the next review be helpful to you?	What do you want to find out about next? What questions do you need to ask now? What will you do first?

(Continued)

Table 7.2 *(Continued)*

Stage of learning conversation	The tutor can:	Tutor prompts to support reflective learning of student	Tutor prompts to support development of student's subject knowledge/skills/ …
4. Stand back from the conversation and consider how it helped or hindered learning (meta-cognition)	(See items for stage 1)	What did you notice about this conversation? In what ways did you find it effective? Describe the changes in your feelings during the tutorial. In what ways are you finding talking about your learning more effective? Is there anything you are noticing about my role that is helping or hindering you?	What did you notice about this conversation? In what ways did you find it effective? Did you learn anything new during the session? In what ways are you finding talking about this topic helpful?

Source: adapted from Carnell and Lodge, 2002b

Activity 7.7   Planning, enacting and evaluating a *learning conversation*

This is an individual activity aimed at developing your understanding and skills of academic tutoring. You may find it useful to review how well the activity worked with another beginning or experienced teacher and identify what you might do better next time.

a) Read the article by Carnell and Lodge (2002) 'Support for students' learning: what the form tutor can do' in *Pastoral Care in Education*, 20(4): 12–20.

b) Study Table 7.2 that sets out the four stages of a *learning conversation* with students. The aim of using this type of structured approach is to help students to focus on their learning: to think about how they learn and what helps or hinders them. In completing this activity you should develop your understanding and skills of academic tutoring.

c) Now, identify a suitable opportunity (for example in preparation for a parents' meeting, or at the start of an extended piece of individual work with a student) in order to use this approach with one or more individuals in your tutor group or one of your teaching groups.

Using the framework, plan an agenda and write out a list of appropriate prompts for each stage for a 10-minute 'conversation'. It is important to keep (i) the questions and prompts open-ended, inviting responses and discussion; and (ii) to allow time for students to think before answering. If possible, try out your plan at the designated event.

d) Evaluate the activity. You should consider:

- Did it help or hinder to have a planned agenda?

- What worked well?

- Was the student able to talk about their learning confidently or did you need to use a number of prompts?

- Did you feel pressed for time or was 10 minutes long enough?

- What changes would you make when using this approach again?

e) Think about what you have learned about this approach from your reading and practical experiences. Make a list of what you think are the advantages and disadvantages of using this approach to help students as learners and discuss these with your mentor.

Reporting to parents and carers

As a result of changes in emphasis on academic tutoring it is now less usual for schools to run the more traditional parents'/carers' meetings in which student progress is reported and discussed with different subject teachers. Drawing on a range of evidence of progress from other teachers, the form tutor reports and discusses a wide range of issues relating to academic and personal progress. They focus on how the school, the teachers and the parents/carers can work together to support the student's continuing progress. This approach draws on research into home–school relationships such as that of Askew (2000) which suggests that schools need to develop more collaborative models of working with parents which include consultation and shared decision-making. Findings from his research suggest that schools should recognize rather more the particular expertise of parents in supporting learning and work with them.

Web activity 7(3) – Reporting to parents and carers: tutors or subject teachers?

Developing skills and attitudes for effective tutoring

Having what is described in therapeutic settings as **unconditional positive regard** for each student lies at the heart of the range of counselling and tutoring skills that you may draw on in both your class and form tutor work in schools. It can be very difficult to achieve this state, not only in relation to each member of a tutor group, but for individuals in all the classes you teach. You will meet a few students who seem actively to seek to be disruptive. They reject help and support and often betray trust. They break promises and can create difficulties with other staff with whom they repeatedly come into conflict. Tutors who work at getting to know their students are likely to find it easier to find something positive about each of them; there will be some redeeming feature to make the effort needed on your part to support them worthwhile. In very difficult circumstances your focus must be on the poor behaviour and not the student himself or herself. With growing experience you will learn that repeated, challenging student behaviour is often explained by their life outside school. For most these are discrete, one-off incidents; for others a chaotic home life may be the norm – school and its boundaries for behaviour may be the only point of stability in their lives. Occasionally a form tutor may identify other behaviours that might suggest the need for specialist counselling or other qualified expert or psychiatric help.

Here we shall enlarge on a group of interpersonal skills which might be referred to rather loosely as counselling skills. There are three aspects that are important to highlight, and Activity 7.8 allows you to work with others to understand these better. Read the brief descriptions which follow first.

Active and accurate listening

This is the most fundamental counselling skill. The tutor has to give their undivided attention, maintaining eye-contact and ensuring the speaker is comfortable and unhurried. It includes confirming with the speaker the facts and feelings expressed so that they hear their own concerns and can check what they have said is really what they mean.

Empathy

This requires the tutor to try to understand the world through the student's eyes.

Honesty and openness

The tutor has to make clear from the outset what information can be kept confidential and what issues require the involvement of outside help and expertise, usually pastoral leaders, senior managers, or the school counsellor in the first instance. It is important that students understand the limits to the help the tutor can give so that they do not build up unrealistic expectations.

Activity 7.8   Developing your counselling skills

This is intended as a small-group activity for groups of beginning teachers.

Listening skills

EITHER

Organize your group of *three* into A, B and C. A and B discuss a controversial subject while C acts as adjudicator. A makes a statement on the subject. B para-phrases the idea, beginning with something like … 'so what you're saying is … ' with no judgement or interpretation. A then tells B whether or not her response was accurate. If there was some misunderstanding A should make the correction and B should feed back her new understanding of the statement. Continue this process until A is sure that B understands. C should monitor this. Change roles.

OR

Carry out the above but act *in role*. Imagine A is a student with one of the following concerns:

'No one in the class is my friend and I want to move out of this tutor group.'

'She has been calling me names and saying things about my Mum.'

Review how successful the listener was in accurately interpreting the statements made by the speaker.

Responding skills

a) Organize yourselves into groups of about 6. One person makes a statement about something which is/has been important to them. Each of the others responds with a comment or question which they think will encourage the client to say more. The first person then says which responses they found helpful and which were off-putting, and the group discusses reasons and possible improvements. You can pursue the exchange further if you wish. Take it in turns to make a statement.

b) Make a composite list of helpful and off-putting responses. Select some responses that you think will help you to gain the confidence of students you work with.

(Continued)

(Continued)

Developing empathy

For pairs/groups of three.

a) Your close friend has applied for at least 25 positions in the past three months and has been turned down for each of them. You know him/her to be a very able person and think very highly of him/her as a person and as a professional. You know that he/she is pretty low at the moment and could well do with some ego boosting. What will you do? Think of a real friend and devise three strategies which could help him/her given the above situation. Discuss with a partner what strategies he/she has thought of and why.

b) Working in groups of three (interviewer, interviewee, observer), plan and then conduct an induction interview with a new student or beginning teacher, to try to discover as much as possible about the likes and dislikes, attitudes and prejudices of the newcomer.

- The interviewer and the observer should write some questions to use in the interview. Provide both *closed* and *open* questions.

- The interviewer carries out the interview with the interviewee. The observer watches and notices: (i) which questions and prompts assist the interviewee to talk; (ii) details such as body language and non-verbal cues which occur between the interviewer–interviewee.

- Together all three draw up a checklist of good interviewing skills which support effective communication.

c) In pairs, discuss how you would investigate a petty theft in your tutor group. You suspect three pupils, with one as the likely ringleader.

Join up with another pair and role-play the interview with one as teacher and three as the suspected pupils.

Review the activity to identify what did or did not work well. Discuss possible ways of eliciting responses from reluctant students.

d) Are there any aspects of juvenile behaviour which you find particularly distasteful or upsetting? In a small group (five to eight), brainstorm different types of unacceptable behaviour. Discuss how to deal with possible incidents in a constructive and non-judgemental way.

Sanger concluded from his research that teachers' beliefs about morality 'play a significant role in their teaching practice and who they are as teachers' (2001: 698). The National Curriculum for England sets out a 'broad set of common values' (DfEE/QCA, 2000: 10) that underpin the school curriculum with the implicit expectation that all teachers will support and promote these values. The preamble recognizes the demanding nature of the statements which is 'demonstrated by our collective failure consistently to live up to them, and the moral challenge which acting on them in practice entails' (DfEE/QCA, 2000: 195). In completing Activity 7.9 you will consider the statement of values (DfEE/QCA, 2000: 195–7) and identify any possible conflicts with your own and prepare yourself for dealing with any moral challenges that you can anticipate in your role as a teacher.

Activity 7.9   Whose values?

This is an individual and small-group activity.

a) Make a list of the *values* that you think schools should promote. Share these with one or more of your colleagues and try to suggest why these may be the same or different?

b) Consult and compare the statements of values in the National Curriculum *Handbook* (DfEE/QCA, 2000: 195–7) and those presented in the CSCS Broadsheet 83 *Some sources of values, religious and secular* (April, 2007).

  • Are there any surprises?

  • Are there any values that you disagree with in these sources?

  • If there are, do you think this will affect your practice as a teacher? How?

  Identify any wider social values that seem to be at odds with the values schools are exhorted to promote. For example, does the current trend to expand the choice of schools for parents (including private schools), the setting up of a seeming hierarchy of schools with fierce competition for places, and public ranking in league tables go against the promotion by schools of the values of social justice and fairness stated in *Every Child Matters*?

c) Find out if/how the values promoted by your placement school have been established and shared with the school community. Ask your mentor or a senior teacher if they have contributed to any discussions about values and ethos in any (other) schools they have worked in and if they think this should be done. Do they think it is taken for granted that the school community holds a common set of values?

THE PERSONAL–SOCIAL CURRICULUM AND ITS RELATIONSHIP WITH OTHER AREAS OF THE WHOLE CURRICULUM

The personal–social curriculum is difficult to define. It is concerned with affective education. Thus, it includes all those aspects of education that, implicitly or explicitly, address the social, cultural, intellectual, physical, emotional, moral, spiritual and economic development of students. These aspects might include careers education and guidance and some elements of education for citizenship, or of religious education or of drama. To be effective all teachers need to understand the nature of affective education and their roles in its delivery.

Personal, social and health education (PSHE)

This section will consider the aims and content of PSHE programmes and consider some of the learning and teaching approaches used in its teaching. There are a number of links to be made with Chapters 2, 3 and 6 in particular.

It was not until a review of the National Curriculum in 2000 that provision for personal, social and health education became a requirement for all secondary schools, and government guidelines (non-statutory) were put in place (DfEE/QCA, 2000). The guidelines were developed to help schools to establish both coherence and consistency in their programmes to ensure continuity and progression. Sex and relationships education (SRE) and careers education are mandatory requirements along with key skills and aspects such as parenting, financial capability, enterprise and entrepreneurial skills, work-related learning and education for sustainable development. Elements of all of these can be found in PSHE curricula. Since the introduction of citizenship in 2002 many schools have included it as part of the PSHE programme (see Chapter 6 for further discussion on this aspect) with no additional time allowance (Ofsted, 2007a: para: 44.19). Where this happens, it is generally to the detriment of both areas. Schools find it difficult to identify sufficient curriculum time to address either area thoroughly. The result can be fragmented programmes focusing narrowly on developing students' subject knowledge and understanding at the expense of developing their skills and attitudes (Ofsted, 2007a: para. 41.18).

What are the values that underpin the PSHE curriculum?

The words in the introduction to the National Curriculum set a challenging and aspirational agenda for all those who exert influence on students (a) by their attitudes towards them, (b) through the educational provision made for them, and (c) by the example set in dealings with them:

> Foremost is a belief in education, at home and at school, as a route to the spiritual, moral, social, cultural, physical and mental development, and thus the well-being, of the individual. Education is also a route to equality of opportunity for all, a healthy and just democracy, a productive economy, and sustainable development. Education should reflect the enduring values that

contribute to these ends. These include valuing ourselves, our families and other relationships, the wider groups to which we belong, the diversity in our society and the environment in which we live. Education should also reaffirm our commitment to the virtues of truth, justice, honesty, trust and a sense of duty.

At the same time, education must enable us to respond positively to the opportunities and challenges of the rapidly changing world in which we live and work. In particular, we need to be prepared to engage as individuals, parents, workers and citizens with economic, social and cultural change, including the continued globalisation of the economy and society, with new work and leisure patterns and with the rapid expansion of communication technologies. (DFEE/QCA, 2000: 10)

For PSHE the challenge to schools is to achieve a balance between the broader aims of education and, as presented in Chapter 6, the increasingly politically-driven aims of recent governments to prepare a skilled workforce for economic prosperity.

In a jointly-written document, *Curriculum 11–16*, the government and HMI illustrated this tension perfectly:

the educational system is charged by society ... with equipping young people to take their place as citizens and workers in adult life ... Secondly there is the responsibility for educating the 'autonomous citizen', a person able to think and act for herself or himself, to resist exploitation, to innovate and to be vigilant in the defence of liberty. These two functions do not always fit easily together. (DES/HMI, 1977: 9)

Since then, there has been increasing attention given to the whole area of enterprise, economic well-being and the world of work. The curriculum review of 2007 identifies personal, social, health and economic education (PSHEE), separating it into two areas: *personal well-being* and *economic well-being* (QCA, 2007a; 2007b). In so doing, it seems to acknowledge the need to support schools in developing curricula that prepare students for a rapidly-changing global world in which the only certainty may be uncertainty. At the time of writing it remains to be seen how these broader agendas for the personal and social curricula can and will be extended within the available curriculum time.

Articulating and implementing the aims of PSHE

It was probably in recognition of difficulties experienced by many schools in planning coherently for PSHE that the revised National Curriculum (DFEE/QCA, 2000) included both exacting aims for personal and social development and a framework and ministerial guidelines (DFEE/QCA, 2000:

188–94). The framework included a statement stating the importance of PSHE in helping students to:

- lead confident, healthy and responsible lives as individuals and as members of society
- gain practical knowledge and skills to help them live healthily and deal with the spiritual, moral, social and cultural issues they face as they approach adulthood
- have time to reflect on their experiences and how they are developing
- understand and manage responsibly a wider range of relationships as they mature
- recognize diversity and show respect for differences and similarities between people
- develop well-being and self-esteem, encouraging belief in their ability to succeed and enabling them to take responsibility for their learning and future choice of career.

These aspects are grouped in the guidelines into three broad areas:

1. Developing confidence and responsibility and making the most of their abilities.
2. Developing a healthy, safer lifestyle.
3. Developing good relationships and respecting the differences between people.

So, how do schools rise to such guidelines? There are many challenges to be overcome: time allocations for PSHE are often limited; numerous approaches and materials might be used; timetabling can result in haphazard, unconnected sets of PSHE lessons which might not focus on developing behaviours and attitudes. Nevertheless, PSHE provides an important framework for planning the whole curriculum. It has the potential also to meet the complex agendas of 14–19 education, personalized learning, and the outcomes of ECM, and so on. Activity 7.10 should assist you in thinking about how different subject areas can contribute to PSHE – in other words, how PSHE might *permeate* a whole school curriculum.

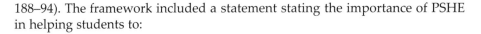

Activity 7.10   How can different subjects contribute to the required core for PSHE?

This can be completed as an individual activity, or with one or more beginning teachers with the same (or different) subject specialisms.

The following list includes the subjects that schools *must* teach that sit within the PSHE programme:

- sex and relationships education: to include teaching about HIV/AIDS and other sexually transmitted infections. Note that parents can withdraw their children from part or all of the programme

- parenting skills

- drugs education to include alcohol and tobacco

- careers education and guidance for Years 9, 10 and 11, with access provided to officers in the careers service. See Connexions website

- explicit opportunities to promote spiritual, moral, social and cultural development (SMSC)

- education for financial capability; opportunities to develop enterprise and entrepreneurial skills to support career flexibility

- work-related learning opportunities such as enterprise activities and work experience; opportunities to develop their understanding of sustainable development

- education for sustainable development.

Although many of these topics are taught in discrete PSHE lessons, most schools devolve some responsibility to subject teachers where they have particular expertise. Consult the National Curriculum *Handbook* (DfEE/QCA, 2000) and the QCA (2007) web-based resources (www.qca.org.uk) 'Opportunities for personal development in the revised programmes of study' to identify what aspects of PSHE your subject has a particular responsibility for.

a) *Select one area* that interests you, from the list above. Plan a lesson for your subject group. Identify how this lesson might differ in content, planned learning outcomes, or learning approach used if you addressed it from a PSHE perspective, rather than a subject perspective. In what ways would the learning outcomes be the same or different?

b) Discuss with your mentor:

   i)   your responses to this activity

   ii) whether the school/department is explicitly required to contribute to the PSHE curriculum

   iii) whether there are systems in place to monitor and evaluate the effectiveness of the contribution of each subject area.

In planning the personal–social curriculum, teachers first need to consider *what* they want students to learn, including the knowledge, understanding, skills and attributes for personal development. They then need to address *how* best to do this by selecting appropriate teaching and learning activities. As part of a secondary curriculum review, the QCA has developed a revised set of aims for a National Curriculum which it proposes should be the starting point for any curriculum design. The suggested three overarching aims are that it should enable all young people to become:

1. Successful learners who enjoy learning, make progress and achieve.
2. Confident individuals, able to live safe, healthy and fulfilling lives.
3. Responsible citizens, who make a positive contribution to society.

In common with all subjects the new programmes of study for personal social health and economic education (PSHEE) set out the key concepts and processes, the range and content and the curriculum opportunities that should be offered to enable students to achieve the overarching aims set out above (QCA, 2007a; 2007b). You can find these and all the support and guidance at www.qca.org.uk/secondarycurriculumreview/. The review offers a number of ways of tackling implementation to meet the revised requirements. These include curriculum planning tools to help schools undertake systematic reviews of their provision for the whole personal–social curriculum to ensure the values they promote their programmes.

The revival of personal–social education

The concerns for young people that have contributed to the development of the *Every Child Matters* agenda (see Chapter 6) support the case for putting those aspects of the curriculum that support students' personal development at the heart of curriculum planning rather than it being a peripheral or fragmented activity. There is concern for the future health of young people and research confirms the risks that they take with their health and well-being (visit the Schools Health Education Unit website at www.sheu.org.uk to access their research on the behaviour of young people). Watkins (2004) sets out the recent trends that resulted in a narrow subject-based curriculum and contributed to the marginalization of all aspects of pastoral care, and makes a strong case for reclaiming its place at the heart of curriculum planning. A further development in 2006 was the creation of a National Subject Association for PSHE, supported by the government and based at the National Children's Bureau in London. It aims to offer a central support network for teachers with opportunities for accredited professional development. The Office for Standards in Education (2007b) also provides a strong steer to schools to recognize the importance of PSHE in the personal and social development of their students.

Emotional intelligence (EI), or emotional health, is referred to in Chapter 2 and concern for this aspect of personal development has also contributed to the revival of PSHE. The article by Qualter et al. (2007) introduces research in this area of EI and highlights potential benefits to schools. The SEAL project (Social and Emotional Aspects of Learning) supported by the DfES as part of the *Primary and Secondary National Strategies* provides guidance and resources for the explicit development of social, emotional and behavioural skills. The website provides information about the project and its resources:

http://bandapilot.org.uk/secondary/. The initial evaluations of the project have seen successes in improving behaviour and reducing incidences of bullying. Perhaps, not surprisingly, the greatest impact has been on teachers' attitudes and understanding of students' social and emotional development (Ofsted, 2007b).

There are two factors that have made school governors and senior managers of schools more aware of their responsibilities in PSHE than previously. These are separate but complementary. The first is the *National Healthy Schools Programme* (see Chapter 6). In order to meet the standards to gain *healthy school* status, schools must show that they have an effective PSHE programme. It requires demonstration of a whole-school approach that deals with the four core themes: PSHE (including SRE and drug education); healthy eating; physical activity; and emotional health and well-being (including bullying).

The second factor relates to the way in which PSHE is reported by Ofsted when it inspects schools. A shorter Ofsted inspection framework relies on judgements, largely based on evidence provided by the schools, on how well they make provision for the personal, health, social, moral and cultural education of their students. This evidence is checked against the practice observed by inspectors, and their discussions with students about student experiences. The questions are directly related to the five outcomes of ECM and indicate clearly where provision needs to be improved in this area.

How is PSHE provided in schools?

Because PSHE cannot be confined to specific timetabled time a variety of forms of provision are appropriate and used in combination at different times. Provision is likely to comprise some or all of the following:

- a formal programme in a regular timetabled slot and most commonly taught by the form tutor
- aspects of the programme ideally taught by a specialist team of trained PSHE staff
- contributions by experts such as local health care staff, careers guidance and connexions, the police, youth workers, the business community
- aspects of the programme taught by subject teachers
- PSHE activities and school events, including off-timetable days. These may include the work of the school council, and planned opportunities for students to take responsibility, for example, looking after visitors.

These contributions may be delivered in discrete lessons; at themed assemblies; on days or weeks devoted to healthy eating and being active; careers guidance or business and enterprise activities; through subject teaching where aspects of the PSHE programme form part of their curriculum. There are many possible examples here: physical education lessons/developing active lifestyles; science lessons dealing with reproduction/pregnancy, genetics/ethical and moral dilemmas; Maths lessons dealing with understanding interest rates/personal finance; history lessons developing empathetic responses to events that may have enduring impact on society; geography lessons considering the impact of globalization on rich and poor economies/personal and social responsibility; English lessons where the texts cover the controversial or personal issues that adolescents may have to deal with (such as alcohol or drug use, abortion, bullying, rejection, aspects of sexuality or discrimination).

You might find it useful to consult *Meeting the Standard in PSHE* (NCB, 2006). It contains a useful diagram that shows how national and international policy has impacted on the development of PSHE. This and other helpful resources can be found in the resources section of the National Children's Bureau website: www.ncb.org.uk.

Activity 7.11   How is PSHE provided in schools?

Part 1. Where do you stand?

Consider your own reactions to the PSHE curriculum and its delivery.

Various PSHE co-ordinators have characterized the reactions of some of their colleagues as follows:

- I'm interested in my subject, that's what I know about

- I really don't know much about it – and I don't particularly want to

- I feel uneasy about the implicit messages in PSHE – the meddling, the manipulation, the promotion of certain values

- I don't feel I can be a teacher in control of a class one minute, and a counsellor or friend the next

- I think it's best left to teachers who like doing this kind of thing

   a) Do any of the above articulate your own views? If none of these statements apply to you, write another sentence to describe your own view point.

   Either on your own *or* in a small group of beginning teachers:

   b) For each of the five statements (bullet points) above, prepare a short commentary (of the sort that a PSHE coordinator might use to try to win over a reluctant colleague, or, to contribute to a school debate in a staff meeting).

c) After rehearsing and/or listening to the arguments presented by others, have your views changed at all?

d) Talk to the PSHE co-ordinator or manager in your school or college.

    i) What problems has s/he encountered in the job?

    ii) How does s/he see the future development of PSHE?

Summarize the points made in the interview and compare these with other beginning teachers in different placement schools in order to identify similarities and differences. Is there general agreement about the importance of PHSE in helping schools meet their overall aims?

Part 2. Identifying possible types of delivery of PSHE

a) Consider the delivery of a personal, social and health education (PSHE) curriculum in your placement school (or one that you apply to teach in). Weigh up the advantages and disadvantages of the structures and organization for it. Consider the extent to which all teachers are expected to contribute, and how.

The following questions should help you explore the main issues:

- Is there discrete curriculum time? (Is there a planned curriculum time for PSHE? Is there a team of specialist teachers who deliver all or part of this?)

- Is PSHE taught through other subjects or curriculum areas? (See *The National Curriculum Handbook for Secondary Teachers in England*, DfEE/QCA, 2000. How is full coverage of the PSHE Framework at Key Stages 3 and 4 ensured? What are the particular contributions of your specialist area?)

- Is it delivered through PSHE activities and school events? (Who contributes to these? What are the contributions from outside visitors? Which students participate?)

- Is it delivered through pastoral care and guidance? (What is delivered in tutor time either formally and/or informally? Do students have access to other health professionals or a school counsellor?)

b) Review your responses with other beginning teachers from different subject areas to this activity. Do you have a better understanding of how schools provide a PSHE curriculum? Make a list of where you as a beginning teacher would be expected to contribute to it.

Characteristics of effective PSHE

There are some well-supported characteristics of effective programmes that relate to what is taught, how it is taught and by whom. These general principles are consistent and could be applied to any subject area.

A whole-school approach

Aggleton et al. (1999) in their research on the National Healthy School Standard, found evidence that a whole-school approach to PSHE can also contribute to school improvement. Curriculum planning tools are provided online by QCA to promote this approach and can be found in the secondary curriculum area at www.qca.org.uk/. The toolkit includes ways of reviewing basic values and school ethos to bring about the commitment of the entire school community.

Identifying students' particular needs

The most effective programmes are tailored to the particular needs of students. Schools with good practice actively engage their students to find out what they think about their school experiences, ensure students know their opinions count and give them power to put them into practice (Ofsted, 2007b). See also Smith (1998).

Quality of teaching and learning

Effective lessons are given by teachers and others who are confident about the area they are teaching. They use a broad range of approaches and plan in detail. They prepare to deal well with any awkward or potentially embarrassing questions. Few teachers are trained specifically to teach PSHE and, where schools have trained their own specialist teams, this is generally the most successful approach. A balance has to be struck between imparting knowledge and developing understanding and supporting students to develop skills that will help them. Lessons that are differentiated can meet the developmental needs of the students and build on earlier learning to ensure progression (see Chapter 2). In some schools form tutors are required to teach PSHE. As a beginning teacher in such circumstances try to access ongoing training and support, particularly in the use of appropriate teaching methods.

Schools regularly monitor, evaluate and assess their provision

Measuring learning and impact in this area of PSHE is a particular challenge. Traditional methods of assessment do not apply easily; many learning outcomes may not reveal themselves for many years. However, without some form of assessment teachers cannot begin to evaluate their teaching or the level of learning. Students, too, need to be encouraged to self-evaluate their learning and to identify (and reflect on) changes in their attitudes. Regis (2000) uses survey findings to report on young people's opinions of their experiences of PSHE. Inman et al. (1998) provide both rationales and practical suggestions for implementing effective assessment practice for personal and social development that you will find stimulating and useful in your own teaching. During 2008 the QCA will be adding guidance materials and examples of effective assessment activities for personal well being to the assessment section of their website at http://curriculum.qca.org.uk/assessment/index.aspx. In addition, providing ways of recording progress and achievement in PSHE such as portfolios or progress files (see Chapter 5) can provide motivation and help *personal development* to be given greater status and value in the school.

Strong links with support services

Schools endeavour to establish links with a range of support services. As an example, some students prefer to seek advice and guidance on some sensitive issues from adults other than teachers. Establishing drop-in centres on the school premises along with other services linked to extended school provision is an effective way of meeting such needs.

An extensive programme of extra-curricular activities

Schools recognize the benefits to the students of providing an attractive programme of extra-curricular activities to enhance the formal curriculum. These can be provided by teachers, youth and community workers, parents, sports coaches and other volunteers and experts. Students can be involved in planning this programme and may be involved in teaching, where they have expertise. Schools should provide opportunities for off-site and residential experiences.

Whatever approaches to the PSHE curriculum schools actually choose, they are likely to have the following elements in their PSHE curriculum. You can use the checklist that follows (Table 7.3) to identify to what extent these elements exist in your placement school and who has responsibility for them.

Teaching approaches used in PSHE

Many of the suggestions for active learning given in Chapter 3 have a place here. You need to use approaches that enable students to discuss, to challenge

Table 7.3 Checklist for examining opportunities in school for contributing to PSHE provision

Elements of a school's PHSE curriculum that provides opportunities for	x-none ✓ – some ✓✓ – good ✓✓✓ – excellent	Where? By whom? – PSHE – Subject area – Other (specify)
Moral, cultural and spiritual development		
Awareness of the common values and how these translate into action?		
Opportunities to think about own beliefs and those of others?		
Opportunities to become aware of the role of tolerance and gain respect for others?		
Good interpersonal relationships		
Opportunities to understand the roles they will have to prepare for as they mature (e.g. being a parent)?		
Emotional development and mental well-being		
Opportunities to become aware of how behaviour affects others?		
Opportunities to learn how to cope in stressful situations?		
Adopting a healthy lifestyle and knowing the risks associated with choosing not to		
Becoming (knowing how to become) active, eating well, basic hygiene, making assessment of risk when making choices? Knowing about the dangers (and choices associated with them) of drug/substance use, including alcohol?		
Understanding how they develop sexually and knowing the risks they take when engaging in sexual activity		
Opportunities to learn how to develop healthy relationships and take responsibility for their actions?		

(Continued)

Table 7.3 *(Continued)*

Elements of a school's PHSE curriculum that provides opportunities for	x-none ✓ – some ✓✓ – good ✓✓✓ – excellent	Where? By whom? – PSHE – Subject area – Other (specify)
Contributing to their own and the wider community		
Opportunities to become more aware of sustainable development?		
Opportunities to participate in sustainable school initiatives?		
Preparation for career choices and the world of work		
Gaining awareness of individual actions in supporting a successful economy?		
Opportunities for enterprise and entrepreneurial activities and a period of work-experience?		
Developing study skills to support themselves as effective and independent learners		
List the opportunities that occur across the curriculum.		

and be challenged, to question experts and peers, to explore their own ideas and values, to acquire a range of complex skills to help them build successful relationships. Often, in a time-restricted programme, teaching approaches have to be selected that can combine acquiring knowledge and developing skills at the same time. All this can be daunting at the start of a teaching career.

Lessons need planning to take advantage of a *Reflecting–Practising–Learning–Planning* cycle. When developing the skills of co-operation, team-work, listening and conflict resolution for example, it seems obvious to use approaches that require students to co-operate, listen to each other, to work as a team to complete a task, or mediate in a simulation.

A summary of suitable and effective active teaching approaches is given below. All these can be used to help students to identify personal response to issues, to examine the values held by them and others, to explore different values and to understand that having a different opinion is legitimate. The best approaches encourage discussion and reporting back. Video, television, magazine and newspaper articles can be used to stimulate debate and, by producing their own media, students can make powerful assessments of their understanding and achievement in aspects of PSHE. Careful consideration needs to be given to types of group work (see Chapters 3 and 4).

Circle time

The group agrees a set of ground rules that encourage everyone to speak and listen and to know that their contribution will be valued. It is common to use an object such as a *say-stick* that gives the holder permission to speak. It can be passed around the circle or simply handed to others who indicate they wish to speak. It may ask students to change places and so helps the group to get to know each other better. Once the routines and rules are established and students appear comfortable and willingly participate, this approach can be used to tackle issues that are causing concern in the class, for example, incidences of bullying or theft. It can also be used to discuss religious, moral, spiritual and cultural issues.

Problem-solving and trust exercises

These are often used early in the year to help develop group identity and interpersonal relationships. Team-building activities – building bridges using limited equipment, or transferring safely members of the group from one place to another – can be used. Many *enterprise activities*, where groups compete to produce the most articles in a given time, can come into this category.

Role play

This approach is used widely in subject teaching. It provides a way of getting to difficult issues quickly, as students assume their roles. It requires students to take on the position of a different person and to explore the feelings and attitudes that they might take. It can help students to accept that the opinions of others are often deeply rooted in their personal experiences and help them to accept difference as normal. It frees students to talk about events, concerns, and personal issues that they might not feel able to do while being themselves. It is important to plan sufficient time to debrief these lessons so that students have time to articulate their feelings and *let go* emotionally of any role that has been taken on or affected them.

Case studies

These allow for approach for engaging students in discussion about controversial or sensitive issues, such as abortion. Different viewpoints can be explored. Dilemma-based case studies can challenge students to suggest solutions or best outcomes for the participants. (See also Chaper 4.)

Thought-showering or word storming

This is commonly used to find out quickly what prior learning students have on the issue. It is normally completed as a whole-class activity and all students are encouraged to make their contribution and all are recorded. The contributions can be used to identify issues to explore further. Students may be given *Post-its* or *stickies* on which to write their ideas. These can be attached to posters and displayed for viewing by the group to provoke further discussion or planned activity. A similar approach, called *snowballing*, is used to share responses to an open question such as, 'Make a list of the qualities of a successful student'. Each student makes their own list. They join another person and compare responses. The pairs join to form a group of four, then eight, and so on. Both approaches enable students to access the responses of many others and can prompt them to reflect on and refine their original ideas.

Clarification of values or understanding

These approaches use a continuum or line on which to locate students' strength of feelings about particular ideas/beliefs. Students are asked to move to a particular part of the line in the room to indicate their response to a question. For example: 'If you agree with the statement "all people are equal", move to the left; if you disagree move to the right'. Thus, students place themselves somewhere on a line from those who 'strongly agree' at one end to those who 'strongly disagree' at the other. It requires students to move towards different places on the line, according to level of their positive or negative response and provides for 'I don't know/I am uncertain' as an option.

The activity can be used to prepare students for further structured activity that might culminate in a short presentation to the class. This approach can also be used to elicit understanding of sensitive issues likes AIDS/HIV by having a list of frequently asked questions which students can respond to.

Ranking or sorting exercises

These can help students to identify what they think are the most and least important aspects of an issue. Students are given individual cards containing statements or pictures and asked to sort them into simple categories such as agree/disagree, like/dislike, acceptable/unacceptable, depending on the statements. The activity is normally organized in small groups to ensure all can contribute. Each group might be asked to identify a small number of statements that they agree on and may be required to share their selection with the rest of the class or other groups. They might be asked to use a number of methods of ranking, or to choose one that they are familiar with. They might be given the option to add their own statements. It is common for students to justify their ranking and to explain how they tackled the task as a group or how they resolved any differences of opinion.

Maps or pictures from memory

Students are asked to replicate a graphic (for example, a map, cartoon, diagram chart) as a group. Each takes it in turns to have a brief look at the graphic and returns to add to the group response. Students are encouraged to develop a strategic approach to the activity and allocate each member with a specific task. The graphic itself will carry important information or ideas. However, the process of completing the task successfully as a team is the main objective. It is important for the group to review the activity and identify what they did well and how they might complete a similar task more successfully next time. It can provide for a *thinking skills* approach or other approaches to explore values and moral dilemmas with students.

 Web activity 7(4) – Planning a PSHE lesson

CONCLUSION

The following statement appears on the front cover of the Ofsted document, *Time for Change? Personal, Social and Health Education*:

> At a time of considerable change for personal, social and health education (PSHE), this report evaluates the current provision: whether it is based sufficiently closely on the needs of young people and how the outcomes might be best achieved. It considers the pressures that children and young people face as they mature and discusses the significant role played by most parents in advising and supporting their children. Schools and PSHE programmes in particular, have a major part to play in the personal and social development of young people. (Ofsted, 2007a)

It is clear that the personal and social development of students should be at the heart of curriculum planning and that all staff should assume some responsibility for contributing to it. In tracing the development of pastoral provision in schools in this chapter of the book, you will now be more than aware that the personal–social curriculum has been, and is, handicapped by its lack of a particular academic discipline. It has been in direct competition for curriculum time with other more distinct (academic) subjects. Its status depends greatly on the expertise and enthusiasms of key staff both in local authorities and in individual schools. It still relies on committed individuals to co-ordinate and to plan the programme. Many of these staff have undertaken additional training in order to plan and teach it effectively and to lead and support their pastoral teams. Meanwhile it continues to rely too often on reluctant or inexperienced non-specialists to teach substantial parts of the PSHE programme.

From now on, schools have great opportunities to find new ways of planning the whole curriculum including personal – social curricula: these will be driven by requirements on schools to address the ECM agenda; by the implementation of a revised National Curriculum from September 2008; and by the additional planning needed to provide access to a full range of academic and vocational courses for the 14–19 aged students. The timing is right to support a root and branch review in each school so that personal and social development can suffuse all provision and all staff can be helped to understand their part in helping students develop as persons.

We return at this juncture to the earlier work of Rogers (1980) and Pring (1984). The person-centred approach developed by Rogers in therapeutic situations has many applications in educational settings. His approach is based on a thesis 'that individuals have within them vast resources for self-understanding and for altering self-concepts, basic attitudes and self-directed behaviours … These resources can be tapped if a definable climate of facilitative psychological artefacts can be provided' (Rogers, 1980: 115). He highlighted three necessary conditions for such work, all of which have a place in your wider tutorial role in schools: genuineness, caring and empathy. Pring, too, identified a number of considerations for teachers when preparing themselves to work with young people on whose personal and social development they can have great impact. You may wish to use this list as a personal checklist. These present an enduring challenge for all teachers to practise personal–social education on a consistent basis:

- Encourage greater mutual respect between teacher and student and student and student.
- Create a climate of caring and fairness.
- Ensure a sense of achievement rather than failure, and of personal worth.

- Develop a habit of deliberation and reflective learning; introduce systematic discussion of significant socio-moral issues; approach learning co-operatively rather than competitively.
- Foster care for the group and eventually the wider community rather than for self-interest.
- Increase group responsibility for decisions taken.

Importantly, the whole area of pastoral care lends itself to more evidence-based research. Hall noted that 'teachers who are really life-long learners retain the capacity to empathise with pupils engaged in the struggle to learn' (1998: 67) and sets the challenge for teachers to add to the evidence through researching their own practice. In the opening paragraph of this chapter we alerted you to the particular challenge you have of interpreting the more general require-ments of your roles and responsibilities such as contributing to the 'all-round well-being and development of the child as a person (and not just as a pupil)' (Best, 1999: 4). To begin to analyse the effectiveness of your contribution here, we suggest that you try to separate the *task-related* and the *person-related* aspects of your various pastoral/tutorial roles (see Harrison, 2006: 444). This would allow you and your mentor to draw on a broad range of evidence for different areas of your pastoral/tutorial work.

Hoyle and John (1995), for example, identified the qualities of a teacher as someone who is tolerant, patient, gentle, sympathetic, socially conscious and responsible. How are professional judgements to be made on such qualities? How can the teachers charged with your assessment in your training year be consistent in how they interpret what these qualities mean in different con-texts? What sort of evidence can *you* provide for particular personal and professional attributes which might be deemed *virtues* rather than *skills*? These are challenging questions for the profession as a whole, as well as for you in your early career.

Within your developing professional portfolio you could begin to focus on a selection of areas of your work which are rooted in good interpersonal relationships and can be exemplified by different kinds of actions. Choose a few classroom-based scenarios to discuss with your mentor. Try posing some questions and then finding evidence for the following (these are examples):

- Are you an adequate role model for your students?
- Are you patient with your students?
- Are you selfish or generous with your time for the students and the school community?
- How do you behave with other teachers and adults in the school community?

Such questions are often not tackled directly in the course of learning conver-sations with mentors since they are highly sensitive. However beginning teachers and their mentors can begin to *model* what we have described in this chapter as effective pastoral and tutorial work with students. As with tutorial work in schools there can be a three-stage developmental sequence to help you progress in relation to key qualities, attributes and skills: *recognition; acquisition; practice/improvement.*

Web activity 7(5) – Time to reflect

SOME FINAL WORDS

We end this book with some words about critical reflection on practice. It should allow your route to proficiency in teaching to be negotiated and for staged help and support to be put in place. Evaluation of your teaching and performance, coupled with learning from evidence (including the effective practice of others) are both key aspects of critical reflection. These aspects will be influenced by your own particular motivations and abilities to take increasing responsibility for your own professional development. Underpinning all that you do are your values: you do what is right, as well as what is technically correct, and so your values influence how priorities are determined for your future actions. We believe that critical reflection on practice provides the way for clarifying values that lie at the heart of successful practice.

REFERENCES

Aggleton, P., Rivers, K., Chase, E., Downie, A., Mulvihill, C., Sinkler, P., Tyrer, P. and Warwick, I. (1999) *Learning Lessons: A Report on Two Research Studies Informing the National Healthy School Standard.* London: DoH/DfEE.

Andrews, D. (2006) 'Non-teachers moving into roles traditionally undertaken by teachers: benefits and challenges – for whom?', *Pastoral Care in Education*, 24(3): 28–31.

Askew, S. (ed.) (2000) *Feedback for Learning.* London: Routledge Falmer.

Baldwin, J. and Wells, A. (1983) 'Uncertain futures: an approach to tutorial work with 16–19 year olds in the 1980s', *Pastoral Care in Education*, 1(1): 40–5.

Best, R. (1999) 'The impact on pastoral care of structural, organisational and statutory changes in schooling: some empirical evidence and discussion', *British Journal of Guidance and Counselling*, 27(1): 55–70.

Best, R. (2002) *Pastoral Care and Personal–Social Education: A Review of UK Research Undertaken for the British Educational Research Association.* Nottingham: BERA.

Best, R., Jarvis, C. and Ribbins, P.M. (eds) (1980) *Perspectives on Pastoral Care.* London: Heinemann.

Best, R., Lang, P., Lodge, C. and Watkins, C. (1995) *Pastoral Care and Personal–Social Education: Entitlement and Provision.* London: Cassell.

Blackburn, K. (1975) *The Tutor.* London: Heinemann.

Carnell, E. and Lodge, C. (2002a) *Supporting Effective Learning*. London: Paul Chapman Publishing.

Carnell, E. and Lodge, C. (2002b) 'Support for students' learning: what the form tutor can do', *Pastoral Care in Education*, 20(4): 12–20.

Centre for the Study of Comprehensive Schools (CSCS) (2007) *Broadsheet 83 Some Sources of Values, Religious and Secular. A Reference Collection, with Questions for Staff Discussion*. Northampton: CSCS.

Department for Education and Science (DES) (1988) *A Survey of Personal and Social Education Courses in Some Secondary Schools: A Report by HM Inspectors*. London: DES.

Department for Education and Employment and the Qualifications and Curriculum Authority (DfEE/QCA) (2000) *The National Curriculum Handbook for Secondary Teachers in England: Key Stage 3 and 4*. London: DfEE/QCA.

Department for Education and Science and Her Majesty's Inspectorate (DES/HMI) (1977) *Curriculum 11–16*. London: DES.

Department for Education and Science and Her Majesty's Inspectorate (DES/HMI) (1989) *Report of Her Majesty's Inspectors on Pastoral Care in Secondary Schools: An Inspection of Some Aspects of Pastoral Care in 1987–8*. London: DES.

Griffiths, P. (1995) 'Guidance and tutoring', in R. Best, P. Lang, C. Lodge and C. Watkins (eds), *Pastoral Care and Personal–Social Education: Entitlement and Provision*. London: Cassell. pp. 75–87.

Hall, C. (1998) 'Fitness for purpose: self-care and the pastoral tutor', in M. Calvert and J. Henderson (eds), *Managing Pastoral Care*. London: Cassell. pp. 53–68.

Hamblin, D. (1978) *The Teacher and Pastoral Care*. Oxford: Blackwell.

Harrison, J. (2006) An examination of the language and interpretations of Standard One for initial teacher training in England: professional values and practice – outcomes or opportunities?, *European Journal of Teacher Education*, 29(4): 431–54.

Hoyle, E. and John, P. (1995) *Professional Knowledge and Professional Practice*. London: Cassell.

Inman, S., Buck, M. and Burke, H. (eds) (1998) *Assessing Personal and Social Development. Measuring the Unmeasurable?* London: Falmer.

Ireson, J. (1999) *Innovative Grouping in Secondary Schools*. London: DfEE.

Jones, P. (2006) 'Status of pastoral care in schools in the 21st century', *Pastoral Care in Education*, 24(2): 64–6.

Lang, P. (1980) 'Pastoral care: problems and choices', in E. Reybould, B. Roberts and K. Wedell (eds), *Helping the Low Achiever in Secondary School*. Education Review Occasional Publication 7.

Lang, P. and Marland, M. (eds.) (1985) *New Directions in Pastoral Care*. Oxford: Blackwell.

Marland, M. (1974) *Pastoral Care*. London: Heinemann.

Marland, M. (1989) *The Tutor and the Tutor Group*. Harlow: Longman.

Marland, M. and Rogers, R. (2004) How to be a successful form tutor. London: Continuum.

Munby, S. (1995) 'Assessment and pastoral care: sense, sensibility and standards', in R. Best, P. Lang, C. Lodge and C. Watkins (eds), *Pastoral Care and Personal–Social Education: Entitlement and Provision*. London: Cassell. pp. 141–54.

Nadge, A. (2005) 'Academic care: building resilience, building futures', *Pastoral Care in Education*, 23(1): 28–33.

National Children's Bureau (NCB) (2006) *Meeting the Standard in PSHE: Briefing 1.* London: National Children's Bureau.

Office for Standards in Education (Ofsted) (1999) *Inspecting Schools: The Framework.* London: Ofsted.

Office for Standards in Education (Ofsted) (2005) *Personal, Social and Health Education in Secondary Schools. HMI Report 2311.* London: Ofsted.

Office for Standards in Education (Ofsted) (2007a) *Time for Change? Personal, Social and Health Education. Report 070049.* London: Ofsted.

Office for Standards in Education (Ofsted) (2007b) *Developing Social, Emotional and Behavioural Skills in Secondary Schools.* London: Ofsted.

Pring, R. (1984) *Personal and Social Education in the Curriculum.* London: Hodder & Stoughton.

Qualifications and Curriculum Authority (QCA) (2007a) *The Secondary Curriculum Review: Programme of Study (Non-statutory): PSHEE – Personal Well-being (Key Stage 3). Draft for Consultation.* London: QCA.

Qualifications and Curriculum Authority (QCA) (2007b) *The Secondary Curriculum Review: Programme of Study (Non-statutory): PSHEE – Economic Well-being (Key Stage 3). Draft for Consultation.* London: QCA.

Qualifications and Curriculum Authority (QCA) (2007c) *The New Secondary Curriculum. What Has Changed and Why?* London: QCA.

Qualter, P., Gardner, K. and Whiteley, H. (2007) 'Emotional intelligence: review of research and educational implications', *Pastoral Care in Education*, 25(1): 11–18.

Regis, D. (2000) 'What do young people think of PSHE? Some recent results from SHEU surveys', *Education and Health*, 18(2): 36–7.

Rogers, C. (1980) *A Way of Being.* Boston, MA: Houghton Mifflin.

Sanger, M. (2001) 'Talking to teachers and looking at practice in understanding the moral dimension of teaching', *Journal of Curriculum Studies*, 33(6): 683–701.

Smith, D. (1998) 'School ethos: a process for eliciting the views of pupils', *Pastoral Care in Education*, 16(1): 3–10.

Times Educational Supplement (2007) 4 May: 288.

Waterhouse, P. (1991) *Tutoring.* Stafford: Network Educational Press.

Watkins, C. (2004) 'Reclaiming pastoral care', *Pastoral Care in Education*, 22(3): 3–6.

Whitty, G.G., Rowe, G. and Aggleton, P. (1994) 'Subjects and themes in the secondary-school curriculum', *Research Papers in Education*, 9(2): 159–81.

APPENDIX

USING ACTIVITIES IN THIS BOOK TO HELP YOU TO ACHIEVE THE STANDARDS FOR QTS

The activities listed alongside each Standard in the chart are designed to support your critical reflection and professional development in particular areas during the university and school/college-based stages of your course.

	Professional attributes	Activities
Q1	Have high expectations of children and young people including a commitment to ensuring that they can achieve their full educational potential and to establishing fair, respectful, trusting, supportive and constructive relationships with them.	1.2, 6.3, 6.4, 6.5
Q2	Demonstrate the positive values, attitudes and behaviour they expect from children and young people.	6.3, 6.4, 6.5, 7.9
Q3	(a) Be aware of the professional duties of teachers and the statutory framework within which they work.	5.10, 6.9
	(b) Be aware of the policies and practices of the workplace and share in collective responsibility for their implementation.	5.10, 6.9
Q4	Communicate effectively with children, young people, colleagues, parents and carers.	5.8, 5.9, 7.7, 7.8
Q5	Recognise and respect the contribution that colleagues, parents and carers can make to the development and well-being of children and young people and to raising their levels of attainment.	4.11, 5.9, 7.4
Q6	Have a commitment to collaboration and co-operative working.	4.11, 7.4
Q7	(a) Reflect on and improve their practice, and take responsibility for identifying and meeting their developing professional needs.	1.2, 1.3, 1.4, 1.5, 1.6, 1.7, 2.1, 2.3, 3.9, 3.10, 3.11, 6.3, 6.4, 6.5
	(b) Identify priorities for their early professional development in the context of induction.	
Q8	Have a creative and constructively critical approach towards innovation, being prepared to adapt their practice where benefits and improvements are identified.	1.4, 1.7, 2.1, 3.11, 6.7, 7.7
Q9	Act upon advice and feedback and be open to coaching and mentoring.	3.11d, 4.1b

Appendix *(Continued)*

	Professional knowledge and understanding	Activities
Q10	Have a knowledge and understanding of a range of teaching, learning and behaviour management strategies and know how to use and adapt them, including how to personalise learning and provide opportunities for all learners to achieve their potential.	2.1, 2.2, 2.5, 2.6, 3.1, 3.4, 6.3, 6.4, 7.7
Q11	Know the assessment requirements and arrangements for the subjects/curriculum areas they are trained to teach, including those relating to public examinations and qualifications.	3.6, 5.3, 5.7, 5.8
Q12	Know a range of approaches to assessment, including the importance of formative assessment.	5.1, 5.2, 5.4, 5.5, 5.6, 5.7
Q13	Know how to use local and national statistical information to evaluate the effectiveness of their teaching, to monitor the progress of those they teach and to raise levels of attainment.	5.11, 5.12
Q14	Have a secure knowledge and understanding of their subjects/curriculum areas and related pedagogy to enable them to teach effectively across the age and ability range for which they are trained.	Your competence in this Standard will be developed primarily through your prior learning, your own course subject sessions which will help you to transform your subject knowledge into pedagogic knowledge and your own teaching. However, many of the activities in Chapters 2–7 will support your developing understanding of pedagogical issues.
Q15	Know and understand the relevant statutory and non-statutory curricula, and frameworks, including those provided through the National Strategies, for their subjects/curriculum areas, and other relevant initiatives applicable to the age and ability range for which they are trained.	3.2, 3.5, 3.6, 3.7, 3.9, 3.10, 3.11, 6.6, 6.7, 6.10, 6.11, 7.10, 7.11

(Continued)

Appendix   (Continued)

	Professional knowledge and understanding	Activities
Q16	Have passed the professional skills tests in numeracy, literacy and information and communications technology (ICT).	3.9, 3.10, 3.11
Q17	Know how to use skills in literacy, numeracy and ICT to support their teaching and wider professional activities.	3.8, 3.9, 3.10, 3.11
Q18	Understand how children and young people develop and that the progress and well-being of learners are affected by a range of developmental, social, religious, ethnic, cultural and linguistic influences.	2.1, 2.2, 2.4, 2.6, 3.2, 3.4, 3.5, 6.3, 6.4, 6.5, 7.2
Q19	Know how to make effective personalised provision for those they teach, including those for whom English is an additional language or who have special educational needs or disabilities, and how to take practical account of diversity and promote equality and inclusion in their teaching.	3.2, 3.3, 3.5, 4.12, 6.3, 6.4, 6.5, 6.10, 6.11, 7.2
Q20	Know and understand the roles of colleagues with specific responsibilities, including those with responsibility for learners with special educational needs and disabilities and other individual learning needs.	3.2, 3.4, 3.5, 3.9, 3.10, 5.10c, 6.8, 6.9, 7.4, 7.5d
Q21	(a) Be aware of current legal requirements, national policies and guidance on the safeguarding and promotion of the well-being of children and young people.	3.2, 6.12, 7.3, 7.6
	(b) Know how to identify and support children and young people whose progress, development or well-being is affected by changes or difficulties in their personal circumstances, and when to refer them to colleagues for specialist support.	3.2, 7.5, 7.6, 7.7, 7.8

Appendix *(Continued)*

	Professional skills	Activities
	These will be particularly demonstrated during school or college placements.	
Q22	Plan for progression across the age and ability range for which they are trained, designing effective learning sequences within lessons and across series of lessons and demonstrating secure subject/curriculum knowledge.	4.2, 4.3, 5.11c
Q23	Design opportunities for learners to develop their literacy, numeracy and ICT skills.	3.8, 3.9, 3.10, 3.11, 4.13b
Q24	Plan homework or other out-of-class work to sustain learners' progress and to extend and consolidate their learning.	5.3
Q25	Teach lessons and sequences of lessons across the age and ability range for which they are trained in which they:	
	(a) use a range of teaching strategies and resources, including e-learning, taking practical account of diversity and promoting equality and inclusion;	2.5, 3.3, 3.4, 4.13b
	(b) build on prior knowledge, develop concepts and processes, enable learners to apply new knowledge, understanding and skills and meet learning objectives;	
	(c) adapt their language to suit the learners they teach, introducing new ideas and concepts clearly, and using explanations, questions, discussions and plenaries effectively;	3.8, 3.9, 4.8, 4.9
	(d) demonstrate the ability to manage the learning of individuals, groups and whole classes, modifying their teaching to suit the stage of the lesson.	4.10, 7.7

(Continued)

Appendix   *(Continued)*

	Professional skills	Activities
Q26	(a) Make effective use of a range of assessment, monitoring and recording strategies.	5.3, 5.4, 5.5, 5.6
	(b) Assess the learning needs of those they teach in order to set challenging learning objectives.	3.3
Q27	Provide timely, accurate and constructive feedback on learners' attainment, progress and areas for development.	5.8, 5.9
Q28	Support and guide learners to reflect on their learning, identify the progress they have made and identify their emerging learning needs.	5.5, 6.11, 7.7, 7.8
Q29	Evaluate the impact of their teaching on the progress of all learners, and modify their planning and classroom practice where necessary.	1.4, 1.7, 2.5, 5.6
Q30	Establish a purposeful and safe learning environment conducive to learning and identify opportunities for learners to learn in out-of-school contexts.	4.4, 4.5, 7.1, 7.2
Q31	Establish a clear framework for classroom discipline to manage learners' behaviour constructively and promote their self-control and independence.	4.6, 4.7
Q32	Work as a team member and identify opportunities for working with colleagues, sharing the development of effective practice with them.	4.11, 7.4, 7.8
Q33	Ensure that colleagues working with them are appropriately involved in supporting learning and understand the roles they are expected to fulfil.	4.11, 7.4

GLOSSARY

Ability: the quality, skill or power to be able to do something.

Academic tutor/ing: intensive support given to students, either individually or in small groups, designed to enhance the quality of their learning. It recognizes that learning is subjective and so its role is to nurture and encourage the intellectual development of each student with the aim of helping them become independent learners.

Accelerated learning: learning based on strategies which are designed to support the three types of learner – visual, auditory and kinaesthetic.

Achievement: succeeding in finishing something or reaching an aim.

Action research: a collaborative form of educational research involving teachers and professionals in clusters of schools or other educational units with shared interests. Importance is given to linking theory to practice, through relating theory to the teachers' own experience and observations and through reflection on observations and own practices. Action research maintains a distance between the teacher-researcher and the study and, in so doing, differs from self-study research.

Advanced skills teacher: (AST) a teacher who has been recognized through external assessment as having excellent classroom practice. An AST has increased non-contact time and a remit to share their skills and experience with other teachers in their own school and from other schools.

Affordances: potential benefits to the learning process through use of a piece of equipment, computer hardware and software or other device.

Assessment: the process of judging the validity and worth of students' work in all its various forms.

Assessment regime: used to indicate a structure of examinations and other assessment formats that constitute a society's main routes to qualifications.

Attainment: something which has been succeeded in, achieved or reached.

Attention deficit hyperactivity disorder: (ADHD) a term used to describe perceived behavioural problems, most often in children. The main behaviours identified are inattention, hyperactivity and impulsive behaviour.

Behaviour management: the various actions and interactions used by teaching staff to enhance the probability of students acting in a productive and socially acceptable manner.

Behaviourism: is concerned with: modelling appropriate behaviours; creating environments that enable or condition students to respond in what are deemed appropriate ways; rewarding positive responses; learning through repetition.

'Big picture': an overview of what students will learn during the lesson at the beginning of a session and how it connects with prior learning and intended future learning

Blogs: otherwise known as weblogs, these are online journals or filters which allow an individual to post ideas and thoughts, or website addresses they feel are useful for a particular purpose. Other users can add comments concerning the content on the weblog thereby making it interactive.

CEHR: The Commission for Equality and Human Rights. Replaced the EOC and the CRE from October 2007.

Classroom management: the teaching behaviours used by an individual to shape and develop conditions which facilitate learning within a group of students.

Cognitivism: cognitivist theory is about thinking and draws on the work of Gagne, Ausubel and Bruner. It assumes that, as learners learn, they draw and build on knowledge they already have, disregarding some prior knowledge when no longer necessary or when new learning makes it redundant.

Common Assessment Framework: refers to procedures for assessing children who are in need of public service intervention for whatever reason. It is a framework that is common to all agencies who are working with children to achieve the aims of *Every Child Matters*.

Communities of practice: Lave and Wenger (1991) conceptualized the idea that these communities are everywhere and have a number of characteristics (mutual engagement; joint enterprise: and a shared repertoire). People learn through participating in practice with newcomers learning from longer standing members and from each other.

Concept mapping: a process of building up diagrams which contain a limited number of concepts or ideas with the propositional relationships which join them written on linking arrows.

Conceptual knowledge: this is concerned with the acquisition of information (knowing this or that about something) and the rules associated with that acquisition or the use of knowledge (knowing how to use something). Constructivist views of learning tend to concentrate on conceptual understanding.

Constructivism: the learner plays a very active role in the construction of his or her new knowledge, skills or attitude. Readers need to distinguish between *psychological* and *social* construction of knowledge, associated with the theories of Piaget and Vygotsky respectively.

CRE: The Commission for Racial Equality.

CSCS: Centre for the Study of Comprehensive Schools (www.cscs.org.uk). The CSCS is a charitable trust, affiliated to the Universities of Leicester and Northampton. Through its activities it seeks to secure high-quality state education for all students.

Curriculum: the group of subjects studied in a school or college or a course of study in a particular subject.

DARTs: Directed Activities Related to Texts (see Chapters 2 and 3).

DCSF: Department for Children, Schools and Families (UK government department with responsibility for children's services, families, schools, 14–19 education, and the Respect Taskforce).

Deductive thinking or **deductivism**: a form of reasoning in which ideas are tested before they are accepted formally. It relies on the logical outcomes of current idea or theory, or an imaginative idea arising from that idea/theory. Scientific knowledge for example is built by deduction through the systematic testing of hypotheses. Any observations are directed or led by the original hypothesis.

Designated senior person: a senior member of the school's leadership team who is designated to take lead responsibility for dealing with child protection issues, providing advice and support to other staff, liaising with the local authority, and working with other agencies. The designated person need not be a teacher but must have the status and authority within the school management structure to carry out the duties of the post including committing resources to child protection matters, and where appropriate directing other staff (taken from Section 157 of the Education Act, 2002).

Differentiation: planning and teaching using approaches to suit the learning needs and prior learning of individual students and to ensure that all are engaged in activities which will challenge them appropriately.

Dis-application or dis-applied: exemption from participation in certain aspects of the curriculum or statutory assessment processes.

EAL: English as an additional language (see Chapter 3).

ECM: *Every Child Matters* (refer to Chapter 3 for an introduction to this policy).

Effect size: a numeric value used to illustrate the extent to which a particular intervention can be identified as having an impact on a given process.

EOC: The Equal Opportunities Commission.

Excellence in Cities: **(EiC)** a major government policy designed to raise standards in urban schools. EiC was organized through partnerships, and each partnership included a local education authority (LEA) and all its secondary schools. EiC had seven key strands:

- support for gifted and talented students
- the provision of learning mentors to support young people facing barriers to learning
- learning support units (LSUs) for students who would benefit from time away from the normal classroom
- city learning centres (CLCs) providing state-of-the-art ICT resources for a small number of schools
- EiC Action Zones enabling small groups of primary and secondary schools to work together to provide local solutions to local problems
- extensions of the existing specialist and beacon school programmes.

Extended schools: (refer to Chapters 3 and 7).

Gatekeeper: A gatekeeper is an individual or an institution which controls access to a valuable asset or resource. In terms of schooling, the school acts as gatekeeper to employment and high salaries through its assessment activities.

Gateway: examinations constitute points of entry into other areas such as further education or employment and at these points some are accepted and some are rejected. The term is therefore used to indicate that at these points of entry for some the gates are open and for some they are closed.

GCSE: General Certificate of Secondary Education.

General Teaching Council of England (GTCE): regulates the teaching profession in England and aims to raise the status of teaching and learning. Similar regulatory bodies exist in Northern Ireland (GTCNI), Scotland (GTCS) and Wales (GTCW).

Hidden curriculum: this includes the caring relationships developed between school and home and includes the physical environment and facilities of the school. It takes account of the notice that students take of the courtesies, concerns, tolerances, and negotiation between people in the school and general care that is taken of its environment. It takes account of the behaviour of the adults, and contradictory attitudes amongst its members. The subtle messages communicated by teachers and others; behaviour to the students have deep effects on what the students actually learn.

HLTA: Higher-level teaching assistant.

IEP: Individual Education Plan (see Chapter 3).

In loco parentis: UK legal term meaning 'in place of the parent'. When parents or carers send their children to school they delegate their authority to the teachers to act in the best interests of the school and the children. A teacher who is supervising or accompanying students on a school trip has overall responsibility for their health and safety and is said to be acting 'in loco parentis'.

Inductive hypothesis: this is a thinking process using logical reasoning that a hypothesis can be made because particular cases that seem to be examples of it exist.

Inductive thinking or **inductivism**: a way of generalizing from a set of observations to a universal law inductively. It is a process used in one form of scientific thinking/reasoning. Scientific knowledge for example is built by induction from a well accepted (reliable) set of observations.

Interpersonal: between people (for example the ability to interact effectively with colleagues in your subject team is an interpersonal skill).

Intrapersonal: within oneself (for example the ability to reflect is an intrapersonal skill).

Key skills: sometimes known as 'core skills' or 'basic skills', these are areas of schooling that are seen as fundamental to the future performance of individuals in the economy. They include numeracy, literacy and ICT, as well as problem-solving, working with others, and managing your own learning.

LEA: Local Education Authority – a term now superseded by **LA**: Local Authority.

Learning communities: partnerships between different agencies within a community (including voluntary sector agencies) to promote learning. Learning communities can be real or virtual.

Learning gain: the gap between that understood by a student before and after a learning encounter.

Learning mentoring: providing support and guidance to children, young people and those engaged with them, by removing barriers to learning in order to promote effective participation, enhance individual learning, raise aspirations and achieve their potential.

Learning to Learn: programmes which seek to give students an opportunity to develop as learners through development of: reflectivity about their learning; thinking skills and ICT.

Lesson planning: the process involved in developing the structure and activities to be undertaken by students within a lesson and the ways in which their learning will be monitored.

Level 3 examinations: these test what might be expected of the notional 16–18-year-old and include for example academic and vocational Advanced level examinations.

Meta-cognition: a form of knowledge. It is knowledge of one's own cognitive processes and includes both strategic knowledge and self-knowledge. It is acquired through the support of others more knowledgeable than oneself (referred to as scaffolding). It provides the capacity for regulating one's own thinking, so an individual can solve problems or ask questions or model these 'conversations with oneself' based on those previously held with others (teachers or peers).

Meta-cognitive frameworks for learning: are where students develop a notion of their learning styles and are able reflect on themselves as learners.

MI: multiple intelligences (see Chapter 2).

Mind map®/mind-mapping: a creative way of organizing material in a visual form that reflects how information is encoded in the brain. A topic or idea is placed in the middle of a page and strands are drawn from it, identifying particular aspects of it. A mind map® is usually more systematic than a spider diagram, with the information being organized logically by strands and sub-strands, rather than just putting down ideas in any order.

NAPCE: National Association of Pastoral Care in Education.

National Qualifications Framework (NQF): a statement of how all the examinations and assessment opportunities in an assessment regime fit together. In the UK , the NQF is expressed as a structure of 'level' qualifications, with different levels corresponding roughly to age cohorts. Note that this does not mean that individuals can only take any level examination at the relevant age.

Neuro Linguistic Programming (NLP) is rooted in both psychology and neurology. It is based on the work of John Grinder, a linguistic professor, and Richard Bandler, a mathematician, at the University of California at Santa Cruz (UCSC), around 1975. They recognized the importance of eye contact and movement in identifying emotional states and how (rather than what) individuals think. NLP identifies six ways in which individuals perceive information which arrives via the senses. These form the basis of what we now know as 'VAK' the identification of *visual*, *auditory* and *kinaesthetic* learners and the need to cater for different learning styles in the classroom. NLP also recognizes the importance of non-verbal communication, particularly eye contact, posture, breathing and movement.

NGO: non-governmental organization.

NHSS: National Healthy School Status.

Observation: the act of recording and noting a classroom experience, predominantly that of another individual.

Ofsted: the Office for Standards in Education, a government agency responsible for the inspection of schools, colleges and teacher training courses.

Pedagogy: a generic term for teaching and learning processes.

Performance data: statistics collected about a school or college that describes the achievements of students in various examinations and other key areas of education. They are usually gathered for purposes of publication to parents, the government, Ofsted and other interested parties.

Personal digital assistant (PDA): a generic term for any form of palm top computer which includes functions such as an address book, memo pad, and to-do lists. They input data through the use of a touch screen or keyboard, and are increasingly being combined within mobile phones.

PLTs: Personal learning and thinking skills.

Podcasts: audio files which are uploaded to the Internet, most commonly in MP3 file format. Once on the Internet, they can be downloaded to personal audio devices.

Procedural knowledge: this is knowledge of ideas and the understanding of principles (examples include: defining the chemical elements; classifying objects; recognizing instances of belonging to a particular group). Specialized forms of this type of knowledge become recognized as a specialist field of study or discipline.

Professional enquiry: includes several academic and social processes, including engagement with research, and the active seeking of evidence and systematic evaluation by one or more professionals in a professional learning community such as a school, or department within a school.

Professional standards: standards for initial teacher training, induction, professional, excellent and advanced skills teachers.

Programme of study: the framework for learning over a prolonged period of time, usually a key stage, which might highlight the content and/or skills to be developed.

QCA: Qualifications and Curriculum Authority. The government-appointed body that has responsibility for all public examinations and the National Curriculum.

Reflective/reflection: the terms refer to the capacity of an individual to think thoughtfully and deeply, to remind oneself of past events and to consider alternative courses of action.

Reflexive/reflexivity: the terms refer to the involuntary or instinctive examination of oneself.

Scaffolding: the construction of structures (such as writing frames and bullet point prompts) which support learners in the initial stages of a task or throughout it and which can be gradually removed as a learner gains confidence (see Chapter 2).

Schemes of work: a series of lessons focusing on a particular area of a subject, or skill.

School ethos: it embraces the aims, attitudes, values and procedures in the school – the 'intangibles' that come from the spirit within the school and its community, including its students, all staff, approaches to teaching and learning, management of the curriculum and of the school as a whole.

SEF: Self-Evaluation Form completed by schools to evaluate leadership, management and capacity to improve. It is the main document used by an Ofsted team when they plan an inspection.

Self-study research: a way of purposefully examining the relationship between teaching and learning so that alternative perspectives on the intentions and outcomes might be better realized. There are similarities and differences between self-study and action research but self-study requires that as a teacher I put myself, my beliefs, my assumptions, my ideologies about teaching as well as my practice, under close scrutiny.

Setted: a system where students are put into groups with others of roughly equal ability. The groups may vary between subjects to reflect the different levels of ability demonstrated by any individual student across the curriculum (see Chapter 3).

SMART: an acronym used in target-setting with the aim of focusing on specific goals. A SMART target is specific, measurable, attainable, realistic and time-based. There are a number of variants on the exact wording.

Social constructivism: focuses on the cognitive processes that occur as people learn through social interaction such as play, listening to and working with others and how these impact on mental development (see Chapter 2). Vygotsky proposed that learning takes place in the zone of proximal development (ZPD) – a simple way of describing the time and place when two or more people are involved in a learning activity.

Specialist Colleges and Academies Trust: trust in existence from Sept 2005 (formerly known as the Technology Colleges Trust and the Specialist Colleges Trust).

Spider diagram: allows you to think about the main idea that, for example, a book is exploring and then how the ideas are seen to be present in many parts of the book. Spider diagrams can combine and extend Venn diagrams (see Activity 6.7) to express constraints on sets (ideas) and their relationships with other sets. A 'spider' is arranged as a tree with branches and a trunk, and is used to explore the connection between one set of ideas (the foot of the trunk) and other sets of related ideas (where the branches touch other sets of ideas).

Storyboard: used by film production crews and others in the media. It is a series of sketches and technical notes showing the sequence of key shots in a scene. Storyboards are also used (in simplified form) in English and media classrooms by students to demonstrate their understanding and interpretation of key events or production features of texts they are studying or creating for themselves.

Streamed: a system where students are put into groups with others of roughly equal ability. The groups remain constant across subjects and do not take into account the variable ability of an individual across the curriculum (see Chapter 3).

Unconditional positive regard: an attitude of caring, characteristic of a person-centred approach to client-centred therapy. It provides the climate for change and

acceptance of whatever immediate feeling is going on – confusion, resentment, fear, anger, courage, pride. Such caring is non possessive and is not conditional.

VAK: visual, auditory and kinaesthetic (see Chapter 2).

VLEs: virtual learning environments. Software applications which are used to organize, aid and assess learning. They are most frequently accessed through an Internet portal.

Wikis: A group of web pages which allows users to add content, while allowing others to edit that content.

Wikipedia: is an encyclopedia on the Web which users can contribute pages to or edit other people's contributions.

Writing frames: outline structures or scaffolds which help learners to shape their ideas or arguments, in particular, written forms such as reports, argued writing or responses to texts.

Zone of proximal development or ZPD is a term first coined by Vygotsky to define the distance between the actual development level of learning and what potentially could be learned through problem solving either with guidance through that zone by a parent, grandparent, sibling, other adult such as a teacher or by collaboration with more capable peers.

INDEX

Added to a page number 'f' denotes a figure, 't' denotes a table and 'g' denotes glossary.